GREG EILERS

A Roller Coaster Through a Hurricane

One Wild Ride: My Journey with Gender Identity

To all who have been cast out

Contents

Foreword		iii
Preface		vi
Acknowledgement		ix
1	In the beginning	1
2	School years and girl fears	7
3	Marriage and children	14
4	Growing into myself	23
5	To the ministry	31
6	Divorce	37
7	Enter Julie	43
8	"It's who you are"	49
9	Tragedy town	53
10	Frustration mounts	65
11	Self-hatred erupts	69
12	The crash	73
13	"I need to be a woman"	77
14	Therapy	81
15	Yes, I will; no, I won't	87
16	Learning why	91
17	Testing the why	96
18	"What's a transsexual?"	101
19	Why do I have to come out?	105
20	WPATH standards of care	111
21	I know why people commit suicide	114
22	HRT and the unexpected	119
23	Supercalifragilisticexpialidocious	123
24	Investigating the harmony	129

25 Outcast   134

26 Gone   138

27 "What do you know about gender dysphoria?"   143

28 Reactions   149

29 "There is no hospital. There is no therapy."   154

30 Time out   162

31 Going insane   167

32 Back to work   171

33 "I have dysphoria"   175

34 Retirement   180

35 Real Life Test   187

36 Going public   195

37 Feedback and fallout   203

38 Presenting Gina   209

39 Family rejection   214

40 Two diversions   219

41 Making Gina legal   223

42 Self-identity   231

43 Controversies   238

44 Meanwhile ...   246

45 Surgery time   253

46 The return to Greg   263

47 It was my hormones all along   269

48 Loose ends and lessons   275

49 Coasting   281

About the Author   285

Foreword

by Julie Eilers

"I would have left in a heartbeat."

The declaration is volunteered by many, men and women alike, upon hearing the story about a transgender husband transitioning to live as a woman. The question I, the wife, expected—"*Did you ever think about leaving?*"—is bypassed, and the listeners fast forward to their own bold assertion about hitting the road. As though even asking the question about staying means there is a sliver of possibility they themselves would have to live through something so unfathomable, so unpleasant. Better to nip that in the bud, slam that door shut. Outta here, in a heartbeat.

How a couple handles a big situation has more to do with how they handled all the little things in all the previous years. Since our wedding on December 30, 2001, I'd learned a lot from Greg Eilers about respect, unconditional love, and kindness. We'd built a pretty deep store of those Golden Rule treasures, so it was only natural that we drew upon it when Greg's gender dysphoria upended our lives.

I couldn't declare "I didn't sign up for this", because this—facing hurdles with my life partner—was exactly what I did sign up to do. I couldn't turn my back on the person I loved, because I knew he, without hesitation, would face any deluge of difficulties I threw his way. I couldn't run the other direction because, I asked, what would I want my spouse to do if I were in his shoes? I couldn't shout "This is not fair!", because life isn't about fairness. It's about being our best for others.

We tend to view relationships as a give and take proposition. That what we give and what we receive is measurable and should somehow balance out the scales. As if every checkmark in the debit column deserves a credit entry on the next line.

What if we saw it this way instead: that both sides of the scale belong equally to both partners, that all the debits and all the credits belong collectively to the team.

Living through a spouse's gender dysphoria and transition from one gender to another seems a very debit-heavy transaction. It is excruciating to watch the person you love experience the torment of being one gender on the inside and another in public. It is painful to see your spouse feel trapped in an unchangeable life and view death as the only escape. It is sorrowful to mourn the loss of the only identity (husband and wife) you've known with this person. It is daunting to fathom an existence where you expect to be condemned and ostracized. It is nerve-racking to think about how your family, your friends, the world will see you.

Life has an abundance of challenges, but the majority of them are understood and accepted. Most everyone will commiserate with you when your spouse has a terminal illness, a disability-causing accident, an affair, a job loss. People can imagine themselves in common situations. They have a frame of reference. You might still feel isolated, but at least you know you're not the only one.

The crossing of gender boundaries, though, is just too weird, too outlandish, too forbidden for most people to wrap their heads around. You don't have the luxury of calling up friends and family, of drawing on a readily-available support network, to help get you through this. This—the "my spouse is transgender"—starts out a closely-held yet extremely-loaded secret—a frightening one to share. And when you do begin to share, it's very often not support you get, but highly-opinionated directives and ultimatums.

It's no wonder most marriages don't survive a gender transition.

Jesus teaches us in Romans 5 that we should "rejoice in our suffering". Quoting scripture doesn't take the hard stuff away. But understanding the point—looking through our earthly suffering to the ultimate spiritual reward God gives us, eternal life with our Savior—helps us take a bigger picture approach to the struggles we have in life.

Despite the trying times, despite the unconquerable mountains and precarious ravines that riddled the landscape of my spouse's gender dysphoria, I always had one thing to cling to: hope. Hope for the four things I desired for my spouse—that he stay alive, that he keep his sanity, that he be as healthy and whole as possible, and maybe even that he achieve happiness. Hope that Greg and I would emerge as a couple—however that looked—stronger, better, and deeper in our love. Hope is a powerful little thing. Hope let me redefine the debits as credits.

It is my hope that Greg's story, and the story of all transgender people, will prompt others to see the bigger picture. To set aside their preconceived notions about what it means to be transgender. To turn their ears and listen to a group of people struggling to be heard. To brave their awkward feelings and step into a space they've never been.

Comfort zones are tough to give up. When faced with an unfamiliar situation, particularly one vastly different than we are accustomed to, our tendency is to recoil, get back to the easy. Something new might pique our curiosity, but we're careful about getting too close, cautious about letting ourselves be vulnerable. Yet, there are some really valuable benefits outside our bubbles: Enrichment. Love. Growth. Understanding. Compassion. Selflessness. Humanity.

Would I leave my comfort zone to stay with Greg? In a heartbeat.

Preface

I was fourteen. Every bit a regular boy, I could be found throwing a baseball, catching a football, or shooting a basketball. My bike got a regular workout. I knew what girls were; they intrigued me and scared me. I was in awe of them. I had no interest in dating them.

I told my mom, "I don't want to get married, but I want to have kids." She was listening. "Do you think I could adopt them? Would they let a single man do that?"

"Perhaps," she replied. "But just wait till you grow up a bit more. I bet you'll want to get married."

"I don't know about that, Mom, but I know I want to have kids."

+ + +

I was sixteen. I asked Mom, "Why do you shop at both drugstores and both grocery stores in town?"

"Since your father is the city manager, I feel I need to patronize all of the stores. I can't play favorites."

This left an impression. I also noticed my parents always bought cars from the same place. I was learning about loyalty.

I took note of people who worked at the same job their entire adult lives. I admired that. It was the mid 1970s, and free agency was entering professional sports. I could not understand why a player would leave his team for a lucrative contract. Where was his loyalty? I wondered.

I decided I wanted to be a loyal lifer—find a job I like and work at it until retirement.

+ + +

I was twenty-one. I was engaged to be married. My fiancé Kim and I were visiting my best friend Tim and his wife Teresa. We were talking about our futures. Our goals. Our dreams.

Teresa said, "I don't want to be that person who never leaves her hometown, who doesn't go out into the world and do big, exciting things. It would be boring to own a house, with a white picket fence, and never leave home."

I was offended. It felt like she was putting down those who had simpler aspirations. I piped up, "That's *all* I want. That sounds like the best thing in the world. Besides, where is it written that a person cannot have a full and wonderful life right here in Montague? That's all I want. Have kids. Own a house. Work at a good job. Never leave."

+ + +

At age twenty-two, I was married. By twenty-three, I was bringing children into the world. At twenty-five, I had a job in my home town, in the company where I intended to work until retirement. And, at twenty-seven, I moved with Kim and our first two children into our own house, which we had first torn down to the studs and rebuilt in a quick six months.

Nowadays, I like to ask people, "When you were in your late teens to early twenties, what were the basic things you wanted to accomplish? Things such as getting married, or traveling the world, or accomplishing this or that." Rarely does anyone recall much. The common response is, "I just wanted to get through college."

I knew. I had my list. It was succinct, but it was complete. I wanted to be married until death parted us. I wanted to have several children. I wanted to work at the same company until I retired. I wanted to live in Montague.

For six years after we moved into our house, after we added two sons to join our two daughters, and after I moved up in the ranks at work, by the age of thirty-three I had checked off each item on my list. I had fulfilled my major life goals. The rest was gravy. I was content. I was supremely happy.

Until I wasn't.

Until I had a yearning to do more.

To do that "more" would mean to leave the job, leave the house, leave Montague. It was the impossible ambition, the crazy idea, the asinine daydream. I tried to stuff it away.

+ + +

There was another impossible ambition, a crazy idea, an asinine daydream which had plagued me since age eleven. This one was so impossible that I could only dream around it, never directly upon it.

Eventually, it was a dream that became a malady, which tried to kill me. To survive it, I had to confront it.

I had already addressed the previous aspiration. Though it meant shelving my priorities list, I had done the right thing. I had found my niche in life. I once again was, as I had thought earlier, set for life.

Until I wasn't.

Until I had to address the malady which now was trying to kill me. And leave the work I loved. And leave the town I loved. And leave the people I loved. And risk losing the family I loved.

And leave even more. Leave the unthinkable.

Leave the male that I was.

Acknowledgement

Few people know that Julie was a journalist before she ran heavy equipment with her dad and then became a tax preparer. She received her bachelor's degree in journalism at the University of Iowa. Thus, when I finished my second big edit of the book and she said, "I'd like to read it," I should have known what was coming.

I said, "I don't want you to be my editor. You're my wife. It would be too hard to have you edit my work." In typical Julie fashion, she let my concerns go unanswered and began reading.

And editing.

She was on the couch. I saw her marking and writing and turning the pages very slowly. I asked, "Are you making notes on every page?" She sweetly replied, "Yes." I fretted.

We sat at the dining room table. Immediately, I had a hard time with how much Xing and word changing she had done. She reminded me that she was a veteran of this stuff. I calmed down. She proceeded.

I knew I had my editor.

Before the book got to Julie, I emailed the first draft to two friends. Thank you to Barb Reese for reading it. Barb's feedback, which included this dandy remark, "I only put it down at night because I had to go to sleep," was vital in motivating me to keep going.

Thank you to Sandy Havel for proofing it for errors and grammatical concerns. I won't tell you how many pages of goofs Sandy caught! Sandy's first words after finishing the book were, "You need to be on Oprah." More important encouragement.

After I went through Sandy's notes, I did a hard edit on the book and then printed it. That's when Julie took over. The adage goes that a man who acts as his own lawyer has a fool for a client, and one might think there is application to his wife acting as editor. But, here's the thing about Julie. She has this marvelous ability to act objectively toward me. I already knew it, from the years of her hearing my sermons and the feedback she provided.

My only other experience with an editor was for my 2016 article in Indianapolis Monthly magazine. As I found him to smooth out that article, Julie did so in every chapter of the book. She removed the chaff. She corrected grammar. She made great suggestions for packing better punches. When we debated things, I almost always went with her suggestion.

Thank you, My Heart, for giving my writing a professional shine.

When we arrived at the final draft, we asked two of Julie's friends to read it, seeking their reactions and insights. Thank you, Tahira Damon and Jill Schroeder for the generous giving of your time and helpful feedback.

When I was ready for a book cover, I did not hesitate to turn to my son, Alex. He'd shown some inspiring work on various personal projects, including music album covers. I explained my idea to him. A few hours later, he emailed his first draft. I was sold. Julie loved it. Thank you, Alex, for a cover which achieves what I wanted for the book.

+ + +

I kept these thanks to those who helped with the book because I could not imagine doing a proper job of acknowledging all the people in my life who have blessed me.

We are the sum of all the parts of our lives, and every person and experience make us who we are and got us where we arrived. I pray that you all know the deep love and profound gratitude I have for you all.

1

In the beginning

I was born Gregory John Eilers, in the spring of 1957, to John and Floye (nee Vogel), their third son and fourth child.

I am from Montague, Michigan. When your hometown numbers 2,300 citizens, a town of 50,000 qualifies as the big city, which is how I saw Muskegon, the county seat of Muskegon County. Muskegon had the hospitals, so I was born in the big city, twenty minutes south of home.

Montague is a West Michigan town in the lower peninsula. If you hold up your right hand, palm facing you, you are looking at our map: the Michigan Mitten. To find Montague, eye the spot below your pinkie.

Montague is bordered on the north and west by countryside, and on the east and south by White Lake. The lake flows five miles west where it empties into Lake Michigan.

Where I grew up was small town, Midwest America, the kind of place where people say that everyone knows each other and looks out for each other. Indeed, they did and they did.

Before being wed to Dad, Mom had a short marriage with Lowell "Pike" Omness. Only a year into their life together, Pike succumbed to cancer. Pike and Dad had grown up north of Montague, farm boys on the gently rolling hills of Claybanks Township. Making many visits to the farm as a kid to see Grandma Eilers, then as an adult going out to the farm's beech tree woods for deer hunting, this land grabbed my heart. I thought I would retire in Claybanks.

Dad was a pallbearer at Pike's funeral. As an adult, a favorite joke of mine was, "Nice job, Dad, picking up a chick at her husband's funeral." Of course, it was not crass like that, but it did follow that John began dating the now-available woman with the unique first name of Floye, a name she often despised, especially when she was called Flo or Floyd.

When they married, John and Floye rented a small apartment in Montague, the upstairs of a two-story house. Four blocks away, Dad began building the house in which he lived until he died. What began as a two-bedroom bungalow soon was expanded to four, because the family was growing quickly. Dad cut a hole in the center of the back wall, turned the initial kids' bedroom into a dining room, connecting it to the kitchen by removing the wall between the two rooms, and neatly placed three bedrooms in a row across the back of the house.

My folks were now set for my two younger brothers to arrive, one the next year and the other four years after that. 4931 Wilcox Street was as much The Eilers as the people who dwelled there.

My folks were devout Roman Catholics. Whenever we whined about our names, as in "Why didn't you name me such-and-such?" Mom replied, "We gave you kids good saints' names. James Frederick. Thomas Joseph. Susan Mary. Gregory John. David Louis. Mark William." She recited our names with appropriate reverence. We dropped our appeals.

As my firstborn would never enjoy the growing-up years of a splendid home, such was the case for my parents' first. When Jim was an infant in 1952, he contracted both whooping cough and encephalitis. The doctor improperly medicated Jim, damaging his brain and leaving him unable to speak or walk. He suffered seizures. They said he would only live to be a young boy.

Jim was in need of a tremendous amount of care. Nineteen months after Jim, Mom bore Tom. Sue came along a very quick eleven months after Tom. Mom then had two miscarriages. One day, I would learn that those miscarriages likely altered the course of my life.

When Jim was turning five, Mom was pregnant with me. Here is how

Mom would speak of those days: "With Greg coming, I knew that I would not be able to care for Jimmy and three other children. John and I made the hardest decision of our lives, to sign Jim over to be a ward of the state. The day we did that was the worst day of my life. I felt like a terrible mother."

When I was a child, it seemed exactly the thing my parents had to do. When I became a father, and I buried my firstborn, I finally understood the pain, the loss which is unique to parents.

Jim was first placed in Coldwater, a few hours south and east of home. By the time I can remember making the trip, Jim had been moved a bit closer, but still was two hours away. We made the trip about every other month to Fort Custer, the former army base near Battle Creek, which after World War II had been converted into a home for the disabled.

The residents at Fort Custer were those often "put away," many of whom society had dubbed "monstrosities." They were deformed. Wheelchair-bound. With too-large heads, or severe Down Syndrome, or deaf and blind. Some could talk, but mostly they made noises, which, to a young kid, sounded monstrous.

I recall one fellow, who could talk and was mobile, who always dressed in the manner of the gas station attendants of the day. He freaked me out for awhile with his chatter, but finally became a friend. He would visit with us in the yard, where we set out our lunch on a picnic table. We tossed a ball with each other.

All he wanted was to have friends. We became his friends.

These visits to Fort Custer stand as the initial impression in my life. First, our parents taught us that Jim, and every resident, was a human being, beloved by God, no different from us, and we were not better than them. Second, we simply got used to being around people who were different from us. We learned they were not going to hurt us; quite the opposite, they only wanted friendship. Affection. To be noticed. Human beings, indeed; not monsters.

I became comfortable around them. As a result, I grew to be a person who was comfortable with anyone and everyone. I grew in compassion and empathy. This would serve me well in every phase of my life.

In the mid 1970s, Muskegon County built a facility appropriate for Jim's needs. Now, he would be near home, only a half-hour away. After a few years in that facility, he was moved into a group home, in North Muskegon, where he still lives. Despite the dire predictions about Jim's longevity, not only is he still with us, having made it well into his sixties, but he has also enjoyed a good life.

For practical purposes growing up, Tom was my oldest sibling and oldest brother. Sue was my only sister. Because of the spread of years between Sue and me, Dave, Mark and I were dubbed "the little boys."

Life on Wilcox Street was grand! Dad served as Montague's Chief of Police—he had joined the police force after returning from serving in the US Army in World War II—and Mom was the consummate housewife—there was no "stay at home mom" language in the 1960s. My folks were set: job, house, family.

In his mid-thirties, Dad had an itch to do more. He was offered and accepted the job of city manager for the city of Hart, a half hour nearer the base of the pinkie. Two months into my second-grade year, we pulled up stakes and settled into the Oceana county seat, a town only slightly smaller than Montague.

My folks sold our house to a young couple just starting out. They sold it on a land contract, meaning Dad and Mom still had control of it. That would come in handy four years later.

We rented a house on Main Street. Hart's downtown was a block to the west. The neighborhood kids were a block to the east. Hart Lake was in our backyard. We five kids had just landed in heaven.

My father was not one to play ball with us kids, but he generously gave his time by taking us fishing, patiently helping us with tangled lines and fish that swallowed the hook, and surely ruining many an outing for himself by looking out for us.

We could not afford a boat. The owner of the bait shop had a sunken row boat. He told Dad he could have it. Dad resurrected it from its three-feet-of-water grave and generously lathered it with tar. He dubbed her The Mayflower. We made many a fishing hole pilgrimage in her.

I never thought myself a particularly introspective kid, but I recall thinking that Hart felt like a vacation. Everything was good. School was a breeze. Friends and activities were aplenty. My parents made a wonderful home and life for us kids. The only things I feared were our spooky basement and the occasional wrath of brother Tom.

All vacations come to an end. After four years, when I was eleven and entering the sixth grade, we moved back to Montague, Dad having tired of city politics and now working for the Muskegon County Road Commission. As I grew into my teen years and adulthood, the vacation-like feel of Hart deepened. I often pined for those days—a young boy at play without a care in the world. If only my life continued just as during the Hart years, before the unwanted desire made its home in me.

We moved back to Montague and back into our house. This action was so natural that I did not question it. I thought, "Of course, we moved back into our house. It's our house. Dad built it." It was only when I was in high school that I learned how unusual was our return to Wilcox Street, and the perfect timing it took for us to do so.

The young couple were divorcing. They were glad that my folks would take the house back. As an adult, I would ask Dad about it. "How did that happen, exactly?" With a chuckle, he replied, "We were damn lucky, that's how it happened."

I re-entered Montague public school. I thought I would pick up where I left off, with the same friends as in second grade. I was wrong. Not only would I move on from grade school to middle school, but my friends had also moved on. They were still there, but they had formed new bonds.

Thankfully, making new friends came easily. Some lasted through the rest of my school days. A few remain to this day.

It was in sixth grade that the mysterious thing began, the thing that I would never be able to shake, the unwanted desire that would occupy my thoughts every single day of the rest of my life, until I was forced to address it head on.

A sixth-grader cannot possibly know that something like this would eventually be a life-changer. At first, and for many years, this new thing was at times comforting, at times a nuisance, and always troublesome.

Finally, forty-five years after it began, it was making demands. It wanted my life.

2

School years and girl fears

In Hart, our house had three bedrooms, two for us five kids. Sue, being the only girl, had the tiny one to herself. Thankfully, the other was huge, and in it was housed all four of us boys.

Back in our old Montague house, we had four bedrooms, three for us kids. Sue would again get the smallest one to herself, while we boys were paired in the ones that flanked hers. Oldest, Tom, was matched up with youngest, Mark, to share a queen-sized bed. Dave, only fourteen months younger than me, and I had the trundle beds, sort of a half-bunk bed where the top one isn't as high as a bunk and the lower one's foot slides under, forming an L.

It's a good thing Dave and I didn't share a bed. He slept like a corpse. He would lie on his back, tucking in the blankets around himself and, it seemed, never moving. Ever. All night long.

Me? I slept as if I were riding the Tilt-A-Whirl. I began on my stomach. I turned to my side. Then to the other. Now try the back. Back to the stomach. Round and round I went. The trundle beds spared Dave his sleep and surely kept us from fighting.

In Hart, my sleep was troubled with my being scared. I always thought there was a monster under my bed. I would fall asleep with my head under the covers, as if they provided castle-wall-like protection. Indeed, they must have; those monsters never got me.

Now, back in Montague, and eleven years old, I no longer feared monsters under my bed. In their place was the visitor which would refuse to leave, which would become the monster I could neither outrun nor outgrow. No covers could protect me.

In sixth grade, I finally noticed girls. I saw how they were different from boys. I liked their prettiness. What they wore. Their hair. How their behavior was different from boys.

There were two girls in my sixth-grade class who caught my eye. They fit everything I admired in a girl. They were cute, and nice, and friendly, and dressed attractively.

I found myself imagining that I could make myself look like either of them. We could stand side-by-side and no one could tell the difference, and everyone marveled. I was so happy about this. I put myself to sleep every night with this thought.

I have one memory before this. It was a year or so earlier when we were at a family gathering of my mom's side of the family. All of the boys were playing outside, but I remained in the house. I found the girls' play more to my liking. And safer. The boys, some older and some younger, seemed wild. And frightening.

Grandma Vogel said, "Greg, why aren't you out playing with the boys?" Here is what I heard: "Greg, go outside. Your behavior is wrong."

I went outside. Intimidated by the way the boys played, I kept my distance. I learned to adapt, but mostly stayed away from boys who were too rough. I hung around with guys who were fun and goofy and into sports.

A year or so later, when I began having the fantasies of being a girl, I knew I had to keep it a deep secret. Even more, I had to conform to boy behavior, so my outward life was boy, boy, boy. Baseball. Football. Basketball.

I wasn't faking it. I loved sports. I loved running. I loved the challenges which sports provided—catching a sideline pass, running down a fly ball, sinking a tough basket.

Two more things happened, which stayed with me through my formative years. First, I knew that I liked girls in a manner that, even though I didn't yet know the word, was heterosexual. Second, I knew that I wanted to be with the girls as a girl. It was a confounding mixture which made me in awe of girls so much that if I had a romantic interest in one I was petrified to be in her presence or talk to her.

Decades later, I would learn that my desire for, and fear of, girls was typical of those who would eventually suffer gender dysphoria. In my fifties, I would come to learn so many things about myself which finally would help me understand why I was the way I was in my youth.

It was sometime in the three years of middle school that I took up the mantra that I would chant to myself thousands of times, even after I married and had kids. In frustration over how I felt, I would lament, "All I want in life is to be a girl." Almost immediately, I would correct myself: "Come on, Greg. You want way more than that. You want to be married. To have kids. Besides, you can't be a girl."

I would leave the moment and try to forget it. Until the next time. Often later that same day.

So troubled was I about my intense desire to be a girl, and so seriously did I take everything I heard in church and weekly religion classes, which Mom made us attend all the way through high school, I experienced great guilt. Oil and water mix easier than devout Roman Catholicism and gender confusion.

In my sophomore year of high school, my falling-asleep routine changed from my fantasies to distress over my eternal fate. I became convinced I was going to be damned forever.

I would go to bed, say my prayers, and then ponder eternity in hell. All of the biblical imagery. The fire. The brimstone. The gnashing of teeth.

The aloneness was horrifying.

I would tell myself that the horror would have to end eventually because everything comes to an end—the school year, summer vacation, the agonizing wait for Christmas Day. But then I would remember that hell is eternal. I would lament, "And it will be one more day. Then one more day. Then one more day ..."

Because I was doomed, I would stop at that point and resume my fantasies. I followed that routine, every night, that entire school year.

My desire to play sports and not date girls made me appear as a classic late bloomer. Even more, I was slow to grow. The odds were that I would grow tall. Dad was 6'3". Tom, now a graduate and having joined the Navy, matched Dad's height. As a high school freshman, I was 5'1", and one of the shortest in my class.

In fifth grade, I took up Dad's trombone and joined band. In sixth grade, the Montague move saw me shift instruments, from trombone to bass for concert band and tuba for marching. I was a sight wearing the tuba for marching band, the instrument consuming scrawny me. My home-room teacher, Mr. Kemp, dubbed me "The Little Bighorn." Everyone laughed and I loved it. I was the cut-up. I learned to milk it. I was a natural entertainer.

I marched that tuba with the zeal of the guy who dots the I in OHIO at Buckeyes' football games.

The band room was shaped like a bowl and the bass players sat in the elevated top row. I had an easy view of the clarinet section. Junior year, a freshman girl was one of the clarinetists. She was brunette. I found her gorgeous. I was infatuated.

Early in my senior year, I knew I had to ask her out. I had not yet asked out a girl. I was scared stiff of the thought of it, and could not imagine knowing what to do on a date. Even so, I simply had to ask her out, had to let her know my feelings.

On a Wednesday night, I mustered every last bit of my courage and called her. I was earthquake-quality shaking. There was nothing I would say in that conversation that would make anyone want to go out with me.

I didn't need to worry. The call was over in seconds.

"Hi. This is Greg Eilers. You know, from band. I play tuba."

"Oh. Uh huh."

"I was wondering if you would want to go to a movie on Friday."

"Sorry, I have to wash my hair that night."

"Oh. Uh. Okay. Bye."

Hanging up the phone in relief, I felt more spared than rejected.

I never again talked with her. I didn't need to worry about making eye contact with her in band or in the hallways. She never once looked my way.

By senior year, I finally had sprouted. I grew a full twelve inches by graduation, and even added one more inch the next year so that I wound up at 6'2". I had grown in other ways. During my junior year, I found gainful employment. The job would result in a friendship that grew quickly, deepened into our being best friends, and continues to this day.

Montague had two drug stores. A few years earlier, sister Sue began working at Lipka Drug, on the south corner of downtown. In January 1974 I was hired at Todd Pharmacy on the other end of the block. I was initially hired to clean at night. Soon, I was learning checkout and stocking shelves.

It's a wonder that I got the job. I handled that phone call about as well as when I phoned for the date. Jim Todd, one of the owners, called me about the application I'd submitted, and asked if I wanted the job. "I guess so." "You guess so? You applied for a job here. Do you want to work here or not?" "Yes, I do. I want the job."

Tim Todd was Jim's nephew. I knew of him, but he was elusive to me. Not only was he a grade ahead, he also was outgoing where I was shy, popular where I had a small circle of friends, and a natural in public where I was deathly afraid of speaking to a group.

Todd Pharmacy brought us together. Tim and I share many personality traits. He is gentle, kind, and goofy. While he sees politics and our shared Christian faith more liberally, from the beginning we were able to discuss these things respectfully. And we both love the Detroit Tigers.

As we moved through adulthood, we would see each other through every stage of life, some of them tremendously tough and tragic. After Tim went away to college and then became a teacher, we never again lived in the same town. He returned to Montague, to teach in our high school, the year after I left. He's still there.

Though Tim and I shared everything, I kept my terrible secret from him. As many times as I felt guilty holding back, I could never picture myself telling him that I wanted to be a girl. Surely, he would find me queer. Surely, he would reject me. Surely, I would never tell him.

He knew I was, outwardly at least, a regular guy interested in girls, but terribly shy. He knew of a girl in my class who would go to senior prom with me, so he challenged me to ask her.

Early in my senior year, Mom and I made a bet. She was sure I would go on a date before I graduated, and I was sure I would not. I never told her about my one feeble attempt to make a date.

As prom neared, Tim told me that Lori, who was one of the prettiest, most popular girls in my class, would be my date to prom if I asked her. Though I had the guarantee, I could not imagine myself with her—oh, I was interested in her!—or even going to prom. The whole thing—prom, pretty girl—scared me into nervous worry. I let the chance slip away.

A week before graduation, Tim and I planned to go to a movie on a Saturday night. I was the dutiful Catholic boy, who went to Mass every Saturday evening, so I could open the drugstore Sunday morning.

After Mass I walked the two blocks to Tim's house, expecting him to drive us to Muskegon for the movie. He said, "Let's pretend that we have dates." "What? Why?" "Just play along. It will be good experience." "Sure. Let's do it," remembering how we commonly did goofy things, such as the time we threw an imaginary football around the parking lot of a favorite hangout.

So we opened doors, ushered our "dates" into the car, made appropriate conversation with them and, as we drove the next several blocks, giggled like idiots.

We had to drive through Montague, cross White River, and go through Whitehall to get to the freeway to Muskegon. As we were leaving Montague, Tim made an incorrect turn. "Where are we going?" "Just wait." "What do you mean, 'Just wait'?" "Just wait."

I got nervous. Within a block, I gulped, "This is the way to Lori's house." The prom girl.

Tim said nothing.

We turned into Lori's driveway. "Timmmm!!!!!" He assured me all would be fine.

Out bounded Lori and another girl, a classmate who also worked at Todd Pharmacy. We drove to Muskegon. Somehow, scared to death though I was, I managed small talk. I was scared to death.

Did I mention I was scared to death?

I was scared to death.

We went to "Lenny," the bio-pic of the late comic Lenny Bruce. Dustin Hoffman starred, so it had to be a good movie, right?

We were nicely settled in when Valerie Perrine's character got into a lesbian love scene with ... I have no idea who the other woman was because I am quite sure my red cheeks puffed so large my eyes were forced shut. I thought, "Lori will never, ever go out with me again after this."

Did I mention that Lori's father was the pastor at Montague's Lutheran Church of the Missouri Synod, which is a traditional, conservative branch of Lutherans? Oh, this was rich! I was doomed! The Catholic kid who took the pastor's daughter to a dirty movie.

Despite my earnest concerns, I did not suffer a fatal heart attack, nor did any trouble brew because of the movie. We headed to a favorite Muskegon pizza joint, The Village Inn.

Though my *scared to death* had eased to *this is fun but I sure will be glad to get home*, I do not recall being all that chatty during the ride back to Montague. The girls were. Tim probably was, that bon vivant. He always was cool with the chicks. As he was on stage. And in whatever he did.

I hated him.

Truth be told? I wanted to be like him. It would be awhile before I was.

As for my bet with Mom, she argued that I had, indeed, had a date before I graduated, while I argued that I never would have had Tim not arranged it. We agreed to disagree. She continued to allow me at the supper table so, in the long run, I won.

As for Lori, I managed to ask her out, all by myself. She thought I'd known I was going on a date that first evening, and felt bad about the trick. We ended up dating all summer. She went away to college, which strained our relationship. By early the next year we fizzled.

She was a wonderful first girlfriend. She would one day become a good friend.

3

Marriage and children

As I moved through high school, my desire to be a girl intensified. Getting into my teenage years also made me a bit more daring.

I longed to wear female clothes. I waited a year too long to be able to fit into my sister's things. In my junior year of high school, I had sprouted enough that my forays into her closet found every item too small. What to do?

Mom's clothes seemed forbidden. She was my mother, for Pete's sake. Even so, I found myself digging through the dirty clothes for things to try on, the hamper being in the safety of the bathroom. Then, when I had the rare occasion of being in the house by myself, I hit her dresser and closet.

Mom was average height but large. Though her things didn't fit right, I could get into them. It was wonderful. I would live at home until I was twenty-two, when I got married. Mom's clothes were my refuge.

And I never got caught. This continues to blow my mind. Only once was there a close call, when a brother came home before I expected. On that occasion, I was able to hide in my room and when all was clear get the clothes back into Mom's bedroom.

Free and clear as far as anyone finding out, I was desperately caught in the trap of being a guy who wanted to be a girl. I longed to date—after Lori, I would take out a few girls—but I really wanted to get married. I wanted to have kids before I ever was interested in dating.

14

I graduated high school in 1975. I had no idea what I wanted to do, but almost everyone who didn't go away to college, or have the armed forces or a job lined up, enrolled at Muskegon Community College, so I did, too. Having no direction, I had no interest in my classes. By the end of the second semester, with a GPA under 2.00 and told I was on academic suspension, I dropped out. I went to work full time at Todd's for a year, then for six months at a candy and tobacco wholesaler in Muskegon. Hating the thirty-five minute drive to and from work, I grabbed an opening at the iron foundry in Montague, a three-minute drive from home.

I loathed everything about the foundry. The building was old and ugly. It wasn't heated, so on winter mornings you froze until the two iron furnaces picked up heads of steam. By afternoon, it was hotter than midday at the equator. When we poured iron, which I did during the months I was a mold maker, the heat rising from the ladle was almost unbearable. Add to the heat the black sand used for forming the molds. It got into your skin—to speak nothing of what was happening in our lungs—leaving every pore looking as if it were a blackhead.

This place was as opposite to me as it could be. I hated the work—pure, physical labor. Since it was the best money I ever made, and my job prospects were nil, I stuck it out. I learned the value of hard, hot, sweaty labor. I went from being a skinny kid to a well-built adult.

And I found a girl.

Kim entered my world because of her friend, who was interested in my buddy. Brian and I were in a bowling league, and they visited the lanes so that Kim's friend could try to get near to mine. Brian wasn't interested, but she persisted.

Thanksgiving evening, Brian and I went to a movie. The girls learned of it, found us, and sat with us. Kim, who had not warmed up to me at all the several times the girls visited the bowling alley, remained cool. As we chatted before the movie, she shushed me. "You're so loud." I also knew she felt I was too demonstrative, from comments at the lanes. After nailing a strike led me to do a happy dance, I heard, "You're a show-off."

After the movie we went to a disco. This was 1978. Discos were all the rage, even in Muskegon, Michigan. The four of us sat in the kaleidoscope-light-drenched room enjoying one Bee Gees hit after another, when Barry Manilow's "Copacabana" came on. I casually remarked, "I have every Barry Manilow album."

Kim turned toward me. Barry Manilow changed everything. I became a person worth Kim's attention. Now we were chatting up a storm. I wound up driving her home. We sat in the driveway of her house and talked and talked.

I asked her out. Soon we were in love, with talk of marriage. In April, we were officially engaged. We were married in December 1979.

Before we married, there were two things to conquer. Kim went to a Nazarene church. I was Catholic. We both were devout, but we could not see our becoming a family and going to separate churches. She said she would not become a Catholic, and Nazarene seemed too big a stretch for me. We resolved that we needed to find our own congregation. Therefore, after Easter, we planned to visit every church in the area which we found a compromise.

I asked my good friend Rick Hughes to take me to his Lutheran Church—the same church where Lori's dad had been pastor but, worry not, he had moved on and so had Lori. I liked the service because of its similarity to the Mass, and the pastor preached an excellent sermon. I took Kim the next week. She, too, found it a good thing. I asked, "Where shall we go next Sunday?" Her surprising reply was, "Let's just go here for awhile and see what we think."

We never visited another congregation. Our wedding was held in her church. As soon as we were married we took the pastor's instruction class to join the Lutheran congregation, which we did the spring after we married.

About that time, Kim became pregnant. I wanted to start a family soon, but she preferred to wait a few years. She was only nineteen, and had zipped her way through a college secretarial program, graduating a week before we got married. When she got pregnant, she had only just begun a good job. Late in her pregnancy she quit the job and would be a stay-at-home mom.

I haven't forgotten about the other thing I had to conquer before we got married. I could not rope Kim into a union without her knowing my terrible secret. I needed to tell her before we were engaged.

On the Ides of March, we sat face to face on her parents' living room floor. It was a near-impossible task for me to stop hemming and hawing and get the words out, "Kim, I'm a transvestite."

"What is that? You like to wear women's clothes?" "Yes."

This troubled her, but she listened to how it affected me. She loved me and this was not too big to fracture that love. She was interested in learning more. Over the next couple of years, she tried to allow it into our relationship. For many years, she would once again give it a try. I could never ask for more than the effort she made. Now that I know how many women drop their guys on the spot when they admit to being a crossdresser, or when the secret is discovered, I give Kim all the credit for trying her best.

She would allow me to keep a box of clothes, which I hid away, and dress occasionally when she was away or had gone to bed. That is how the rest of our twenty-one year marriage went. Ultimately, it would be the wedge which kept us from celebrating more anniversaries.

Before we marked our first anniversary, Kim was one month away from delivering our first child.

+ + +

It was early evening, January 13, and Kim was timing her contractions. We did not want to be premature about going to the hospital, but it was a half hour away in Muskegon and we didn't want to wait too long either.

I was watching Happy Days, anticipating Laverne & Shirley. As the first of the two 1950s sitcoms was wrapping up, Kim announced, "We need to go." Laverne and Shirley would have to Schlemiel and Schlimazel on their own.

As first-time labors go, Kim's was typical, yet Kim was anything but. She rode the waves of spasms with quiet dignity; I mostly spent the time reading the newspaper. We heard another mother in the room next door not having such success. She was just plain screaming. Kim didn't utter a peep. She never would, in all five of her labors. I would tell her she was a horse. It sounded like a compliment in my head, but I found myself falling all over myself trying to explain what I meant. I went back to reading the paper.

Labor went into and through the night. I stood by with my encouragements, but felt as useful as snow boots in a swimming pool.

Just after 5:00 a.m., the big moment arrived. Kim pushed. I watched in fascination, standing right over her so I didn't miss a thing.

The top of our child's head appeared. And out popped his entire little person.

"It's a boy!"

And he was perfect.

And I bawled louder than he.

We rejoiced. We placed calls to our parents. We debated whether we should name him Gregory Johnathan (my middle name is John, so we would not make him a Junior), or Johnathan Gregory. We decided that we wanted him to have his own name, so Johnathan it was.

Kim needed to rest, so I drove home to shower, make phone calls, and catch breakfast at my folks'. In the early afternoon, Mom and I headed to the hospital.

After enjoying our first visit as a little family, I readied to head back to Montague with Mom. Johnathan had been taken back to the nursery. We stopped for a final look.

I peered in at my boy. I hesitated to speak. I was immediately scared. I did not want to be scared.

Me, voice cracking: "Mom, he's breathing hard."

Mom, calmly: "Go get a nurse."

I would not make it back to Montague that day.

I was sitting with Kim when a doctor entered. He told us they had cultured Johnathan to learn what infected him. It could be this, or that, or any number of things. Every one of them scared us. Our joyous day was now the worst of our lives.

Despite not yet knowing what had overcome our son, he needed to be taken from Muskegon to Grand Rapids, forty minutes further from

18

Montague, to Butterworth Hospital and its neonatal ICU.

Having just given birth, they did not allow Kim to travel. She was desperate to be with her child, but heeded their advice and stayed put. Her folks drove me to Grand Rapids. It was now well into the evening.

Soon after arriving at Butterworth, we learned that Johnathan had a strep infection. Though Kim had not been ill, they determined that the germ resided in the birth canal. Had he been delivered via C-section …

It does no good to play that game.

Where an older child or adult gets only a sore throat, the strep infection overwhelmed Johnathan's little body. The doctor stated they had Christian nurses who will baptize, should a baby appear near death, and would I want that? "Yes. Thank you," spoke my wavering voice. "Please, don't let it come to that," pleaded my heart.

I had been up for forty hours. Thankfully, some good friends lived near the hospital. I would sleep there. An hour before midnight, we sat at their kitchen table. As I ate a sandwich, I babbled like a drunkard. Sleep-deprived, I was daffy.

The next morning, I was on the phone with Mom when I heard a beep I'd never heard before. The hospital was breaking into the line. A nurse spoke. "Please, come now."

Johnathan lived twenty-seven hours. He had been baptized.

The hospital allowed Kim to be discharged. I had not yet talked with her. Her folks brought her to Grand Rapids. Entering the ICU, fear and hope battled to occupy her face as she pleaded, "How is my baby?" "Oh, Kim …"

A nurse suggested it would be helpful to hold Johnathan. We did. It was. But he was cold. And still. And everything in our world was wrong. We headed home with the weight of a thousand worlds crushing us.

We rebounded as best we could. Eager for a child, Kim wanted to try again even before her doctor gave her the go-ahead to be sexually active. Soon she was again pregnant.

We welcomed Erin before the year was out. This provided me with a fun bit of trivia, which I bet I've told a hundred times. We had two children in the same calendar year, yet did not have twins. While I have known folks, including my own, to have two kids closer than twelve months, I've yet to meet any who did it in the same calendar year.

Second daughter Jaclyn arrived two years later, in 1983. Another son, Addison, graced us in 1986. Finally, Alexander rounded out our gang in 1989.

+ + +

What do you count as the best experiences or events of your life? I have been blessed with a host of situations which could vie for number one, but just as no tune has been able to top my favorite pop song—from 1975, 10cc's silly "I'm Not In Love"—nothing has been able to knock off the leader board the births of my five children.

The birth of one's first is a momentous event. Because we lost Johnathan, the coming of child number two was huge. After Kim once again wowed me with her ability to ride out every contraction, Erin's appearance brought the same tears of joy as ten months and ten days earlier. Sadly, Erin would soon be sick.

I had returned to Montague to make the joyous phone calls when Kim rang our house. "Greg, Erin is breathing hard. The doctor thinks she might have the same thing Johnathan had." This news was almost too much. I was on fire with anger. As hard as I could, I threw pillows at the wall of the baby's bedroom.

Once again, we were headed to Butterworth. This time, Muskegon General immediately discharged Kim so that she could be with her baby.

Thankfully, we had a better diagnosis for Erin. She had wet lung pneumonia, not uncommon in newborns. She rallied and in a week we brought her home. Finally, baby cries came from the bedroom which Kim, using her artistic abilities, had brightened with a huge hot air balloon, filled with animal characters, painted on the largest wall.

Being two-for-two with sick newborns, Kim's doctor put her on amoxicillin the final week of her pregnancy for Jackie. When Jackie popped her head into the world, after the doctor coolly had Kim stop pushing because the cord was around the baby's neck, emotion once again overcame me. While Jackie would not get sick, the antibiotic had been hard on her little body. She became jaundiced, and her need to stay under a bili light for a few days meant that for the third time we would not be taking our baby home when Kim was discharged.

With two healthy girls, we were happy but aching for a boy. One winter Sunday afternoon, as we sat at my folks' kitchen table with our usual game of cards underway, the conversation turned to kids and I was filled with a troubling ache. I cried out, "What if I never get a son?" and bawled. Soon, Kim would be carrying our fourth child and it would be a boy, our Addison.

Sadly, my mom did not get to see him. In March, just as she was to begin chemotherapy for bone cancer, she suffered heart failure and died. She was only sixty-two, but over her life she had experienced enough illness and heartache and grief for ten people. With great sadness, we laid her to rest. With great thankfulness, we rejoiced in all she was for us.

We now followed a familiar pattern. Kim was on amoxicillin. As with Erin and Jackie, her labor was induced. We calmly made our way to Muskegon, Kim quietly and stoically endured labor and safely delivered the baby, he became jaundiced and needed a few days under a bili light, and we went home empty-handed.

In the 1980s, we did not know what sex our children would be. The doctor's call, "It's a boy!" brought me a fresh and profound wave of joyous tears. Addison was healthy. I was happy. We were a family of five. Wonderful!

Kim again desired to have a child and I readily agreed. Soon, we were counting down the months to her delivering.

At the first four births, I broke down in tears and elation every time. As Kim labored and I read the newspaper, I paused and pondered how I was going to react this time. I was genuinely concerned that number five would feel routine. We had run the gamut of experiences. How could this one ever be special?

It came time for Kim to push. I stood by, absorbed in the scene as always, but with no emotion on the horizon. I thought, "If I don't react as I did with the other kids, will I be cheating this one?" I was troubled at the thought.

I need not have been troubled. The appearance of Alexander, child number five and son number three, was phenomenal—a one-of-a-kind appearance when I had feared the mundane. Nearly thirty years later, I can still feel the wad of emotion well in the pit of my stomach, rocket with ferocity through my chest and into my face, landing in my forehead with a stabbing pain.

No pain was ever so welcomed. I exploded in tears of joy over the birth of our son, and with elation that he would not be cheated by his dad. And, you better believe it, I have told him this story many times.

In the coming years, I would be with young people in many settings. Something would come up which led me to tell them that they will never know how deeply their parents love them until they have children of their own. It is a unique love. A love so profound that you would die for them in a heartbeat.

That is why I place the births of my five children at the top of the best experiences in life.

+ + +

Over these years, I noticed how the Lord was using the tragedy of Johnathan's short life for my good. I believed Johnathan was with the Lord and, trusting in the promised resurrection to glory because of Jesus Christ's own death and resurrection, I could say that his short life was not a tragedy since all life is too short and should not end in death, and in our resurrected bodies we will live in the heaven-on-earth paradise, forever.

My trust in Christ was growing deep and wide. I became involved at church. Only a couple of years into being a Lutheran, I would watch my pastor in the pulpit and think, "I would like doing that."

For almost a decade, that would be my next great secret: I wanted to be a minister. But how could that ever happen with four young children and my needing so much schooling? Besides, we finally had everything we needed and wanted.

How could I give it all up?

4

Growing into myself

Johnathan's death and Erin's illness were not the only struggles Kim and I faced in the first years of marriage. The recession of the early 1980s was especially hard on Michigan. The auto industry was in a slump. Our state took the brunt of it. I was laid off from the foundry for two long stretches.

Our first house, a tiny two bedroom bungalow on the north side of Montague, was a rent-to-own. Our folks helped us make ends meet. Dad was good friends with the owner of the house, who would display lots of grace when we had trouble making the rent.

During the job layoffs, I shingled a roof, painted a house, worked a summer on my friend's dairy farm, shoveled snow from roofs, picked apples for my uncle, and put in some hours at Todd Pharmacy.

It was November 1982 and Erin was nearing her first birthday. I was painting the inside of Montague's post office. I was barely half done when my friend Rick, who took me to the Lutheran church that first time, called with a job offer.

Rick had finished college and taken over his grandfather's company. Located on the edge of Montague, MasterTag manufactured plastic labels for flowering annuals and perennials, vegetables, house plants, and shrubs and trees. Business was booming and they needed one more person on the night shift to print the black-and-white plant label known as Quick Tag, aptly named because it could be printed and shipped in short order.

The Quick Tag department had two small printers, run by hand. The hours would be 6:00 p.m. to 6:00 a.m. This shift would be manned only with Bill, the department head, and me. Because the ink would dry out if the printers were idle, during breaks and lunches one person would have to run both printers. Picture Lucy and Vivian trying to keep up with the chocolates coming down the conveyor belt.

Rick could only offer work for a handful of weeks, not wanting to make a promise of longer employment. I had the post office to finish. I didn't want to ditch them. I was ready to thank Rick and turn him down. I'm not sure what changed my mind, but I took him up on his offer.

It was one of the most important decisions I ever made.

After two months printing Quick Tag, that department's orders were slowing down for the season. The shipping department was buzzing, so I was moved there. By late spring, shipping slowed down because of the seasonal nature of plant growing, but now the office was booming with paperwork that backed up when everyone was busy with order taking and customer service calls.

I was appointed to file invoices. As mundane as that work was, it had me in the office, and I was able to observe how things were done. As summer settled in and work slowed down, I was thankful that they found me a useful employee and didn't want to lose me to another job by laying me off, so they found all the work for me they could.

I began working the phones. As summer settled in, so did overdue customers' bills. I was asked if I would like to call these customers, to prompt their paying up. As my head said, "No way!" my mouth said, "Sure, I'll do it." Trepidation turned into getting comfortable with it, which turned into excelling at it.

By autumn, it was obvious I was good with customers. I now had all of the customer service calls (read that: problems with orders) sent my way and was made credit manager. The company was growing quickly. The next year, I was named their first customer service manager, and two part-time workers were hired to work under my direction.

Soon, we needed more. A proper marketing director was hired. I was placed under him and over an expanded department. We divided the country into four territories, hired four full-time employees to take orders, handle customer service, and make outgoing sales calls. I was their boss and, over the next few years, I was put in charge of the yearly catalog, was the liaison to our Canadian and British distributors, traveled the country working trade shows, and got to work with and understand every facet of the company, from horticulture to printing to packaging to shipping to sales to marketing.

I had the job that I had in mind when I was younger. I saw myself at MasterTag the rest of my working life. I saw opportunities and growth galore before me. I still didn't make a lot of money, but that was coming and I had good benefits. I worked in my hometown. I was married, had four children, and by now owned a home. I had met all of my life's goals. I liked the people with whom I worked. I enjoyed my work.

Until I didn't.

+ + +

In the 1980s, I began performing in Montague's music and comedy revue, "Showboat." Jim Todd, co-owner of the drugstore and Tim's uncle, needed a new front man for a nautical themed foursome called "deckhands," to replace a retiring member. The deckhands told jokes and performed skits between the musical and dance numbers.

When Jim asked me, it was akin to my being asked to call delinquent customers at work, where my mouth overruled my head. He challenged me by saying, "You can be funny around the store, but I bet you couldn't do it on stage," and walked away. I was miffed, knowing exactly what he was up to.

I sucked it up and told Jim I wanted to give it a shot.

I learned the value of practice, practice, practice. That lesson was cemented at MasterTag, where I would eventually speak in front of groups of customers. Intense rehearsal made me confident for the task, and I proceeded to perform well.

I was terribly nervous the first ten minutes of my first show. Those jitters would be the last time in my life I would experience anything more than the typical low-level nerves one has when faced with a new or big situation.

I fell in love with performing. Over the course of four Showboats, I became head deckhand, in charge of all jokes and skit writing. I would play the roles no one else wanted, including a wacky waitress in a diner skit. I relished dressing for and playing the part of a woman, and had a heyday exaggerating her in voice and mannerisms. I also wrote and performed a seven-minute stand-up routine, and it was well-received.

I had a taste for more. I wanted to stretch my wings. I booked myself at an open mic night at a Grand Rapids comedy club. I bombed, but I had confidence that I would learn how to play to the crowd. I really wanted to take a stab at being a professional comic.

I continued to daydream about becoming a Lutheran minister. Both jobs—comic and pastor—seemed impossible. Besides, I had all I wanted—marriage and kids and job and house and it all was wrapped up in Montague. I was set. Why would I mess with that?

I didn't tell Kim.

It was now the summer of 1990 and I was miserable with myself. I had grown completely discontent with my job at MasterTag. Nothing changed there, but everything changed inside of me. Inner growth. Personal expectations. Desires for so much more.

That summer our children were aged eight, six, four, and one. A few months earlier, in my yearly performance review at work, I decided my job had changed enough that my value to the company had exploded. I asked for a fifty-percent raise. I hoped I might get as much as twenty percent, never dreaming I would get the whole thing. I got the whole thing. Finally, after years of struggling, we had a good income and could catch up on our debt.

Yet, I wasn't happy. Even more, there still was no way I was going to tell Kim.

Become a stand-up comic? Are you kidding? Most never make it. Many, who sort of make it, never make any money and are never home. The few who make it—well, the odds are the same as a high-school sports star succeeding in the pros. Infinitesimal.

Become a minister? Are you kidding? I first had to finish college, which I barely started after high school with two poorly-undertaken semesters at community college. Then, I would face four years of seminary. And that would mean what? No income and lots of expense, which would add to the pile of debt we were finally getting out from under. And, when I received my first church, my starting income would surely be less than I was currently earning at MasterTag.

None of it seemed doable, achievable, reasonable. I was set for life, so why couldn't I just be content with all I had?

I still never said a word to Kim as I continued to stew about it. I never would have said a word to Kim, unless …

Enter a marvelous lady named Jan Pobursky. (For years, I could not reveal Jan's name, only her good deed, so humble was she who insisted, "A good deed isn't a good deed if you tell people you did it." I only began using her name after she fell asleep in Christ.) Jan was a member of our church, recently widowed when her beloved Al succumbed to heart disease. In September of 1990, she asked if she could come over and talk with Kim and me.

We sat at our dining room table as Jan laid out her idea. She told us how she thought I would make a good pastor. With Al gone and being set financially, she was going to take a job as church custodian and save the money. Then, if I ever decided to go to seminary, she would help us with a monthly check.

Kim and I were speechless and I was in trouble. Because of Jan's vision and generous heart, I was going to have to tell Kim what was going on inside of me.

Jan left. Kim and I sat at the dining room table. I mustered the gumption to spill the beans. Kim was shocked. Sure, she was sad that I had not told her what I was feeling, but she understood how I thought it could never happen. She agreed; we were set for life just as we were.

Every day, we would talk about the possibility of pulling up stakes and heading for seminary. One day, we were sure we could do it; the next day, we were not. One day, we knew the Lord would provide; the following day, we were filled with doubt.

Round and round we went. By November, we were talked out. Exhausted. I was prayed out, so I found myself praying the same prayer every day: show me your will, Lord, and help me to follow it.

I thought my prayer would never be answered.

Enter December 7, a Friday, and the day I have come to call my own Pearl Harbor Day because of the bomb-like news dropped on me from out of nowhere. My boss told me that he and the company owner Rick would like to see me about an exciting proposition. I could not imagine what they had in mind.

Our company had a division in England, started in the early 1980s. It never got off the ground as Rick had hoped, and its general manager had recently left. I already was the connection to our British branch, even having visited there on a nine-day trip, and I had experience and knowledge of MasterTag unlike any other employee.

Barely comfortable in our chairs, Rick opened the payload doors. "Greg, we want to send you and your whole family to England, for what we think will be two years, to teach the British branch how we do business and finally get them off the ground. After you get things in place and the right people hired, we will bring you home and plug you back in here."

Rarely am I at a loss for words. I was at a loss for words. I was equal parts flattered and scared to death. After Rick and my boss fleshed out the proposition, they told me to go home and talk with Kim. I left, but I could not imagine this conversation with Kim, especially with our three months of struggling whether or not to leave home and head to the seminary.

Kim received my news with amusement and real interest. We had a Christmas dinner planned that evening at Dad and Louise's, widower Dad having married widow Louise six months after Mom died. All of my siblings and spouses would be there, and now we didn't want to go. We did go, but our minds were in England. We made eyes at each other the entire evening.

We got home from Dad's and talked some more, late into the night, until we were worn out. It really felt possible, that we could do more than head out of state to seminary, but actually leave the country. We both were shocked that we were taking seriously this job offer.

The next morning, I headed outside to do my usual winter Saturday chore: throw firewood into the basement. Dad had convinced us to put in a wood-burning furnace when we bought our house and remodeled it before moving in, in 1984. He and I spent many winter Saturdays cutting trees, splitting the wood and stacking it so it would be seasoned for the next winter. Behind our house was a shed, at the rear of our back yard, filled with the fruits of our labor.

Though it was only December 8, we already had a foot of snow on the ground. This being West Michigan, in the snow belt near the coast of Lake Michigan, that was not uncommon. I went outside around 9:00. I beat a new path in the forty-foot trek from shed to basement window, loading my arms with five or six pieces of wood at a time and dropping them into the basement through the removed windowpane.

A half hour into the chore, I realized something. The entire time I was carrying wood I was only thinking about one thing, and it wasn't going to England.

On the way back to the shed, at the halfway mark, I stopped in the path. I felt the cold. I looked over the shed into the clear blue sky. I wouldn't move.

I realized I had not spent a moment thinking about England, but only about the seminary. That's when it hit me.

These are the words I spoke to myself: "I am going to the seminary and everything is going to be just fine."

In that moment, every question, every concern, every fear was gone. It didn't matter that nothing had been answered; everything had been answered. The Lord would provide. I knew it just as sure as I knew anything.

The Lord had answered my prayer, and I knew His will for me.

I returned to my chore, using the balance of the time to figure out how to tell Kim.

A half hour later, I found her in the living room. I knelt by her chair. I said, "I know what I am supposed to do, and it isn't England." I explained what I just experienced and wrapped it up, "This one time, please, we have to do what I am saying and trust that it will work out." She replied, slowly and calmly, "Okay. I'm scared, but okay."

Boy, were Rick and my boss surprised, not to mention my family and friends. I told Rick, who was my fellow Lutheran, that the Lord had used him to get me to recognize I had to do something, that staying home in my current job was not an option. By then, stand-up comedy was no longer part of the mix. It was either England or the ministry—and it wasn't England.

The sense I had that December day came true. I never had a single moment of doubt. The Lord paved the way for everything to work out. Even with new hardships that would come along, my confidence never wavered.

But what of my crossdressing, my desire to be a female? Everything continually deepened. My desire to be a woman was my daily visitor. But now I had the perfect plan to put this out of my life. I would go to seminary, immerse myself in the Bible and learning theology, and crowd out all thoughts of being a woman.

I burned my box of clothes before heading to seminary. It was a cleansing moment. I was confident in my decision. For the first time, I had hopes of closing the door to my visitor and of being a regular guy—and a Christian minister at that.

5

To the ministry

Big things had to take place before we could pull up stakes for Concordia Theological Seminary in Fort Wayne, Indiana. Thankfully, two things shortened my path by a few years. Because I was older than thirty-two, the seminary would accept life experience toward two years of college, so long as I had two years of education in liberal arts. I never dreamed any of the classes I had taken my first year at community college would be counted, but several were.

In January 1991 I returned to the place where, April 23, 1976, I declared I would never set foot again. Because I was still working full time at MasterTag, and I needed to get adjusted to college, I signed up for only one class, sociology.

I did well. I was ready for full time. Thankfully, Rick supported me. I was able to work part time, about thirty hours a week, though I had to go back to punching a clock as an hourly employee. That was fine with me. Who else could continue to do his job and have his company pay his tuition as part of their continuing education program, as he looked for and hired his replacement and was still a year and a half from leaving the company? The thought that Rick would do that for me still floors me.

We would need to sell our house. We did that in but a moment. My younger brother was in search of a place. He bought it.

Because we had remodeled it ourselves, having purchased a rundown

31

place for a pittance, we had a small mortgage. We were able to pay that off and have enough savings that, with Jan's monthly $500 gift, we didn't have to get a loan the first two years of seminary. Third year seminary students serve a vicarage—an internship in a congregation—and the small salary and provided housing kept us from anything but an average amount of credit card debt. It was only in the fourth year, back at seminary, that we needed to borrow $10,000 to make it. Kim added some cash by cleaning houses and I did chores for some elderly folks. Jan's faithful, monthly gift kept coming.

From the spring semester of 1991 through the spring semester of 1992, I was a full-time college student at good ol' Muskegon Community College, and kept working thirty hours a week at MasterTag. I took as many night classes as I could. I finally made it as a college student. I was focused. My grades improved as I grasped how to write papers and study for tests. My final semester, I pulled down a perfect, at-one-time unimaginable, 4.00 grade point average.

I was ready for seminary.

I left my job the end of May 1992. I entered seminary in June.

The drive from Montague to the Fort Wayne school was three and half hours. I had to study Greek, the language of the New Testament, before I could take regular classes. They offered it during the summer as a ten-week course. As I studied Greek, my family remained in Montague. I drove home every Friday for the weekend.

I enjoyed living in the dorm and getting to know the guys, but I didn't like the time apart from my wife and kids. The days of the internet and easy communication were still several years off. Greek successfully under my belt, I was ready for regular classes and we prepared to move at the end of August.

With an assortment of pick-ups and a van, we packed them up and headed south. The way Dad's truck was stacked reminded me of the opening sequence from The Beverly Hillbillies and Granny Clampett sitting on her rocker-cum-throne. We were a sight.

Our little family adapted well. I made loads of friends and had my studies, and the kids connected with new pals in school, but Kim was in a foreign place with no friends. One day in the first weeks she lamented, "Even at the grocery store, I don't see the same people twice." She hung in there, eventually made friends with other wives, and busied herself with the work of a mother and homemaker, both things at which she excelled.

We were flourishing. The third year, in June 1994, we headed to a country church outside the small town of Osage in north-central Iowa for my vicarage. We had as dandy a year as a family could hope. We didn't want to leave, but the fourth year of seminary called and we returned to Fort Wayne in August 1995.

Vicarage is placed in the third year so the student gains practical experience, and many fourth-year classes are designed to make use of the acquired practical knowledge to further prepare for first calls into the ministry. My vicarage definitely prepared me—I preached every week, officiated two funerals, and was privileged to baptize two elementary-school-aged kids. I loved the fourth year of seminary. In May 1996 I was ready to graduate and, in June, head to serve my new congregation.

And my plan to conquer my desire to be a female had worked out just as I had planned, right? Not even close. It worked for a week, then I found myself pining to be a woman with the same intensity I had before burning my box of clothes.

Eventually, Kim would allow me to buy a few things, and keep them and my dressing hidden. Guilt rose up and I tossed them out. As the shampoo bottle suggests, I would wash, rinse, and repeat.

One November, Kim went on a shopping trip with her friends from back home, and she left the kids with her parents. Having the house to myself, I bought a full outfit and cheap wig. I spent the entire weekend in those clothes. I hid them away, but once again the guilt got to me and I placed them in the garbage.

I had to figure out how to beat this thing. I constantly repented to the Lord, asking His forgiveness and seeking His strength. Soon, I would be a minister. Being a pastor and a crossdresser did not mix.

+ + +

I received my call to a dual parish, Trinity Lutheran Church in Guttenberg, Iowa, and St. Paul Lutheran Church in McGregor, nineteen miles to the north. The parsonage was in Guttenberg. Both towns are on the Mississippi. The road between them climbs the bluff out of Guttenberg, follows the ridge until forced down into a hollow, then climbs back to the top—wash, ridge, repeat—causing the drive to take twenty-five to thirty minutes. The longest straight and flat stretch was nine-tenths of a mile.

Yes, I clocked it. Many times.

The two small congregations, in the two small towns, were a perfect fit. They received me well as their pastor. Kim found her way as a new minister's wife, getting busy in both congregations. The kids quickly made friends and did well in school.

My guilt over desiring to be a female intensified. Now, I felt that I had to hide it from Kim. I was so blind to what my longing to be female was doing to me, I did not recognize the depths of Kim's aching. I had never been good at initiating romance—I would only learn why many years later—and this strained our intimacy. And this strained everything.

Even as we continued to get along well, she grew discontent. She could be easily riled, especially by the kids. And so I thought it was all about the kids. It really was all about us. About me. I would not learn this until October 2013.

Kim was going to turn forty in September 2000. Hindsight tells me that this was weighing on her. She was contemplating her age and her future.

In the spring, she began making comments, indicating her frustration with our marriage. She never went to the heart of the matter. No matter, I should have gotten it. We resolved to be more purposeful about doing things together; you know, date your mate.

Then the craziest thing happened and, surely, it set into motion her decision to divorce me.

Kim had attended Thursday morning Bible class at the McGregor congregation, then headed across the Mississippi, to Prairie du Chien, Wisconsin, for some shopping. Overnight, it had rained hard. The ground was drenched.

One crosses from Prairie du Chien into Iowa at Marquette, then follows the highway south to McGregor before hitting the bluffs and hollows on the way to Guttenberg. The road south from Marquette runs with the river immediately on one side and the steep bluff on the other.

Kim was tooling along at the forty-five speed limit. She could have no idea that, ahead atop the bluff, a forty-foot-tall, fourteen-inch-in-diameter tree had pulled loose from its rain-drenched mooring. Down the side of the bluff it came, landing squarely across the windshield of our van then, miraculously as Kim hit the brakes, bouncing off and landing on the highway.

Kim was both shaken and stirred, but not physically injured. The van would need significant repairs, but would be fixed. Kim's heart, however, was forever altered. Her comments to me, displaying her frustration, increased in intensity.

One day, as we drove home from eating out, she asked a question, a query which turned out to be the one question I had to answer correctly, and I did not. She asked me not to forget about her as I grew more and more into the work of the ministry. A year later, she would tell me that my answer did not cut it for her. It was too casual. I remember it well: "Of course, I won't."

And, of course, it wasn't the ministry that was the problem. The ministry never was. I was not overly busy. It was a just-right level of work, not too many evening meetings, and plenty of time for family. But my heart was not deeply enough into Kim. She needed more. I can now say that she needed only what she deserved. She deserved for me to be her husband, to love her as a husband is supposed to love his wife, with all his heart—emotionally and romantically.

We always were the best of friends, but the other two never stacked up and were fading further into the shadows.

The summer of 2000, Kim was making plans to leave me. Coincidentally, a friend from the church of her youth, a guy she dated casually, was divorcing his wife. I never learned the specifics, but one of them contacted the other, and Randy visited.

Kim grew distant. One day, she took one of the kids to Dubuque, forty-five miles south, to a doctor's appointment. She did not say goodbye. That evening, I brought it up. She finally spilled her heart.

She intended to leave me. She wanted to explore a relationship with Randy.

I begged. I pleaded. We talked and talked. Thankfully, we had always talked through things and could do so in a respectable manner, and it paid off. By January 2001 she was determined to stay in our marriage and set Randy aside.

Then everything changed.

6

Divorce

There are two events in this book of which I write most delicately, my divorce being the first. While I provide enough detail so as to make sense of things, I am not some tell-all author with an agenda to scathe those about whom he writes. Quite the opposite, I am not interested in burning bridges. I long to remain in good relationships with these very people, one of whom is my former wife who has been tremendously gracious to me so that we regained a marvelous friendship.

I write with no anger or bitterness. Though I hurt deeply by being divorced, I eventually grasped why Kim could not remain in our marriage. I am very thankful to Kim for everything she was to me and for me, and continues to be.

Through the tumultuous second half of 2000, I never could get Kim to tell me the details, why she wanted out of the marriage. The most I could coax from her was, "I just don't love you anymore," and "It's been growing for many years." It would be thirteen years before she would be able to give voice to what was behind it. By then, it would make perfect sense.

That, in 2000, she never provided explanation, and that she began a relationship with Randy before she divorced me, kept me in the ministry.

In a new church, a new town, and back in Michigan.

While in my first parish, I received calls to be the pastor at other churches. In the Lutheran church, a congregation without a minister will extend a "call" (the spiritual version of a job offer) to another pastor. That pastor, after prayerful deliberation, decides to accept or decline the call. One of the churches calling me was in Iowa, the second in Wisconsin, and the third in Michigan—only two hours from Montague. In each case, I knew I was to decline the call and remain in Guttenberg and McGregor.

Those three calls all came the summer of 1999, after I had been in the ministry three years. The fourth would come on January 14, 2001, the anniversary of Johnathan's birth and a day on which I always reflect on the events of his short life.

The pastor who was assisting St. John Lutheran Church in Port Hope (where the dickens is that?), Michigan phoned me the day after Christmas to inform me I was on their call list and to see if I were available to receive a call. After a friendly chat, Ken and I hung up and I had a revelation: St. John is going to call me and I am going to say yes to this one.

I don't put much stock in premonitions. My mom was famous for hers. Almost none of them came to pass, so I rarely listen to people who begin declarations with, "I feel that so-and-so is going to happen."

But I felt that so-and-so was going to happen. Three weeks later, it came to pass.

January 14 was a Sunday. The next Sunday, after telling my two congregations in Iowa of my new call, I headed to Michigan, a six-hundred-mile, ten-hour drive, for a visit to St. John. I was greeted by various church leaders, given a tour of the church and parsonage and town, then ushered into the church's K-8 school lunchroom for a meet-and-greet with whomever wanted to come.

They packed the place. Fifty or so came out on a wintry evening to check out the prospective pastor. I gave them the basic intro, told them some of the things I was sure they wanted to know about how I would minister, and then fielded questions. I love an audience and played to them as if I were the stand-up comic of earlier desire. They laughed. I liked them. They warmed up to me.

It grew late in the day. On the drive out of town, to get a couple hours under my belt before finding a hotel room, I phoned Kim. I felt strongly about the call, but felt queasy about the town. Village, really. About three hundred residents. The streets concluding at Third Street. A public school with barely over one hundred students from kindergarten through 12.

And in the deep snow of January it looked dumpy.

It seemed to have nothing going for it. On what I would come to dub "The Hangnail of the Thumb," it was a corner of Michigan you didn't go through, because only Lake Huron is on the other side. It was a half hour from the nearest Walmart, and eighty minutes from the nearest mall. Surely, this had something to do with several previous pastors declining St. John's call.

The call process used by Lutherans is interesting. At first, the congregation holds all the cards. The district in which the congregation resides provides the church a list of ministers who are seen as good fits for the congregation. Working from this list, the congregation reads the pastors' resumes, discusses them, prays, and votes, narrowing the list until one wins the majority.

The congregation immediately telephones the pastor they've called. They then mail him the call documents, which include information about the salary and benefit package, a description of their expectations of the pastor, and demographics about their parish and community. When they issue their call to a minister, they pass the cards to that man, who now has full control over whether he stays where he is or goes to the new place.

I immediately informed my two Iowa congregations of my call to Port Hope. Many members expressed their opinion. Most of them were of the "please don't go" variety, but a couple of folks recognized it might be time for me to move on and, certainly this church, being larger than the two congregations in Iowa combined, along with having a K-8 school, would provide new and exciting challenges.

Was I ready for the larger church and the school? That weighed on me, but I was confident. Plus, a fresh restart for Kim and me sounded good.

So there I was, driving away from my visit, Kim on the phone, me detailing each part of my day. She summarized things nicely, noting how the important aspects about the call—the people and the work—were positive, and only my first impression of the village negative. And, even more, she was sure that once we lived in the town we would love it just as we loved everywhere we had lived, from the small towns of Montague and Guttenberg, to the city of Fort Wayne, to the country on vicarage.

Because I would remain pastor in Iowa only through the month of February, what to do with the kids and school until June? Erin had graduated from high school, but Jackie was a senior; it would not be fair to move her. Addison was a freshman and Alex was in sixth grade.

A discussion with church leaders quickly resolved the problem: Kim and the kids could remain in the Guttenberg parsonage the rest of the school year. Erin decided to accompany me to Michigan.

Were Kim and I concerned about our newly rekindled dedication to our marriage? Indeed we were. We were determined to talk often on the phone, and one make the trip to the other as often as possible, which she did by attending my installation on March 4, and a couple of weeks later I did to see Jackie and Addison in the school's spring musical.

While I did not at that time, and do not now, believe that Kim had in mind our being apart as opportunity to revive thinking about Randy, was she put into a weakened position? Easily, any person could be.

I should have known something was brewing in March when we were speaking on the phone one Sunday afternoon. It was NCAA basketball tournament time. The Michigan State Spartans were about to start. I told her I wanted to get going, to watch the game. I offended her.

She never talked with me the same after that, but she also did not speak of leaving me or seeing a lawyer.

On April 2, I received a letter from Kim. "Dear Greg: I have filed for divorce …"

Appeals to Kim changed nothing. No, she was not interested in counseling. Yes, she had resumed her relationship with Randy.

The end of May brought Jackie's high school graduation. We all were together in Guttenberg. We treated each other respectfully, we even were friendly, but it was terribly uncomfortable. Many church members and friends visited for Jackie's open house; we tried to make it as festive as it possibly could be.

Where I list the births of my five children as the best experiences of my life, I easily count this day as one in which I carry great guilt. Jackie tied with two classmates at the head of her class. Even if she had not attained this lofty status, she deserved way better than the lousy situation her parents had her in. Though she has forgiven me, I continue to mourn that Jackie did not receive the fabulous day she had earned.

The next day, Kim headed to Indiana with Randy, while I set out to finish packing the house. Several folks had brought trucks from Port Hope in February to move enough stuff so Erin and I had furniture in our new home. A different mix of them now returned to Guttenberg to finish the job.

Erin and Jackie had summer plans, so only Add, Alex and I went to Port Hope, with the girls joining us later. Jackie soon would head to college; thus our new household most often consisted of three of the kids and me.

Me, trying to do my job, take care of my kids, and fight off depression. I suffered terribly from being rejected.

Divorced pastors and biblically-traditional, culturally-conservative church denominations, which is what my church body, the Lutheran Church—Missouri Synod (LCMS) is, don't go together. But, because of the circumstances of my divorce, I received little concern from the synod and did not even face a suspension.

Even so, I was concerned how my new congregation would view this. First, I offered my resignation to Ken, the pastor who helped with the call. He said it was not necessary. Despite that, I felt I needed to offer it to the congregational leadership. They were not interested. Finally, in late April at the church meeting at which I made public my divorce, I said, "I have been told that I do not need to resign, but if you find me a disgrace I will do so immediately."

Not only did they not reject me, they threw their support behind me. After the meeting, I never heard nicer words than those spoken to me by Ken: "I don't know what you have done here in your first two months, but these people really love you."

I was pleased to have a job, and a house, and stability for my kids. I continued to fight depression. I didn't want to go to bed at night. I didn't want to get up in the morning. I wanted to eat ice cream every evening.

I ate a lot of ice cream.

It was now June. I was lonely. I was sad. I continued to experience an extremely deep sense of rejection, which was exacerbated by Kim's not providing me specifics why she was no longer happy with me. I continued to be blind to how it was my fault.

I have always had a regular routine of prayer. I added a Psalm verse to my daily petitions, turning it into an appeal. The verse is the final one from Psalm 27, which I prayed this way: "Lord, I am waiting for you. I am strong in your love and I take heart in all of your promises, but I am hurting so badly. Please, don't make me wait too long to feel better."

7

Enter Julie

Living in a rural area, our church's members were spread out. Because we were in a small village, services such as hospitals and nursing homes were miles away in larger towns.

A regular routine for Lutheran ministers is to provide Holy Communion, generally monthly, to those who are homebound or residing in nursing homes, and to make regular visits to those hospitalized. Driving a half hour, one way, to see folks was common. Even more, living in the Hangnail of the Thumb of Michigan, the larger hospitals—in Port Huron, Bay City, and Saginaw—were drives of seventy to ninety minutes each way.

I burned a lot of time on the road.

I listened to a lot of talk radio.

Dr. Laura Schlessinger had a popular show in those days. I liked her take on many things—"It's not an engagement unless there's a ring AND a date!"—so she had my ear when she told a man, who was sole parent of a couple of young kids and was wondering about dating, that his job was to focus on his children, to forget about women until he got them through high school.

It was the summer of 2001. Addison would be going into his sophomore year of high school and Alex into seventh grade. Their mother was seven hours away. I made up my mind that Dr. Laura's advice for that father-caller was wisdom for me.

One day in early August, the boys and I were making the half-hour drive into Bad Axe. (How's that for a town name? Legend has it that, in the 1800s, an axe was buried in a tree, marking a boundary. The axe had a broken handle, hence, it was bad. When the spot became a town, Bad Axe stuck.) I told the boys I had made a decision, that my job was to take care of them, that I was not going to date, not even look at women, until I got them through high school.

Before the week was out, I wished I'd kept my big trap shut.

For the reason, I need to back up fourteen months. In the summer of 2000, still in Iowa, I had an article on the topic of husbands published in a church magazine.

Julie Johnson lived on the opposite side of Iowa, tucked into the northwest corner of the state near the tiny village of Ocheyedan (o CHEE den). Julie, a lifelong Lutheran in the Missouri Synod, subscribed to the magazine. She wrote me a letter, seeking insight into the doctrine of marriage. Addressing her concerns and fleshing out our Lutheran theology, we exchanged three letters each. In my final letter, I told her about an email magazine—this was pre-blog days—in which I posted sermons and other items of interest. She subscribed. That was that.

In May 2001 I wrote briefly about my divorce, and the struggle of now being a single parent and the new pastor in a new town. I stressed how we need to reflect on the tough times of our lives, and see all of the hurdles the Lord helped us jump so we do not despair but are able to see we will jump the tough ones we now are facing. Julie emailed saying how she felt for me, commenting that she sensed she knew me through our letters and the email magazine. We began to write emails, about one a week. Julie admitted that she, too, was going through a divorce. We used email to lift up each other.

By August, we found ourselves writing in a more personal way. We were like a couple of middle schoolers who pass notes through their friends. Neither of us wanted to go too far in what we wrote. We both were divorcing. We lived nearly one thousand miles apart. We had never met in person, or spoken on the phone, or seen each other's picture—social media was still a few years off. Yet, we were dropping hints that our fondness was growing quickly and deeply.

I had meant what I told my boys, yet I found myself thinking about Julie a lot, once again the tuba-playing boy gazing across the band room at the cute clarinet-playing girl.

Things progressed. Fast. Only days after talking to the boys, I was sensing that Julie was falling for me as I was for her. I decided to take the plunge. On August 21, I wrote her a long email telling her I was finding myself attracted to her, that I hoped I wasn't stepping out of bounds for saying so, and that if she lived in Port Hope I would ask her out. I sent the email in the morning. Awaiting her reply, I sweated out the day.

And the night.

I knew she was putting in long work days, so the logical side of me could understand the lack of reply. The emotional side of me was a wreck.

Late the next morning, I got her reply. A long one. A wonderful one. Her subject line was, "Wow." Her opening words were, "Um, wow."

She said she was feeling all the same things I had expressed.

We began emailing with great frequency. She worked outside and not near her computer, but I was often in my office and prone to popping into my email. I sent her as many as twenty a day, mostly of the "I can't wait to see you in person" variety.

I asked if I could phone her, but she didn't want to talk until she had my picture. We put photos in the snail mail.

In our emails, we were already talking about marriage. We didn't want to date for dating's sake—besides, how does one date a person who lives fifteen hours away?—but only wanted to pursue a permanent relationship. We were in love before we ever spoke on the phone or saw each other's picture. We knew we would be married simply by our written words.

The fifth day after we opened up to each other, I couldn't stand it any more. I begged her to call me. I knew she had told her parents about me. I found their phone number. I called their house.

I suppose it didn't hurt my cause that I was an LCMS minister and they were lifelong Missouri Synod Lutherans with pastors in the family tree. Score one for the future son-in-law with his mother-in-law-to-be.

When Julie's mom answered the phone, I said, "If I told you this is Greg Eilers, from Port Hope, Michigan, would you know who I was talking about?" She reacted with laughter. Julie arrived as we were chatting. She was grungy from work and hungry, so she quickly ate and showered, and called me back fifteen minutes later.

We talked for three hours. There was no Skype or Facetime in those days, and no cell phones with unlimited talk. In the coming weeks, I nearly went broke paying the phone bill.

That we talked so long is no surprise, but how our first-ever conversation began was one-of-a-kind. Here comes just about the neatest story about my life that I have to tell.

Since it was nine at night, the odds of my office phone ringing were slim. When it rang, I answered: "Julie?"

"Yes," came her lovely voice, the first word I ever heard her speak.

I asked, "Do you have the rest of your life ahead of you?"

She replied, "I do."

I requested, "Will you spend it with me?"

With no hesitation she filled my request: "I will."

The first words I ever spoke to Julie were to ask her to marry me. And she accepted—sight unseen!

Two days later, we received each other's pictures. I was more dazzled than ever. Thankfully, at the sight of me she didn't run away in horror, or change her answer to my proposal.

The only thing left was finally to be in each other's company. With my job and the kids it was hard for me to plan a trip, so Julie would be the one to travel. It was late September before she could head to Port Hope.

As she neared town, I walked outside to wait in the driveway. She pulled in and jumped out. The moment we saw each other, everything came together. My first words to her were, "Welcome home." We kissed as if we had been kissing for months. We hardly said a word. Before we could, I whisked her next door to the church.

I took her to the altar, to stand in the spot where I united couples in marriage. I had hidden a ring on the altar. I grabbed it, returned to her, and repeated our first words.

"Do you have the rest of your life ahead of you?"

"I do."

"Will you spend it with me?"

"I will."

I placed the ring on her finger and we stood there and kissed like a couple of teenagers.

Thankfully, my kids immediately fell in love with Julie, saving me a huge meal of crow.

Because Julie worked with her dad, using heavy equipment to prepare ground for buildings, and digging ponds and the like, she would not be able to move to Michigan until the ground froze. She loved running excavators and scrapers, and anything that falls into the heavy equipment category.

She was able to return to Michigan one more time, in October. Two times, we met halfway, near Chicago, for a day. That was the extent of our dating life. Though we had so little time together, we were rock-solid in our love and affection for each other. We had no doubts about getting married, and soon.

The first of December, I drove to Iowa to retrieve her and brought her back to Port Hope.

On the fifth of December, during the first Wednesday evening service of the Advent season, I announced to the congregation that we were engaged and would not waste any time. Amazingly, no one suggested to us that we were rushing it.

We were married on December 30. I was the first St. John minister to be married while pastor there. Julie's folks and two sisters, and my dad and Louise were there. My best friend, Tim Todd, served as wedding photographer.

The congregation filled the church. Everyone supported us marvelously from day one.

As I fell for Julie, and as my kids fell for Julie, so did the members of St. John. And, as she took a job in the village's convenience store, so did the entire community.

The Lord had answered the prayer of my lonely, rejected heart—"Please, don't make me wait too long"—in mind-numbingly dazzling fashion.

And, in the process, I successfully leaped the one hurdle which I feared would trip up Julie.

8

"It's who you are"

I should have told Julie before she moved to Michigan. It wasn't that I thought, "Once she has moved, it will be harder for her to reject me." No, I didn't think it through in that manner. It simply was that I was afraid to tell her, to hurt her, to hurt us.

But I knew I had to tell her before we got married, just as I had to tell Kim.

Surprisingly, I don't have the date etched in my mind when I told her, but I know it was very soon after she moved to Port Hope. What I do have firmly planted in my memory is where we were sitting—on the floor, legs crossed, on the far end of the living room—and what I said, and how she reacted.

In my fear, I hemmed and hawed and hesitated for minutes, letting her know that it was hard for me to tell her this thing about myself. She remained patient. Finally, I got it out. "I'm a crossdresser. I don't understand why, but I have always had a strong desire to wear women's clothes."

Julie didn't flinch. She asked some questions. I answered them fully. She finally asked the biggest one: "Do you think you will ever want to become a woman?"

"I don't think so," I began. "I want to be your husband. But I know this thing has grown worse over the years, so I don't know how I will feel in the future. But, right now, no, I don't want to be a woman."

Julie didn't flinch. Her attitude that day, and for all of our years, was found

49

in her reaction in that moment. She continued, "I can tell this is part of who you are. I don't know anything about this, so I will want you to tell me about it."

Julie and Kim would have opposing approaches to my gender identity issues. Whatever I say about either of them, I never mean it as criticism to Kim. She worked hard to grasp this, to understand me, to accept that I could not shake this thing. She did better with me than most women who, at the news from their boyfriends, fiances, or husbands, drop them with ferocious swiftness.

Reflecting on my marriage to Kim allows me to see that she was a champ. I was a chump in not being the husband she desired and needed. Julie, however, is built in a manner in which few people are constructed.

Soon, we were shopping for clothes for me. Though I was elated we were doing this, and that Julie was fine with my wearing these things in front of her, guilt was my constant visitor. I didn't want to be this way. I wanted to be a man. Her husband. Free from this insidious desire to be a female.

I always downplayed that. After our initial conversation, I never was completely honest about the level of my need to be female. I tempered how much I enjoyed it when I was dressed in women's things. I did not let on how strong was my longing to be approached and adored and loved as a woman.

The amount I revealed of my secret felt dirty enough. The entirety of it seemed positively filthy.

We settled into a wonderful life. I loved my work as pastor. As I gained experience having a larger congregation and a school, I grew as a minister. Julie and I bonded as a couple exactly as we believed we would. The kids took to her as if she had given birth to them, and she, for never having had children, parented them in a manner which was truly astonishing.

Jackie, in those early days, summed up Julie perfectly and succinctly: "Julie is amiable." Is she ever.

After the kids flew the nest and would phone us, I would joke how a typical conversation would go when I answered the phone. After a quick catch-up on life, I would hear, "Is Julie around?" When she was, their conversations went on until the cows came home to roost.

I never thought people believed me when I told them that the kids loved Julie with no "step" in the "mother." Who is so blessed to have such a lovely bond as this? My family, that's who.

The kids did their growing-up thing. Erin remained home, found work, and also found a guy on a game site on the internet. Jackie graduated college and went to work for her alma mater. The boys graduated high school.

By the fall of 2007, we were empty-nesters. Jackie was married in 2006. Erin had moved to Georgia to be with her guy, and they were united in 2007. The boys moved to West Michigan, near Montague, with Add going to work and Alex to college. In 2010, Add would be married, and in 2013 Alex would follow suit. I was pleased to be able to officiate each wedding.

Then came the grandchildren. Where many young people wait to have children until they get established, often for many years, my kids took the plunge right away. First Jackie, then Erin, then Jackie again, then Add, and Add again, then Alex, then Erin once more gave us seven grandchildren in under eight years.

But, oh! They all lived so far away! Erin was in Georgia, fifteen hours away. Jackie had moved to Indianapolis to get her master's degree and remained there, six hours from us. After West Michigan, first Add, then Alex, headed to Austin, Texas. Finally, Add was back in my home town Montague's sister city, Whitehall, nearly five hours away, and Alex landed in West Virginia, near his wife's parents, a ten-hour trip.

When you are a minister and working every weekend, travel is not easy to plan outside of one's three weeks of vacation each year. I grew lonely for the kids. Thankfully, Julie and I were tight.

After the convenience store, Julie became our church school's secretary, then quickly added a seasonal job as a tax preparer for the Bad Axe H & R Block. After a few years she dropped the secretary job, continually took on a greater role at the Block office, and would work there ten years, until we left Port Hope.

Port of Hope. That was its original name. The story from the 1800s goes that some men were struggling in bad weather and rough waters on

Lake Huron. Before all was lost, they neared land enough to see the natural harbor that lay before them. Making it safely to shore, they dubbed that cove their port of hope.

As the spot became a settlement became a town, the "of" was dropped. Port Hope never grew much larger than it was in the years we lived there, despite its enjoying prosperous endeavors. In the 1800s, it thrived on salt brine taken from the shallow rock layer underground, along with a lumber mill which made boards of the pine trees that littered the landscape, and finally the grain mill and co-op which were kept busy after the land was opened for farming. All around the village were farms, the usual dairy cows and corn and hay fields. The big cash crop in the area? Sugar beets.

Port Hope's citizens took on the character of the village's name. It came to claim for itself the slogan, "The Little Town with the Big Welcome." During my years there, all of us in the village would have to rely on our hopeful nature and welcoming spirit. As with those men in the boat on the rocky waves, Port Hope would be buffeted about fiercely. I often found myself the captain of the teetering and tottering ship.

9

Tragedy town

I came to call myself the Disaster Pastor.

The first tragedy came crashing when I had been St. John's pastor for only three months. The seventh tragedy kidnapped us ten years later. I often include what happened to me as bookends to these seven, with my second personal trial bringing to a conclusion my pastorate after thirteen years (after I had taken to joking that I intended to be their minister until the local funeral home came to pry my dead fingers from the pulpit).

For most of my life, I lived a peaceful existence. My first personal tragedy was Johnathan's death. The second, just as I began in Port Hope, was the death of my marriage.

I now recount, for a number of reasons, the seven tragedies through which I led the folks of Port Hope. First, for as tiny is the village and how rural is the countryside, that we suffered seven in ten years is way out of whack statistically. I would ask my brother pastors of the sixteen other LCMS congregations in the Thumb if they experienced more than one tragedy. I never heard anyone claim as many as three.

Second is the collective nature of the events, and the way they seemed to escalate in severity. Three of them were the stuff of movies.

Third, as I ponder the idea that we humans are the sum of all of our experiences, I would spend a lot of time wondering if what happened to me was brought on by, or at least exacerbated by, being the guy to whom everyone looked to hold together a grieving village.

Holding it together for others, was I unable to hold it together for myself?

On June 8, six-year-old Carly was riding bikes into town with her teenaged uncle, Adam. They were only a block from the village's edge. A block from our church school's playground. Measly yards from where the speed limit drops from fifty-five to twenty-five. A car approached from behind, striking and killing her.

The lethal combination would be an elderly woman who perhaps did not have the vision or reflexes she once had, a young girl who didn't have the experience of an older biker, and a section of road where the shoulder immediately falls off into the ditch.

Adam was fifteen that year. So was my son Addison. They were classmates in one of Port Hope's smallest-ever classes. Their grade began high school numbering seven. Only five would graduate. And, at age thirty, Adam would die suddenly. The Port Hope Class of '04 now numbers 04.

One classmate left short of their senior year. Chelsea, only two years after Carly, became the second tragic death in my Port Hope pastorate. Three weeks shy of starting her senior year, Chelsea was driving home from a friend's when—we never knew why; did she swerve to miss a deer?—she went off the road and so violently entered the ditch that she was thrown out the rear window and left brain dead. I was with her parents when they had the awful task of deciding when to turn off the machines after signing papers to donate Chelsea's organs.

Just over a year later, the third auto death included so much more than the accident. It was the 2004-05 school year. One of our congregation's boys was on the varsity basketball team, which included other boys from our church. Was it tomfoolery or sexual assault, the day the other boys took after Derek in the locker room? The District Attorney decided there was no foul play, just boys being boys. A man, who was on the school board and an outspoken critic of the school leadership, counseled the family. They filed a civil suit against the school and each member of the team.

In a tiny village, the old saying is true. Everyone knows everyone's business. How much more that is the case in a situation such as this, which turned into a mess, folks taking sides. Because we had St. John members on both sides, very often I found myself in the middle.

Soon after they filed the lawsuit, I sat down with the parents and the young man. Derek described the incident. Secretly, I tended to think his teammates meant no harm. Yes, I thought they went overboard, but they intended no malice. I kept this to myself, working to be supportive of the family, yet striving to be supportive of those being sued, many of whom also were my members.

The next Sunday, I preached about the situation. I had let Derek's folks know I was going to do this. The entire family sat very close to the pulpit. As I developed as a minister, I decided that it was best to bring things out into the open, to face them and deal with them, than try to pretend they don't exist and allow folks to whisper about them. That Sunday, I spoke of how there are many aspects involved in the situation, how none of us was there so we should not make judgments, how we should let the case be heard by the court, and how we must treat each other the way we want them to treat us, remembering that we are united in Christ.

We had eight days of relative peace. Halloween night, my phone rang at 11:00 p.m. It was Derek's mother. Her very first words were, "They got him." She sounded as if she had expected it, the way people will comment on a team's victory when they were huge favorites, "Yup, they won."

Derek had died in a one-car accident, going into the ditch on a country road not far from their farm. By, "They got him," she was saying she believed those being sued had rigged his car to break down as he was driving, or that someone ran him off the road.

The police could find no evidence that Derek had been run off the road. A nearby hunter, who also was our church member, had seen Derek's truck and no other. There was no suspicious mechanical failure. The case was closed as an untimely single-car accident.

Not surprisingly, the family did not accept this. Who could blame them? Well, plenty did, but if they had tried to put themselves in the family's shoes they might have grasped how fishy this seemed to the family. I kept my ideas to myself.

The church is always packed for the death of a young person. Derek's was the largest funeral I would ever officiate. The packed pews overflowed to the entryway where folks had to remain standing. We connected a TV in the basement to the camera in the church's balcony, in case we needed it for seating. We did. It was packed primarily by Derek's classmates from neighboring Kinde, the school to which Derek had just transferred.

There were threats that violence might break out, so the police were stationed at the church. In my sermon that day, I pled to those congregated:

Now, to address how we move on from here. It grieves me to feel utterly compelled to speak of the following things in a funeral sermon, so I will frame them in a way to respect Derek's name and give honor to our Lord Jesus Christ.

Derek was a man of peace. He had a friendly smile for everyone. He spoke a kind word. He did not use his tall stature to bully people. He was a teddy bear of a guy.

What would Derek say to the threats that are being made between his former and current classmates? What would Derek say to the allegations that are being tossed about since Monday? What rules your heart these days? Will you let anger control you, or will you control yourself and live in peace?

My dear friends, is it not tragic enough that we are burying this fine boy, today? Do you really think the right thing to do is to make threats to your fellow man that you are going to get even? That you are going to do bodily harm? That making threatening phone calls—even if they are prank calls—is smart? That sending harassing letters, whether signed or anonymous, is pleasing? Do you really think that is going to help? Would you want to be treated in that way? Would that bring Derek back? Would that make his family feel better?

My dear friends, if you want to honor the memory of this man of peace whom we lay to rest, then live as men and women of peace. Each and every one of us needs to make the Golden Rule the rule of our lives, that we will only treat others as we would have them treat us. There is no other behavior which is acceptable.

If there is unlawful behavior after this day, you better know that you will be found and punished to the full extent of the law. That goes for everyone. Especially to you who belong to our church, if you perpetrate evil words or deeds in the coming days, you will have both the law and the Lord to deal with. As far as the Lord goes, you have to deal with Him through me. The time for peace is now.

Yes, the TV news found us. One of the reporters for a Saginaw television station zealously covered the story. I found her to be sensationalizing in how she interviewed the parents in front of the funeral home. When I returned to Port Hope from Derek's wake, I found her, with her news van, at the edge of town. I mustered my gumption and approached her. I explained how torn our little village was. I begged her to tone it down. She hemmed and hawed that she was being responsible. Responsible or not, she was following suit with the sensationalist reporting style of the day.

We remained a village in turmoil for many months. I entertained person after person in my office and on the street, who shared his or her opinion on the matter. My reply was always the same. Keep your cool. Understand that none of us knows all of the details. Remember the Golden Rule.

When I left nearly ten years later, there remained tension. All of the individuals and families involved still live in and around the village, generally avoiding each other. The civil suit was still active, though no action has been reported on it for many years.

The mother of that son had the sad opportunity to reach out to another mother the very next summer, as we were struck with a fourth auto death. An elderly lady blew through a stop sign at over fifty miles an hour, nailing the driver's door of a thirty-year-old mother of three, her infant daughter in the back seat. The mother was immediately killed, while the baby, protected by the car seat, suffered only a few scratches.

Amy was only five hundred feet from her destination, her in-law's house.

At the time of the crash, I was visiting a member in the Harbor Beach hospital, only eight miles south of Port Hope, when another of our members who worked there found me, directing me to a room where the husband and two sisters were awaiting a definite answer whether or not Amy was alive.

Soon after I entered the room, the sheriff's deputy arrived. Amy was dead. Each of the three family members reacted differently.

One denied it: "No. It's not true. She's a fighter. You don't know her."

One got angry: "I hope the bitch who did this dies."

One simply melted into uncontrollable sobbing.

I accompanied the family to the other hospital, in Bad Axe, where Amy's body was. After it was all over, both family and hospital staff told me how I was a rock for the family. At the time, I felt completely underqualified for the moment. Who was I to be the one to whom grieving people looked for strength? And why was I regularly finding myself in this spot?

For months afterward, I ministered to the parents, the son-in-law widower, and the entire family. Some serious issues developed. I was stretched to the limit in my capacity to share God's Word and impart His wisdom so they could go about their daily lives.

That was August 2006. In just over five years we experienced four deaths by car accident. Since we were such a tiny village, I was hopeful that we had played out the string on these things during my time there.

The worst was yet to come. At least we had more than four years to catch our breath. We caught it, then it was sucked out of us with three quick, deep blows.

Blow number one: I got home from church the last Sunday of March 2011 to find my office phone machine blinking, which was a rarity since most folks who call my office would be in church. But not if they were in the hospital.

It was one of our members, the mother of four teenagers. A divorced mom, she and the kids lived with her mother, the kids' grandmother, a woman already familiar with tragedy—a car/train accident that killed two daughters and left her with a lifetime of health issues.

A new hell visited the family. Mom's message was that her youngest child, only fourteen, had delivered a baby the day before, all by herself, in the bathroom of a friend. The boy was born dead, and she, being scared, hid him in a closet. It was only when her older sister saw all of the blood on the floor that the truth came out.

A lot more truth would soon come out.

She thought the baby was born dead. Later, it was determined the baby was born alive, and had breathed on his own for a short time.

Who was the father? The newspaper reported it was a family member who lived in their house. At the same time, her brother was removed from the home and placed in a group home.

Quickly, it was a known secret to everyone in Port Hope who the father was.

That wasn't bad enough. Mom had trouble with social services in the past, losing her kids for a number of months. Social services once again leaped into action. Entering the family home, they found it to be generally uninhabitable. The son who had been taken into custody told authorities they had not had electricity or water for some time.

The county would not let them re-enter the house, except to get some clothes and personal items. They had nowhere to go. The sheriff's deputy requested I go out to the house to offer my support. I called Julie to ask if she were okay with my taking them home with us, since we had plenty of room and they had no money for a hotel room. That evening, they moved in with us. They would stay for two weeks.

The mother had to go to court. Her mother and I attended with her. When the judge was going to immediately remove the remaining children from her, I found myself raising my hand to speak. I was emboldened because it was an informal hearing. The judge recognized me. I explained we were going to have a funeral for the baby in two days, and could he please delay the action until afterward.

He was very considerate. He got the mother and grandmother to promise they would not divulge to the children that they were to be removed from their mother the afternoon after we were done with the funeral and lunch. At their promising this, he turned to me and charged me with seeing to it that no one blabbed. I asked how I could be responsible for what they might say. He was very encouraging that I could do it.

That was a Thursday. The funeral was set for Saturday. On Friday, in our parsonage we celebrated the other son's birthday as if nothing were awry.

The funeral was attended by a few of our loyal members, a few close friends, and the immediate family. I hosted the luncheon at the parsonage.

All went well.

Lunch ended and social services arrived. Realizing what was up, the oldest child tried to run for it. I caught her and held her tightly until she relented. There was great sobbing, promises from Mom of "I'll get you back," and the ensuing, seemingly unending court dates.

Ultimately, Mom lost the kids. By 2014, the two older ones, a daughter and a son, were able to return to her. Of the two younger, the daughter who gave birth was moved to an unknown location. The third youngest, a son, was taken into a good home, not far from Port Hope. During his high school years, I chatted online with him many times. He was always upbeat and sounded well. Indeed, I have had friendly social media contact with every member of the family, right up to the present day, for which I am thankful.

When Thanksgiving arrived, the group home, to which the older son had been remanded, contacted me. They wondered whether we could have him at our place for the holiday, since he had nowhere to go. Of course, we said. After that, he came for Christmas, and then for Memorial Day weekend, and we talked on the phone many times. When he turned eighteen, he was released. He located his mother and went to live near her.

That was the most intense ministering I ever did, especially during the two weeks they lived with us. It was tax season, with Julie working long hours, so I was completely in charge of taking care of everyone. It was good for me. While each day was long and hard, it was fulfilling work. The word "minister" means "to serve." I was blessed in the serving.

Having gone through all of these tragedies, one at a time is enough. But, two days after this punch was delivered came blow number two of 2011.

On Sunday was the call that greeted me after church. On Tuesday was the call that came too early in the morning for me to know the phone's ringing was bringing nothing I wanted to hear.

It was a member, the grandmother of a young man who also was a member, who was a Marine stationed in Afghanistan. Joey had stepped on an IED and first reports were that he had been killed. They were wrong, but that news spread to friends before it was retracted. He was alive, but he had lost a leg. Soon, the correct news came that it was both legs.

For our tiny village, these twin tragedies might as well have been the twin towers of 9/11. By the afternoon of that Tuesday, it was suggested to me to hold a special service at church. It was Lent, so we already had a Wednesday evening service on the schedule. We just happened to have our monthly board of elders meeting that Tuesday, and the group agreed we would hold a special service after our regular Lenten service. Word of mouth and Facebook got the news around in the one-day lead time.

I worked feverishly on a framework for the service. How could I make sense of these two situations? Everyone always wants to know where God is at these times, just as was asked after 9/11. Being the only resident pastor of Port Hope, I was the guy who was supposed to have the answers. To be able to provide comfort. Peace. Hope. Calm.

The Lenten service was twice as full as usual. Even more poured in for the special service, many from town who were not members of our church. The place was packed. The parents and family of the Marine were there. Grandma and one sibling of the young girl were there.

I fashioned a program weaving hymns, Scriptures, explanations, encouragements, and prayers, one round each for both situations. The crowd was attentive, and I believe we struck the right tone.

Joey was a classmate of my youngest, Alex. Joey's and Alex's co-best friend, Shawn, made a trip with Julie and me to see Joey in Washington D. C., at Walter Reed Army Medical Center. There, we were humbled at the sight of many men in various states of limb loss and stages of recovery, and invigorated by their determination to overcome their injuries.

Joey, I am pleased to report, has done good things despite his bad break. And that mother's kids all returned to her. The encouragement I once heard has proven true. We get better.

Before 2011 was out, however, Port Hope would grow worse. The final blow was one not imaginable, a one/two to the gut and the head. Indeed, it was so inconceivable that for months afterward I would mutter, "I can't believe I am the pastor of a person who was murdered."

Rhonda found our church by way of her daughter, whom she had enrolled in our school. Soon, the two of them became regulars in worship. In the summer, I would go out to her house once a week to instruct her in the faith. She joined the church and I baptized her daughter.

At Rhonda's house, I usually saw her husband. I already knew Gary; his entire extended family were part of our church. I officiated the funerals of both of his parents.

Gary had fallen away from church decades earlier. He no longer was a member. He and Rhonda had previous marriages. Gary had no children with his first wife; Rhonda had three, who did not live with them. When Rhonda gave birth to their daughter, Gary was over the moon.

Their marriage was on stable ground for about five years. I never had the opportunity to learn what happened but, by late 2011, they were estranged. By the time I learned of it, she was moving out and, the next day, was nowhere to be seen.

And neither was Gary.

Gary's brother-in-law, a faithful member with whom I was very close, came to my office to tell me that he and his wife were watching the daughter and they had not heard from Gary or Rhonda since the day before. He was afraid Gary was going to do something bad, that Gary had commented if he could not have their daughter under his roof, then neither could Rhonda.

We would learn that Gary had kidnapped Rhonda. When their minivan was found outside a hotel in a small town a few hours south of Port Hope, there was a chain, with a lock on the end, that had been bolted to the floor by the passenger's front seat. One wonders how he chose the town he did, but as I was searching the internet for news stories in the first few hours after we got the news he had shot Rhonda and himself to death, I found a story from the week before in which another man had done the same thing in the same small town.

Coincidence? Maybe. It sure didn't feel like it.

Indeed, this had me hoping against hope that there had been a mix-up in the news, just as we got the wrong report that Joey had been killed when he was still alive. Nope. By mid-afternoon, we received firm news. Both were dead.

I went out to the house of the members with whom the daughter was staying. Soon, Rhonda's mother and step-father were there, along with some of Gary's siblings and other family. I was asked to break the news to the five-year-old, who would never see her parents again in this world.

She and I sat face-to-face on the floor, the family encircling us. Somehow, I found the words that I needed for the terrible moment.

Once again, I would be facing a church packed with grieving family and friends. They would be longing for me to make some sense from this most senseless of acts. Rhonda's two older children were teenagers and the third was a tween. I decided to make good use of that. Here, in part, is how I helped them grasp this tragedy and still apprehend that the Lord is a God of love:

Why does God allow these crimes and tragedies to happen—to happen to Rhonda, and to happen to her children, to her mother, and to everyone to whom Rhonda meant a lot. The easy answer is that we live in a sinful world. That's why bad stuff happens. God doesn't like it any more than we do—in fact, He hates it—but He allows it. That we are sinners is our fault. We know God's commandments. We know the laws of the country. We know how to keep them, and we know how to break them, and God lets us live our lives.

Why does God let us live like this, if it means we will hurt each other? God lets us live like this because He loves us. This takes some explaining.

What do we Americans value the most? We value our freedom. What does a teenager value the most? You, Rhonda's children and your friends, you want to be free to live your lives, right? But, it is at this age that parents become concerned. Teenagers are now smart enough to go out into the world, to drive, to get jobs, to date—you name it. They can do a lot of good—work hard at their education, earn some money, excel in sports, lots of stuff—but they can also get into trouble. They can get hurt.

What are parents to do? I have the solution! Don't let your kids leave home. Place a protective shield over your kids and you never need to worry because nothing bad can ever happen to them, nor can they go off and hurt anyone else.

Now, how would these teenagers feel about their parents? They would hate their parents' guts.

No one, of any age, wants to have his freedom taken away. Just as my parents allowed me to grow up and go out into the world, so I allowed my kids to grow up and go out into the world. You folks equip your kids with knowledge and wisdom, get them an education and some valuable experiences, and then you set them free. And they love you for it.

God works exactly the same way. People always ask why God created Adam and Eve if He knew they would sin and turn this world into the mess that we inherited. God created Adam and Eve out of love, which means He gave them the freedom that we give to our children—a freedom to choose the right way, and a freedom to choose the wrong way.

Think about your own lives. How many times have you chosen the wrong way? Every time you are about to do something wrong, do you want God to stop you? No, you don't want God constantly interfering in your life any more than you want your parents interfering in your life. You want freedom to live. But, if you are going to be free to choose right from wrong, it also means you will be left wide open to other people doing you wrong, as Rhonda was done wrong. Yet, parents will continue to give freedom to their kids in the way that God gives freedom to you and me.

So, to answer the question, how can a loving God allow such terrible things to happen? A loving God gives us freedom. And, because we all do wrong, and are done wrong, God our loving Father, through His Son, Jesus Christ, makes everything right ...

We laid Rhonda to rest, thus laying to rest the tragedies that we would experience together during my pastorate at St. John Evangelical Lutheran Church, Port Hope, Michigan.

And then I came apart at the seams.

10

Frustration mounts

New Year's Day of 2012, I found myself in a mood that was one part frustration, one part anger, and one part every other nasty feeling that could possibly accompany the first two.

Julie noticed that I was surly. Surly is easy to see in me because my nature is easy-going. Upbeat. A spring in my step. A smile and a quick quip always at the ready.

As usual, I tried to dismiss, deny, deflect. She managed to get me to divulge.

My rage emerged like water from a fire hose that was shot from a cannon.

I took with great seriousness my work as a Christian minister. I loved preaching and teaching and calling on the sick and helping wherever and however I was needed. I have always been a goal-oriented person. When I undertook a project, a friendship, a job, I was in it all the way or not at all. I expected results, especially from myself.

Recall that I had announced my divorce when I was only in Port Hope two months, and how the congregation rallied to me, and how that pastor had commented that he didn't know what I had done in my first weeks there but that the people sure did love me.

They sure did love me, and when I so quickly introduced Julie they loved her and us as a couple.

Only six weeks after I announced my divorce we suffered the first tragedy, the death of six-year-old Carly. As I led the congregation through this saddest of times, I needed to show them what their new pastor was made of. I felt good about how I ministered to them. The members confirmed it with their kind words.

With every tragedy came the same compliments. My Sunday sermons, my teaching, the way I ministered to the sick and dying—they found me to do the work of their pastor as well as any.

The faithful remained faithful. The middling members and the less-than-faithful, however, did not move off the dime. They were driving me nuts.

After perhaps five years in Port Hope, I was lamenting to two of our women who worked in the village's bank. One of them said, "Pastor, it might be that we are so laid back that even you can't change us." It felt like a compliment. It was wrapped in resignation. I would repeat the comment many times.

I was not shy to let my members know what the Lord expected of them in their worship and the way they lived their lives. Gossip and excessive drinking were two bugaboos in our community; I addressed them often. Laziness with their dedication to be in worship was a common topic. Living as children of God, showing each other and the world that we were interested in fulfilling the two greatest commandments by how they live—love the Lord your God with all your heart and soul and strength, and love your neighbor as you love yourself—was my ongoing theme.

Nothing ever changed.

On January 1, 2012 all of my frustration and anger ignited. Surely, as over these five weeks I was daily muttering to myself, "I can't believe I am the pastor of someone who was murdered," it seemed this event was the igniter of the flame which turned into an inferno.

For me, it boiled down to this: either I was a failure as a minister or my flock was the most deaf and dumb and blind of sheep.

Julie responded exactly as almost everyone would. You can only do so much. St. John's congregation is no different than almost every other twenty-first century American church. You do your job. You do it well. How the people react is on them, not on you.

Not on me? But I'm a goal-setting, results-oriented person who pours his entire heart into everything he deems important!

At this time, both of our boys lived in Texas. Addison was now married. Alex lived with them. Julie said, "You haven't seen the boys in awhile. Go visit them."

I had a seven-week window of relative peace until Ash Wednesday and the busy season of Lent. I planned for eleven days away, but so I would only be gone one Sunday. Four of the days would be consumed with the long drive.

It was a wonderful vacation. Good to be away. Great to be with the kids. I didn't want to return home. Nothing was different. I was miserable.

Two weeks later, I found myself in a spot where I was tempted to do what virtually every pastor would caution a brother pastor never to do. As the first of Sunday morning's two worship services progressed, all of my anger and frustration was fomenting in me. By the end of the service, I knew that I had to tell them what was going on inside of me.

Where virtually every pastor would find it a terrible idea, my people knew me as a person who talks about sensitive issues. I mince no words even as I find ways to explain things in such a manner that a member once commented, "You say things to us that we don't want to hear in a way we want to hear them." I considered that the highest praise. Through crises, through how I addressed difficult situations head-on from the pulpit, they knew me not to flinch in the midst of the most thorny of spots. I wanted them to find me a stand-up guy, an honorable man, and so I did and said what it took to be that man.

I finished the post-worship announcements. I then told them what was behind my taking the impromptu vacation to Texas.

"I am so frustrated. I've been with you more than ten years and nothing ever changes around here. I do not assume that it is you. Maybe it's me. Maybe I've been doing a lousy job. If that is the case, I need you to tell me. Is it my sermons? Have they grown stale? Something else? What is it that keeps most of you from responding to the work that I do here?"

Through tear-laced bitterness I continued, "Yet, you tell me that you love my sermons. That after ten years they are fresh and interesting and helpful. You've always been kind in your assessment of my work. So, is it you? Is it true what one of you told me several years ago, that you are such a laid back community of people that even the likes of me can't rouse you?"

Nearing the end, I slowed down. Calmed down. Wrapped it up on an encouraging note, bathed in the Lord's love for us in Jesus Christ.

And then nothing changed. Worship attendance didn't even receive a temporary boost. Some reached out to me while I surely ticked off plenty. 2012 proceeded the way every other year had.

Of course, to a large degree it was them. They were typical Americans. They had so many weekend opportunities that, as one pastor once said to me as I lamented lousy worship attendance, "It's a wonder anyone at all comes to church."

While I cannot truly answer the question, I suspect that if folks were more faithful in their worship—and if comments such as the following, which really happened, "Pastor, you might as well stop harping on us about our drinking. We aren't going to change," had turned into, "You're right, Pastor. We need to be responsible drinkers,"—then, yeah, I think I could have been content.

Maybe. For awhile.

But not for long, because to a much larger degree it was me. Not them. Even if we had one hundred percent of our members in worship one hundred percent of the Sundays, I still would have been exactly where I found myself.

Because it was not about the ministry. Or them. Or anything else.

It was because I hated myself.

11

Self-hatred erupts

In 2007, I turned fifty. A few weeks later, I experienced chest pain. I flunked a stress test. Before I could have the scheduled heart catheterization, my chest pain became serious.

I had my first-ever ambulance ride when the doctor at the small Harbor Beach hospital was confident that I needed an immediate catheterization. To Saginaw we went where, the next day, I received two stents, both blockages not terribly severe at seventy percent, but on a bend and right next to each other.

My weight, which has been up and down my entire adult life, had ballooned to the highest ever. On the way home from Saginaw, Julie asked in that loving and innocent, always amiable manner of hers, "Now what are you going to do?"

Without hesitation, I replied, "I am going on a diet." Then, from where I got the number I have no idea, I proclaimed, "I'm going to eat 1,800 calories a day. I am going to count them. I am going to lose weight and get healthy."

And I did. I counted calories the way Scrooge counted his money. As soon as I was cleared to run, I was back at my routine of jogging—an activity I took up in 1980 and kept at—and soon was running five miles a day, five days a week.

In six months I lost seventy pounds. By the third year after I got the stents, I no longer made annual visits to the cardiologist. Our family doctor did another stress test. I passed. My blood work was great—low cholesterol, good blood sugar, every number on the chart where it should be.

My physical health was dandy. My emotional health was in the toilet.

In 2012, I noticed something that had been going on for a few years. I couldn't look myself in the eye in the mirror. At first, when I did that, say when I was finished brushing my teeth, I would make a funny face. I would screw up my face into some *hey kids don't I look goofy* way. I would not be able to leave the mirror without doing that. I had to make a face.

That went on for a year. Maybe two. If I were inspecting my hairline, which was creeping up my forehead, I would say to myself, "A lot of men look good this way. Dad did. My hairline is following the path of his." But the episode concluded with making the face.

Until it didn't.

Eventually, I could not look at myself. Eventually, my hair had receded too much. Eventually, everything about my face was wrong. Eventually, I hated myself.

No longer could I look at myself. I saw an aging man. I despised him. The rare times I allowed myself to make eye contact, I cursed myself.

To where had my gender identity issues gone over the years since Julie and I married? The first ten years, all was relatively stable. Now, in 2012, I found myself speaking to myself a notion which had never before met my lips. "You're not a crossdresser," I would say. "You're a transsexual."

This was more for consoling me than it was realization. It was not spoken to Julie, but I would say it out loud as often as I would think it. "You're not a crossdresser. You're a transsexual."

Not transgender. Transsexual.

Transgender has replaced transsexual as the common term for those who experience a mismatch of gender and sex. Nowadays, when transsexual is used, it is almost exclusively reserved for those who have surgery on their genitals to conform them to their identity. Mostly, it is a term which has been discarded. But for me, in 2012, I needed the totality of the word transsexual.

I was not thinking about transitioning from male to female. Not only was that an insanely ridiculous idea, it was also so foreign I could not even begin to entertain it. Throughout my life, as much as I thought, "All I want is to be a girl," my fantasies did not approach my transitioning. The dream I had, which was the furthest I ever took my pining, was to imagine I had grown up in a non-religious, dysfunctional family from which I ran away to Chicago and became a female impersonator.

Still a guy, mind you. Only a part-time girl. My upbringing and worldview did not allow me to concoct dreams of my transitioning to female.

My desires had made my guilt grow so deep that I had ceased fully dressing in front of Julie. I saved that for when I was alone. I rarely got into full female dress, with clothes and wig and makeup. It was too much for me, emotionally.

I had years earlier found a community of people like me on the internet. They became my kindred spirits. I admired the men who crossdressed to perfection. I marveled at the drag queens who made themselves gorgeous, so long as they didn't go over the top and become caricatures of women. I envied the true transsexuals, the males who had surgery.

Because I am a Christian—and as a minister I was by-the-book to the traditional doctrine of my church body—all my envy and coveting and hating myself found me constantly seeking forgiveness from the Lord, begging for strength, longing to shed myself of this affliction.

I hated myself for hating myself.

I kept my legs shaved during the winter. I now took to shaving my arms for the same reason I did my legs. They looked way more feminine with no hair.

As autumn 2011 approached, I could hardly wait to shave. I had always held off until I came home from our family deer camp. I never wanted to take a chance on one of my brothers or other relatives at deer camp seeing my bare skin, asking what was up with that. So shaving did not take place until late November. But, in the autumn of 2011, I could not wait. I shaved in October. I took my chances at deer camp. No one noticed.

All summer in 2012, I had my eye on early October to shave. It grew cool enough as far up in Michigan where we lived that I switched over to sweat pants and sweatshirt for jogging, so no one would see my bare arms and legs. So anxious was I, I could not even wait for October to arrive. Friday was my day off, and on September 28 I took on the arduous task of clearing my arms and legs.

To have my body smooth again provided great joy and relief.

Julie did not bat an eye at it. My behavior had not changed, so there was nothing to alarm her. She knew that I preferred my body hair gone.

As 2012 came to a close, I didn't have a clue as to what would occur early in 2013.

12

The crash

All my life, though my desire to be female was daily, I was only an occasional crossdresser. At the most, I did so once a week. Generally, it was way less often than that.

In 2013, several practical things were in place that, when combined, contributed to it being convenient for me to dress way more often. First, because I preferred not to fully dress in front of Julie, knowing when she would return from work was vital. Beginning in mid-January, she would not get home until very late in the evening, right through the end of tax season in mid-April. She suggested that she text me when she was leaving work, a twenty-five minute drive from Bad Axe, so that I knew when to expect her. Often, this was so that I could have supper ready and waiting. This blossomed into daily check-ins, which really helped to keep us connected as she worked twelve to sixteen hours a day, seven days a week, during these three months.

Thus, the first and very important point was that I knew when she would be coming home and I could be back in my guy's clothes.

Second, we had gotten a Kindle Fire, which I dubbed *Sparky*. I now had the internet with me upstairs, in the bedroom. I didn't need to go downstairs and risk someone seeing me from outside the house. With Sparky, I had something to do, other than reading, while dressed.

Third, I had gotten some new dresses and shoes that were simply wonderful. I finally had a pretty respectable wardrobe. I wasn't forced to wear the same things, which quickly grew tiresome.

Fourth, I had the right wig. I had owned other wig styles and colors, and with each purchase I got better at knowing what would look good on me but, wow, this one made me feel marvelous.

These things in place, I found myself wanting to dress, and dressing more often. Once a week soon became twice a week. By the middle of February, I was up to four times a week.

And then it happened.

One night, I couldn't stand the thought of changing back into Greg. During those hours of dressing, I was Gina, the name I had recently selected after years of searching for one that felt like me. Gina was the girl of my dreams, and my dreams were a reality in a way they had never been before. I was in the clothes which felt right. I looked as much a woman as ever in my life. I felt that I was a woman.

Yes, I felt that I was a woman. I was realizing the feelings I always had about myself: I should have been born a female.

I noticed that I no longer thought of myself as a transsexual. I now was thinking of myself as a woman. I would stand in front of the mirror and tell myself, "You are a woman. I am a woman."

The night I dreaded the thought of changing back into Greg, I pleaded with myself not to do it. I flopped onto the floor and sobbed.

The next time I dressed, I experienced more of the same. And the next time, and the next time. There were a couple of times that I was able to dress without hysterics in getting undressed, but those soon evaporated. By early March, I was lost. I had to be Gina. I never let an opportunity go—evenings with no meetings, my day off, a quiet afternoon when I could quit working early—making use of every last chance to be Gina.

I had finally found the girl I had been searching for all of these years, and I couldn't stand not being her.

I came to say, "When I am Greg, I always want to be Gina. When I am Gina, I never want to be Greg."

I was now in crisis mode. I went through a series of experiences each time my several-hour session of being Gina was nearing an end. One Friday night stands out as the worst. Over the years, I prayed the Lord would take away my desires to dress. I was praying that now, but I also was praying that He would let me be a woman. Knowing how traumatic that would be for my family and so many others, I then prayed He would let me go crazy so I could be a woman and no one would blame me, or be angry with me, or be hurt by me because, hey, I went nuts. My other prayer was that He would give me a split personality, a legitimate insanity, a way I could become a woman. No one could hate me and I would not be responsible for hurting anyone because it wouldn't be my fault.

I lay on my bed and prayed and bawled and writhed in pain. I even entertained the notion I might be possessed by a demon. I hollered at the devil and told him to leave me alone. At one point, I screamed so loud I was afraid anyone walking down our block could have heard me. I screamed at the devil to leave me alone, that I was a child of God, and that he had to get the hell away from me.

Nothing happened. I was now sitting on the edge of the bed, looking into the full-length mirror at this man-ish woman whose mascara was running down her face. I was exhausted. I prayed once more: Lord, please, take this away.

Most folks know the phrase, "A thorn in the flesh." It comes from the Bible, from when the apostle Paul experienced a terrible situation which he called a thorn in his flesh. He doesn't say what it was, only that it was a messenger from Satan to torment him.

He pleaded with the Lord to take it away. The Lord said, "No," telling Paul, "When you are weak, I am strong. My power is made perfect in weakness."

In that moment, sitting on the edge of my bed, it seemed as if this is what the Lord was telling me. All these years of praying, asking Him to let me be a regular man, with it having reached this summit, I felt the Lord was saying to me, "I want you weak, because when you are weak you rely on me and not yourself for your strength, and then you tell others and glorify me as you strengthen them in their faith in me."

I believe it. All of my adult life I have had the sense that if I did not have this

75

desire, which has made me feel everything from terribly flawed to horribly guilty to awfully stupid, I would be too cocky of a person, too filled with pride about what a great guy I am.

I was a great guy in many ways, but not due to anything I made myself to be. The Lord blessed me with everything for which a person could ask. But if I didn't have this *thing* that made me a complete weakling, I was afraid that I would be full of myself. With this *thing*, I was humbled.

I was experiencing the lesson I often used with my members. Just when you think you are in control of your life, something comes along to humble you. A terrible snowstorm blows in. The electricity goes out. The snowdrifts make travel impossible. You are stuck where you are and you have no control over the situation.

I found myself stuck. Woefully weak. Utterly powerless.

I could not remain where I was. The time to act was now.

13

"I need to be a woman"

This is how I assessed myself in March 2013: I hate Greg. I hate my life. I hate who I see when I look in the mirror. I hate being a male. I hate my male voice. I hate wearing men's clothes. I hate having a penis. I hate that I am stuck in this mess of a life. If I have to be a man, I would rather be dead. I long to begin a new life. I love seeing a female face in the mirror. I love wearing women's clothes. It feels right to be soft and feminine and pretty. I love feeling that I am a woman. I long to be, to be seen as, and to be treated as a woman. I love Gina.

Suicidal thoughts were now my common companion. They always went this way, "You hate being a man. You can't be a woman. Just kill yourself."

I was pretty sure I would not kill myself. I wanted to live, to beat this thing. I did not want to put the Lord to the test, as Scripture teaches us we are not to do. I especially did not want to harm my family and congregation and friends.

I didn't think I'd hurt myself, but I also could not stop what became my mantra, "You hate being a man. You can't be a woman. Just kill yourself."

I formed a plan. If I were to kill myself, I knew how I would do it.

I longed to tell Julie what I was experiencing. We talked about everything. We did not keep secrets. I was guilty of keeping a secret, but I did not want to burden her during tax season.

The evening of Thursday, March 7, I dressed as Gina. The evening ended more horribly than ever. I knew the time had arrived, that I had to tell Julie what was going on with me.

Friday morning began as usual. It was my day off, and I lingered over the news and sports websites that I read every day. When Julie came into my office for our routine *we don't have much time so let's catch up on life* chat, I broke down. Soon, she had to be on the road for work, so I got to it.

I took her through the previous several weeks. Then I told her what I had never told anyone before, exactly this way: "I want to be a woman. I *need* to be a woman. If I don't transition, I might not survive."

Bless Julie's heart. We can talk about anything. She takes everything with calm and understanding. Just as when in 2001 she received with grace my news of being a crossdresser, now she looked at me with the deepest concern and profound love. She said, "Then we will figure it out."

My wife! My heart! My joy! When I needed her the most, she came through for me. When the vast majority of wives freak out, when they say, hey, I didn't sign up for this and cut and run for it, my Julie turned toward the flames and entered the fire with me.

I would not be alone! I would have my mate! My strength! The person on earth who loves me the most, whom I love the most, with whom I have the greatest connection!

For better or for worse, in sickness and in health, she would be there for me. With me. And, as the months and years unfolded, very often leading me.

So that we could talk that evening, she said that she would leave work by suppertime, four or five hours earlier than usual. I would get dressed up completely, so that I could express everything to her.

That evening, we ate our usual Friday pizza and then talked and talked. After awhile, we went upstairs. I showed her how I would talk to myself in front of the mirror. I wanted her to see how I spent my time. Now that I had come clean, I was determined to tell her all, all the time. I needed her to trust me. I needed to honor her as she was so marvelously respecting me.

When it was time for me to undress, I freaked out. I lay face down on the bed screaming, "You have to leave! You have to leave!" meaning, "Greg, you don't get to have this body anymore, now it is Gina's turn."

Julie sat next to me. Observing. Learning. Soaking it in.

Meltdowns would become routine for me for the next year. Many of them occurred in front of Julie, when she would recognize by my demeanor—no smile, few words, quickly passing through a room—that I was hurting. She would ask me what was going on. Not wanting to give voice to my distress, yet no longer able to hold it in, I erupted in great, emotional tears, writhing in pain, pounding the arms of my chair or the floor.

Julie sat by. Observing. Waiting. Ready to get me talking when I finally wore myself out. She said, "I wish I could spend a day in your brain, so I would understand your pain."

The Saturday after my Friday tell-all, Julie was in my office before leaving for work. We had our typical chat over coffee—me in my chair, her sitting on the desk—when she said: "You can be a woman. That's what you are, so that's what you need to be."

I couldn't believe it. In fact, I argued with her. Debated, really. I couldn't see it happening. Too many obstacles. She replied, "We will address each of the obstacles."

So that we could visualize the obstacles, Julie made a pro and con list. In total numbers, the cons won. Each con felt like an obstacle of Mount Everest proportions.

Pro:

1. I will be at peace with myself.

Cons:

1. What happens to our marriage?
2. The kids will be hurt.
3. Can one be a Christian and be transgender?
4. Too many others will be hurt.

5. I will have to quit my job.
6. We will have to move to a large city, perhaps farther away from our family, from whom we already live too far, to a city that is trans-friendly.
7. We will take a big financial hit.
8. We will be ostracized.

The list constantly on my mind, ten days later I told her I was not interested in climbing this mountain of cons. We both breathed a sigh of relief as if that were that. We would figure out how I could cope as Greg and Gina, not giving up either one but getting them to coexist in me.

Nice try.

I could not see myself continuing as a pastor. Being a pastor meant being Greg. Being male. Being a guy to the world. I wanted out. Immediately.

I told Julie I could only hang in there till Easter, which in 2013 was March 31, so unable was I to fathom remaining male for even a second longer.

I settled into a regular course of meltdowns. Every three to four days, I would get into such a funk I would be inconsolable. I would cry. I would scream. I would pound my fists or feet into the chair or floor. Julie and I would talk it out.

Wash. Rinse. Repeat.

I needed a therapist.

14

Therapy

I would have to drive a ways to see a therapist. I could not risk anyone seeing me going to one, and I could not imagine there being a therapist in any of our tiny, nearby towns experienced with my condition for which, finally, I had a name: gender dysphoria.

This was a fairly new term, having been adopted by the medical community to replace gender identity disorder, so that the condition would not be seen as an illness. I had never thought of myself as having gender identity disorder, but now I was dealing with dysphoria, a Greek-derived word meaning "ill feelings." The person with gender dysphoria has ill feelings that his gender, or personal identity, does not match his sex, or how he was identified at birth.

Before I ever set foot in a therapist's office, I knew my diagnosis. For the first time in my life, my desire to be a female extended to my needing to interact with people as a female, for everyone to see and treat me as a female, and for my body to conform to my brain.

I located a therapist in Flint, a two-hour drive from Port Hope, who was experienced with gender dysphoria and transgender folks. My first appointment was only thirteen days after I broke the news to Julie.

I sat down with her and minced no words. "I need you to tell me whether I am transgender or just a crazy crossdresser." She asked me to sketch my life for her. I liked her. Because Holy Week—the days leading up to Easter, a pastor's busiest week of the year—was the next week, I made an appointment for two weeks later.

The long drive home found me crying most of the way. Before I arrived in Port Hope, I knew I would cancel my second appointment. This all was so insane. Idiotic. Besides, I knew I would not be able to deal with either of the answers I had determined, and I saw no other possibilities. If she deemed me a crossdresser who had gone off the deep end, how would I be drawn back up? And if she determined I were transgender ...

There was no way I was going to transition.

The con list was too long. Too ugly. Absolutely, positively not going to happen.

At the decision to cancel my second appointment, Julie and I once again heaved a sigh of relief.

+ + +

Many years ago, I switched from being a night person to a morning person. I grew to love the early morning. Over the years, I rose earlier and earlier, to where I was getting up at 5:30.

I had developed a splendid morning ritual. After putting on the coffee, I had my morning devotions of prayer, reading through the Bible and one of my books on doctrine. I then hopped on the internet, catching up on obituaries from all the places I have lived, then the sports sections from Detroit—my lifelong love for the Tigers and Lions never waned—and then other news and email.

Now, early mornings found me sitting at my computer in tears. I was at a complete loss.

Easter was fast approaching. I knew I was not going to quit the day after Easter even as I did not know how I could continue as St. John's pastor. I was constantly torn in two. At one moment, I simply had to be a woman. In the next, I needed to get my act together, be a man, be the husband and father and grandfather and brother and pastor that I was.

The noise in my brain never let up. It was constantly on fire.

As Julie and I talked about the possibility of leaving Port Hope, we thought we could do it that summer, when school was out and I was not needed for teaching duties. It would be the off season for taxes, and her boss would have time to replace her. The church would be given a vacancy pastor in time for autumn.

I only saw one way for me to leave. I would have to resign my call, but I was loathe to do so. Resigning had failure written all over it. Embarrassment. A black eye not only for me but also for the congregation. Besides, what would I tell them? Why was I quitting?

I have never been a quitter. Resigning was out. I was stuck.

March entered like a lion. It left like a pride of lions, and they were pursuing me.

I thought of that condition called walking pneumonia and concluded I was having a walking nervous breakdown. Somehow, I managed to do my job without fail. I never took a sick day. I prepared and preached every sermon, taught each of the half-dozen religion and Bible classes every week, attended church meetings, and called on the sick and shut-in members.

The Lord gave me the strength to suck it up so the work of the ministry was carried out. At home, I was a wreck, often falling apart as soon as I entered the parsonage.

In April, while sitting on the living room floor after I had finished the umpteenth meltdown, a new realization left my lips. I told Julie, "I feel like this is happening *to* me. I feel that I am going to transition, and I am not going to be able to do anything to stop it."

Out of the mouths of would-be babes.

April 17 arrived and Julie's frantic work schedule eased. That meant that she would have a lot of time at home, and a lot of time to do what she does as well as the finest research scientist. She went to work learning about my condition and finding me another therapist.

Late Thursday morning on the eighteenth of April, I returned from calling on a shut-in member and Julie had news for me. "I found you a therapist." My little researcher had struck gold.

She began describing his credentials. He had a broad range of experience.

He was a family therapist, and a child therapist, and a sex therapist. He did not have a large number of patients who suffered gender dysphoria or had transitioned, but he did have experience. The topper to all of this was that he had once been a minister.

The man, whom I'll simply call Doc, practiced in Saginaw, which would be only fifteen minutes closer than the drive to the Flint therapist. That wasn't going to stop me. I called him. Getting no answer, I left a voice mail.

I did not expect a call back that evening, and certainly did not expect to hear from the man himself, but when I answered the phone that night it was him.

He immediately made it clear he was too busy to take me on. I told him I was desperate.

He said he was scheduled into June. I told him I was suffering from gender dysphoria.

He said he could have his assistant call me when there is a cancellation. I pulled out my biggest weapon, "I am a pastor in the Thumb. I am a Lutheran minister in the Missouri Synod, and I am afraid I am transgender."

Without hesitation, he told me his office was closed on Friday, but he would have his assistant call me on Monday and find a time to get me in as soon as possible.

I was in the very next week. Julie was able to accompany me. Even better, when it came time for the doctor to call us into his office and I introduced him to Julie, he was pleased to have her attend the session with me. She would attend almost every session with me until tax season once more reared its busy head.

I explained everything to Doc. Julie added her perspective and things I didn't think of. I told him I wanted him to teach me to cope with who I am, that I couldn't see myself transitioning but that I couldn't stand the thought of losing Gina. To me, losing Gina would mean I had murdered her.

That was a new one. Never before had I said that, nor did I think it, but the moment the words fell from my mouth I knew they were true. To rid myself of Gina would be to kill her, and it would be an unjust homicide.

Doc said he would help me to cope.

Through appointment cancellations, his assistant wove us into the schedule so Julie and I saw Doc nearly every week. The meltdowns continued. Doc taught us some coping skills. I worked at employing them.

They didn't help.

The weeks dragged on. I longed to be Gina, but couldn't give up Greg. The con list was too huge, too hard, too horrible.

Julie was constantly observing me. All couples should talk as much as we were talking. The troubles in life will either make your bond stronger, or they will rip it apart. Julie and I were super-glued to each other.

I held nothing back. From my March 8 disclosure, I kept my unspoken promise not to shade the truth or withhold any thoughts. I resisted any inclination to spare her my anguish. We were in this together, just as we vowed on the day of our wedding.

For Julie, the con list was cracking. In a matter of two weeks she was able to get over the big item: what would happen to our marriage? She came to believe that, no matter what, we would stay together. For her, with that one crossed off, all of the others were manageable, addressable, conquerable. Julie is a planner. She would plan everything, we would work the plan, and we would accomplish this. She believed that I was, in my head and heart, female, and the only remedy for my angst was for my body and life to match my head and heart. She was in.

I was not. Well, I was *in* one day, then *out* the next. Round and round we went, not knowing where the spinner would stop. It was 1990 all over again, when Kim and I were trying to decide whether we would leave Montague for me to pursue the ministry.

Julie came to describe my existence this way: I was a chrysalis riding a roller coaster through a hurricane.

Doc and Julie tried to teach me to make a decision based on me, not based on others. In other words, I needed to do what I believed was right for me to survive, not what others would think about it.

With that, I made a decision. The fourth visit to Doc, I told him I knew I needed to transition, that I was going to, and Julie was with me one hundred percent. (I told Doc I was sure he had a number of visits in mind before I would finally cave. He did. He said it was eight.)

Buoyed by my decision, I had a one-week reprieve from the meltdowns. But the reality of maintaining my male persona in public, while my brain ached to be female, quickly returned. The torturous roller coaster continued.

15

Yes, I will; no, I won't

My decision to transition was genuine. I did not make it under the influence of Julie or Doc. It came from my complete and utter inability to survive as Greg, and my intense desire to be Gina.

But my decision simply would not stick. During our fifth visit with Doc I had to admit I had faltered in my decision. Doc helped me learn, once again, that I needed to be in control of the decision, not let others control it.

As we drove home, I was feeling a new resolve to transition. Indeed, my resolve was so great I decided to make my next visit as Gina. We had talked about this, Doc encouraged it, and now I was ready for it.

My next appointment was scheduled for when Julie would be in Iowa for her dad's eightieth birthday party. I had made an online trans friend in Saginaw over these months, who was only two years younger than me and in the early stages of transitioning. She said she would love to accompany me to my next appointment. I would drive to Saginaw in male garb and get a hotel room to get dressed. She would pick me up and drive us to Doc's.

The plan went perfectly. I was not self-conscious about leaving the hotel room, riding to the office, chatting with Doc's lovely assistant (who always was wonderfully kind to me and anxious to meet Gina), having a few other patients see me, and visiting with Doc. It was a hot, June day and I was wearing a fairly short skirt and low heels. I was appropriately made up.

To me, I looked nice. I felt good. It was an excellent experience.

That June day was a Monday. My euphoria would last for three days. On Thursday, we headed out of town for a big family event.

It was the wedding of our youngest child, Alex. The wedding was in Ohio. We booked a bunch of suites—rooms with multiple bedrooms and kitchenettes—so that we could get as few rooms as possible and make our own meals, outside of the wedding reception and rehearsal dinner.

It was a marvelous four days, and a rare opportunity to see together all of our kids and grandchildren and extended families. Interacting with everyone as my male self—father, grandfather, brother, uncle—there was no way I could ever see myself with them as a woman. No way. None whatsoever. Period. End of discussion.

On the drive home to Port Hope, I told this to Julie. I was adamant. We tried to formulate a new plan. Part of my troubles over the previous five years had been our empty nest, with the kids so far away and never enough opportunities to be with them. Indeed, this would be my cover story when, in September, I would announce my retirement from the ministry at the too-young age of 56: my loneliness simply grew too great.

Retirement? How did that enter the discussion? In the days after the wedding, as I was again struggling with and against myself, feeling I could not go on in the ministry or succeeding in my male life, Julie said, "You know, you could retire. You're over fifty-five. You've hit retirement age."

This news landed upon me marvelously. It sounded good, where resigning felt terrible. I began praying fervently, seeking the Lord's will on the matter. Within a couple of days, I was confident retirement was the answer, an honest and respectable way out.

The final week of July, I met for lunch with Ken, the pastor who worked with the congregation when I received the call to Port Hope. I had no plans of telling him about the gender dysphoria, but only about the extreme loneliness. He was surprised at my news but very understanding.

As I drove home from Bad Axe, I had a bad case of the guilts. I had not told him the entire story and it simply is not in my nature to shade the truth.

I had only told one other person, another pastor with whom I was close, about my gender issues. When, in March, I told him how bad things had gotten, any ideas about my possibly transitioning were met with his strong opposition. Therefore Julie and I had true concern over telling anyone attached to church work.

But I had not been forthright with Ken, and I could not shake it. I decided I was going to tell him all, and only inform Julie after the fact so she could not stop me.

How does one tell others he suffers from gender dysphoria, might be transgender, and might wind up transitioning to female? I decided to open the conversation with a question.

Me: "What do you know about gender dysphoria?" Him: "What's that?" Me: "To have gender dysphoria means that one has ill feelings about himself. His gender, or self identity, does not match his sex, his physical body. I have suffered from gender dysphoria all of my life."

It worked. From this pastor on to everyone I told, no one ever was so shocked or offended that I was unable to roll out my entire story.

That day, the pastor understood why I needed to retire. I decided to hang in there until the next March. I would first inform our congregation's elders, who are the pastor's primary sounding board, and they would agree with my telling the congregation six months before the fact, which would give them time to adjust and plan for my leaving and their vacancy.

The first Sunday in September, here is what I announced after worship:

The beginning of March will be my thirteenth anniversary in Port Hope. Over the last several days, I informed the elders, chairman, and principal that, at that time, I will retire from being pastor of St. John.

While I still love being your pastor, I have been struggling for several years, since the kids left home. With each passing year, my loneliness has only increased. Every time we got to be with family, it became harder to say goodbye. July of 2011 provides a good example of my struggle. After we had all of the kids home, I took Jackie and the two grandchildren back to Indianapolis. I cried the whole drive home.

I never expected that it would come to my retiring. The last six months, I found myself praying very intensely, asking the Lord to give me direction. I prayed the same prayer that I said when I was trying to decide to give up my job, and move my family, to go to the seminary: Lord, show me your good and gracious will, and help me to follow it.

Over the summer, the answer began to come to me: since I was over fifty-five years old, I could retire. Considering retirement seemed odd, since I have no intention of not working anymore, and certainly cannot afford it. But, it began to feel right, so I kept praying.

I thought there was no way that I could leave the ministry. I love preaching and the work of a pastor. I love you, with all of my heart. I never thought I could give this up. Yet, as odd as it seemed to leave the ministry, I finally found the Lord giving me peace of mind.

In trying to choose a date to retire, I liked the sound of putting in an even thirteen years, and it seemed like a reasonable period of time to do two things, which is why I am informing you now, six months ahead of time. First, you folks will have time to find an interim pastor. Second, Julie and I can go about what we need to do, to get ready to move.

Since we can't live in three places to be near all of the kids, we will move to Indianapolis, which will put us in the middle.

While I don't anticipate ever again being a parish pastor, I still feel called to serve the Lord. Right now, I don't know what that will entail, but I will continue to seek His good and gracious will.

I did not like giving this cover story, but there was no way I could reveal everything. Even though I only skimmed the surface, what I said was absolutely true. I was hurting badly enough with my kids so far away that if we could just move closer to some of them and change the kind of job I had, I could satisfy a large part of my trouble—my loneliness and the need to be with family. I could be Greg—I had to be Greg for my family's sake—and I could be content. Maybe, just maybe, not being a minister also would ease my gender dysphoria.

It sounded great. I believed in the plan.

I believed in the plan for two whole days.

16

Learning why

It is common for adopted persons to long to find their birth parents. There is a strong sense of "where did I come from?" A desire to know one's history. Are there siblings? What inherent disease might be lurking?

I experienced a similar sense. Why am I the way I am? How did I get this way? Is there a tangible reason for it? Was I born with it? Did something happen when I was young to bring it on? Did I do it to myself?

I had never asked those questions before 2013. I lived under the assumption, formed from the religion of my youth, that I had a sinful desire that made me feel good, and so I fed it, kept it warm and safe, and nurtured it all my life. I knew nothing of the causes that many ascribe to one's gender dysphoria. I was ignorant as to every last thing because I never asked the question.

I never thought there was a question to ask.

Freed from the burden of tax season, Julie was busy asking every question. In our house, when we wonder something out loud, you will likely hear, "Goog the quest." We all have the internet in our hands, so we pop onto Google with our question.

It was a Friday morning. My day off. I was at my computer, writing. Julie came into my office. She had news.

Julie and I could not be more different in our desire to research things. When she bought her car, she read review after review on cars before deciding and buying. Me? I went to town, saw an Impala I liked, test drove it, and bought it.

Julie had been ordering books. We already had ten or more of them, on every aspect of trans issues, transitioning, crossdressing, you name it. I read four of them, in quick succession, before I hit overload and returned to my Grisham, Patterson, and Baldacci novels.

In her internet scanning, searching every word and phrase she could conjure in order to turn up new and different websites, she hit on something that would affect me so deeply, so profoundly, that it changed me.

Now that we know about it, it is easy to find loads of websites that feature it. The *it* is diethylstilbestrol, commonly referred to as DES. The *point* is what it has done to the fetuses of the mothers who took it.

For thirty years beginning in 1940, DES was prescribed for pregnant women who were prone to miscarriage. It is a synthetic form of the hormone estrogen. It was intended to keep a pregnant woman's body in balance, to keep her baby safe.

The peak years for prescribing DES were in the mid 1950s. My mom became pregnant with me in 1956. She had two of her four miscarriages immediately before carrying me.

Mom died in 1986. Her doctor died a long time ago. I have no way of learning whether she was given the drug. Because of her two miscarriages, and how frequently DES was prescribed in her situation, the odds are good that she took DES.

Julie came into my office and directed me to a website. She found a study of about five hundred males, whose mothers were prescribed DES. After she left my office, I read the entire study, but she directed me first to the pages that discussed the high incidence of transgender in the males whose mothers were prescribed the drug.

Forty-seven percent.

Nearly half of the approximately five hundred males reported some level of being transgender.

At this news, I was smacked in the face. In anger, I hollered out, *"You mean someone did this to me?"* I broke down and cried.

92

Before long, anger was replaced by relief. Finally, there might be an answer to why I was the way I was, and the notion that this need to transition is happening *to* me was taking shape in something real, something tangible, as with the blockages in my heart.

I devoured the report. In reading about diethylstilbestrol, I came across something called androgen insensitivity syndrome, or AIS. AIS has three forms. One of the forms is called mild AIS, or MAIS.

I recognized in me physical attributes that pointed to MAIS. First, I went through puberty very late. When I was in high school, we had gym class every day and the boys showered together at the end of class. I could not understand all this hair growing on my classmates. It was more than a year after the last of them before I grew pubic hair.

Second, I don't have an Adam's Apple. My brothers do, so why don't I? The Adam's Apple forms in males during puberty. It is considered a secondary sex characteristic. It is the result of hormonal activity when the fetus is forming. If the androgen does not process at the right time, the information to form an Adam's apple at puberty will not be put into place.

Third, that I am left handed might be explained by my endocrine system having been disrupted when I was in the womb. The cause of left handedness has not been pinned down, but some believe it is hormonal, explaining why only about one in ten are left handed.

All of these things gave me evidence that my gender dysphoria was likely the result of my endocrine system being disrupted when I was in the womb. My mother being prescribed DES was a plausible culprit. Toward this end I would learn much more about endocrine disruptors and their profound effects on fetuses. I discovered that extreme stress also adversely affects a pregnant woman's hormone levels. My mother experienced significant anguish when pregnant with me, as it was then she was faced with the decision to have my brother Jim institutionalized.

This all did a number of things for me. I learned I wasn't nuts. And I didn't have a sexual fetish. My desires did not stem from how my life was nurtured, but rather by the nature I was given. I have a physical malady in the same vein as many other conditions of the endocrine system.

While in the womb, the fetus's brain undergoes hormone washings. What seems to happen is that, for various reasons—DES being one possible cause—one or more hormone washing is affected. Does the washing not happen at all? Too much of one hormone? Not enough? Any of these? Once? Twice? More? These are as yet unanswered questions and much more medical study needs to be done. I am convinced, based on my own experience and what I've learned, that disrupting the proper balance of hormones surrounding a genetic male fetus can impact the developing brain and its response to the endocrine system. Thus: male body, female brain.

I believe I have been correct in my declaration: this is happening *to* me. I never *chose* to want to play with girl toys or avoid the boys. I never *decided*, in sixth grade, that it would be neat to dress as a girl so well that no one could tell I was a boy. I never *hoped* to get to the point of needing to transition from male to female. Not of my own volition. It happened *to* me.

This doesn't excuse many of my actions. I hid much from both of my wives. I allowed myself to covet. I did things I should not have done.

I own those things. I have repented of those things. I have the forgiveness of both of my wives and the Lord.

My actions are not excused, but now, finally, I was understanding them. This knowledge was powerful in me. Life-changing. As with anyone solving a perplexing mystery, I was tremendously relieved to know there is certainly a real, physiological reason for why I longed to be a female.

Even with this news, I was not able to be at peace with myself trying to remain male. The suicidal thoughts returned as quickly as the grass grows green on the first warm day of spring. I suspected I would transition, or at least try it to see if it worked for me.

I felt so much better about myself, knowing about my origins. As with an adopted child locating his birth mother, I have learned so much about who I am.

I was hopeful this tangible evidence would prove helpful to my kids and siblings, congregation and friends, and everyone else whom I would be informing I suffered gender dysphoria and might be transitioning to live my life as a woman.

Finally, after the months of 2013 feeling I was coming apart, things were coming together.

Despite these answers, there remained questions. What caused me to crash? Why now? Why not ten years ago? Twenty years ago? When I was a kid?

17

Testing the why

Those years I was pondering going into the ministry, my appetite for answers was growing. As a Lutheran Christian, I became confident in the Gospel and that I would be going to heaven, but heaven still seemed daunting. The movies and cartoons depict it in such ethereal and goofy ways. Do we sit on clouds? Have wings? Play harps? Have to answer a quiz from St. Peter to gain entrance? I needed answers.

Entering seminary, I was licking my chops at the prospects of learning the Bible inside and out, of finding the answers to my questions.

I learned the real story about heaven. I found out what happens at death, about the period when our soul is in heaven and our body is in its grave, about Judgment Day, and about the resurrection from the dead and eternal life. Having learned all of this, it became one of my favorite things to teach, that others might have their questions answered and fears alleviated.

For me to long for answers about my physical self feels the same as my desire for theological answers. Indeed, some of them cross paths. Having learned much about endocrine disruption and what I believe happened to me in the womb, I moved on to new questions. The big one, now, was why I crashed when I did.

I learned that I fit a pattern. For males who have experienced a lifetime of longing to be female, it is common for it to turn into gender dysphoria in their forties, fifties, or sixties. That was good to know. In my mind I was less of a freak than I had felt before having this knowledge. But it didn't address the why.

I liken all of this to a slow-growing tumor. At first, you don't even know you have it; I have no memories of gender confusion before I was around ten years old. Then, the tumor might simply be a nuisance; when in sixth grade I began desiring to disguise myself as one of my girl classmates, I didn't understand why but it was barely an annoyance. Next, the tumor is noticeable but still does not make you sick; when I was in high school and I would say, "All I want in life is to be a girl," I still did not hate being a guy. Finally, the cancer behind the tumor grows enough that you are ill, it cannot be ignored and must be treated; this describes what happens to the one suffering gender dysphoria.

That's all a bunch of *what*, not *why*.

The short answer is, I don't know why. All I have are possibilities.

The camp which believes gender dysphoria is a mental illness makes the culprit one of these: sexual abuse, emotional abuse by father, an overly-doting mother, an absent mother, an absent father—the same things to which have been traditionally pointed as to cause homosexuality.

I experienced none of these. Deep conversation with Doc, whom I virtually begged to uncover in me a memory which I had been refusing to allow to surface, came up empty.

Was moving from one town to another, which we did early in my second-grade year and then again right before sixth grade, the cause for my escaping into fantasies of being a girl? Did I create a coping mechanism? I have no bad memories from either move; indeed, everything I can produce is good. Moving, changing schools, and making new friends never felt like a cause for anything negative in me.

Restating an old adage, I'd sometimes declare, "I'm the best stressed pastor in town." This moniker came to me during the years of tragedies while I ministered in Port Hope. I always felt the Lord equipped me with the ability to handle tough situations calmly and coolly. I had become a fierce preparer and I entered the most terrible situations with confidence.

I wanted to be the minister in that spot. No one looks for tragedies, but when they came it was a privilege to be the pastor. I came to say that when it is the bottom of the ninth, in the seventh game of the World Series, and the big hit is needed, I want to be the one stepping into the batter's box.

I never got rattled. I didn't experience sleepless nights. But after the murder, I found myself muttering to myself for weeks, "I can't believe I am the pastor of someone who was murdered."

Within a year, I found myself chanting, "You hate being a man. You can't be a woman. Just kill yourself."

Was the murder the culprit, my tipping point in a series of tipping points, each one chipping away at my resolve and knocking me a bit closer to the edge?

Was my now all-out desire to be a woman really a longing to get out of being a man, so that I had a way out of the ministry? Regardless of how well I handled these years, were they taking this steep a toll on me? Was there any way of finding an answer?

A few months after announcing my retirement, I admitted to the congregation that I had cried more in 2013 than in the previous fifty-five years of my life put together. This was no exaggeration. Even as my retirement date approached, I fought myself over it. If there were any hope that I could hold myself together and remain the pastor in Port Hope, I would have latched onto it.

I determined that, no, I was not running away.

Now that I am retired, there are things I appreciate being out from under. My meals are rarely interrupted by the phone. I no longer return home to a blinking answering machine light announcing the latest thing needing my immediate attention. I want to say I'm glad church meetings are a thing of the past but, honestly, I liked most of them. I enjoyed being with the members of the congregation, whether in meetings, or during a church dinner, or a Bible class, or, best of all, in worship.

Even so, I experience a certain amount of relief that I am no longer in the ministry. Don't fall for that old joke. Pastors do not only work on Sunday. The ministry is a six- or seven-day-a-week grind.

When I considered all of these things and asked myself if the Crash of

2013 had been my way of escape, it gave me pause.

Until I recognized this.

I never really retired.

I did not remove myself from pressure. If stress had been silently growing inside me, I did not walk away from placing myself into stressful situations.

In retiring from the ministry, I always knew that I had a new career in front of me. I planned on it. I told the members who said, "You're too young to retire," that I knew the Lord had another calling for me.

I knew I would eventually go public about my struggles, whether or not I transitioned, because my fellow Christians are so in the dark about gender dysphoria and what it means to be transgender.

I could not have predicted, when I crashed in 2013 and retired in 2014, that by 2015 transgender folks would find themselves in many headlines. Caitlyn Jenner was still Bruce. Bathrooms were being used by trans folks in the quiet, respectful manner they'd always used them. Governments were making no wacky legislation regarding the transgender community.

I had researched whether a pastor from my Lutheran Church—Missouri Synod had ever left the ministry because he was transgender. I found one tiny reference, on a Lutheran chat site, about a man who had done so, but no name was given, no town or dates cited, nothing to aid my search. If there had been an LCMS pastor who had transitioned, he did it quieter than a church mouse.

Quietly was never in my game plan for the reason cited. Besides, in this internet age, I could not see *quietly* being pulled off. No matter how under the radar I tried to be, if I transitioned the news would get out. My integrity required me to be honest and forthright, but I also didn't want to blindside the people and congregation for whom I cared so deeply. The church leaders prohibited me from speaking publicly about my situation while a pastor, and I respected and abided by that directive. It was always my intention, though, to be open and tell my story, which I finally did in 2015.

Since then, I have been writing about the transgender topic in general and about my personal experience. I took every opportunity to educate, putting myself into a variety of situations, both in print and in person. And

I have taken on every person who has challenged me. I have responded to one hundred percent of emails, as well as comments and messages online, from those who have sought information, from those who have shared their own experiences, and from those who have raked me over the coals as a despicable sinner.

And that's my point in this final section, the answer to the questions: was I running away from being a man? Was becoming a woman my form of escape?

If I were escaping the challenges of the ministry, why did I create a new pulpit? And if I were running away from being a man, why have I continued to live my public life in the same manner as I always had?

If I were shrinking away from tragedies, why do I meet each new challenge the same way, with deep preparation and confidence to enter the situation?

If transitioning were my way of escape, I would have found my comfort zone in Indianapolis, settled into my new role as house spouse, and dug into the quiet life.

Reflecting on those tragedy-filled years in Port Hope, I find that they were not my tipping point, causing me to want to run away from being a man.

Reflecting on my youth, there is nothing to which I can point that triggered young Greg into wishing he were a girl.

Reflecting on an oft-pointed-to theory is where I find the likely culprit. Decades of battling ever-deepening gender identity issues is what caused me to crash. I simply could not outrun, outlast, or outlive my condition. In the way myriad conditions, diseases, and illnesses overcome their victims, gender dysphoria finally got the best of me.

18

"What's a transsexual?"

I was a naive child. I was content in my little world with no desire to explore bigger or different things.

When I was in eighth grade, a small newspaper piece announced the murder of a transsexual woman. I was intrigued. I innocently cut out the article and took it to school, to ask about the topic in science class.

"What's a transsexual?"

Bless the teacher's heart, he tried to be helpful. I don't think the poor guy knew much about transsexuality—and why would he in 1970? He simply said that some people, for whatever reason, felt they needed to be the other sex from what they were born.

My classmates did not pick on me for having asked about this. If they were giggling at my question, they hid it. No one suggested that if I were asking such questions perhaps I wanted to be a transsexual. I was the kind of kid who was easily picked on (probably because I had a quick wit and a smart mouth). Someone in that very class nicknamed me Albert Eilerstein (which I thought was cool), but no one called me out over my question. Maybe they were just too stunned.

Two years later, an even greater event occurred in my learning process. Along with so many Americans, we Eilers were fans of The Carol Burnett Show. One evening, she introduced a singer named Jim Bailey who had an unusual gimmick to set himself apart. He dressed as famous women and could make his voice sound like theirs. On the show, he impersonated Barbra Streisand.

Wow! He looked just like her! He sounded just like her! I wanted to be like Jim Bailey!

I could not get that show out of my head. I was already spending every night, as I lay in bed before falling asleep, fantasizing about making myself look like a girl. Now I knew that men were doing it for a living. I was in disbelief that a man would do such a thing as turn himself into a woman and then go on stage. It was crazy to me, yet it was the most wonderful thing I had ever encountered.

Maybe, someday, just maybe I too could be a pretty woman.

After seeing Jim Bailey as Barbra Streisand, I kept my eyes open for others. We subscribed to TV Guide, and I would scour the listings for shows with female impersonators, talk shows about transsexuals, or anything that remotely resembled this. Through my high school years, I saw various programs and movies to satisfy my growing desire to see these people, to learn from them and, little did I realize at the time, to learn about myself.

Way before Oprah, there was Phil Donahue. A few times in the 1970s, Phil dedicated his show to people who had undergone sex changes, to transvestites, and to female impersonators. As my mom was a fan of the show, I watched it with her, so I had to be careful not to gawk. Inside, I most certainly was gawking. The Donahue Show was my greatest teacher in my young adult years.

As much as I marveled at the female impersonators, I most appreciated the regular people who appeared on the show dressed as women, talking about the challenges of their lives. Yes, they kept this hidden. Yes, when exposed they lost wives and girlfriends. Yes, they wished they could do it more often.

Some were content to remain crossdressers. Others longed to transition.

One man, appearing as his alter ego, talked of when the time came that he would die. As he explained that his will called for him to be dressed as his feminine self, he said with bitter anger about his family and friends who would view him as her, "You never got me. My entire life, you never got me.

Well, now they will get me."

Most of my exposures to men-as-women were trivial. In the movie Freebie and the Bean, a female impersonator named Christopher Morley had a bit part. As small as his part was, when he was onscreen I didn't dare blink lest I miss a second of this man who had turned himself into a very pretty woman. Morley popped up on cop shows as the mysterious femme fatale. When he landed a significant role on Mom's favorite soap, General Hospital, which I watched with her when I got home from school, I was in heaven.

Could I do this, too? Why couldn't I do this? I wanted to be a female impersonator!

On the TV show The Streets of San Francisco, the singer John Davidson played a female impersonator who was a murderer. This was interesting to me because John Davidson was heterosexual. He was married with kids. Later, I learned that he was born to two Baptist ministers for Pete's sake. And yet here he was, plucked eyebrows and all, playing a convincing woman.

I was a heterosexual. I intended to get married and have kids. I was a Christian. Why couldn't I make myself into a pretty woman? As I was seeing more and more men dressing as women, entertaining as women, and becoming women, couldn't this also be for me?

In the late 1990s we got our first computer and the internet. This opened up my world. I became a regular on MySpace, Flickr, Pinterest, and other sites filled with photos and information, looking at hundreds of men who were crossdressers, drag queens, and transsexuals. More than to just admire them, I wanted to know their story, to find those with whom I could most identify, that I might have a sense of who I was.

With YouTube's arrival came the chance to see them talk and act. In recent years, many transgender folks have posted videos of their transition. They became my role models, my aspiration, very nearly heroes to me. I admired them, was happy for them, and envied them.

Learning and looking were never enough. But, come on, this could never be me. Besides, I had a great life. Why would I want to mess it up? I would surely destroy it.

Coming out was out. I could never tell my family and friends and pastors and fellow Christians that I was transgender.

19

Why do I have to come out?

Is being transgender something for which a person should be embarrassed?

Or ashamed?

Should I be embarrassed or ashamed?

Did I do something wrong?

Is it a sin to be transgender?

Perhaps the thing I hated most in those months of 2013, in deciding whether or not to transition, was that Julie and I had to keep this secret.

I wanted to tell my world. I longed to tell my world. One day, surely I would tell our kids, my siblings, and everyone else who makes up my world. I had resolved that I would do it face to face.

But there was one group I didn't know if I would be permitted to tell face to face. They might have had to find out about it by word of mouth or through the internet. It was the congregation I was serving.

I was going to leave St. John, retiring as pastor under the pretense I missed my family. While it certainly was true, and all by itself could have led me into an early retirement from the ministry, it was far from the primary reason for my leaving, and should I transition from Greg to Gina and the members were to find out, many of them might experience any number of negative reactions.

"Why didn't Pastor tell us?"

"Why did he run away?"

"He's a chicken."

"He's a liar"

"He's a sinner."

"How can he want to be a woman? He's married to a wonderful woman. Is he gay?"

"Did he lose his faith?"

I have always been open and honest. I have worn my heart for all to see. Only weeks after I became the pastor in Port Hope, I had to tell the folks my wife was divorcing me. I broke down and bawled twice while telling them. They were tremendously gracious, voting overwhelmingly that I remain their pastor.

As a congregation, we experienced seven tragedies together. I showed every emotion that our people felt and did so unashamedly as I led them through these terrible situations. If a particular thing struck a chord while preaching—be it on Christmas, or Thanksgiving, or just a regular old Sunday—I didn't mind if I would choke up, needing to pause because tears had welled in my eyes. In my ninth year in Port Hope, my dad broke his hip and soon after died. I spoke of him throughout the ordeal, getting emotional many times.

I display my heart for all to see and I don't hold back.

When the congregation needed stern talk from the pastor, I never shied from delivering it. I sat with many a struggling married couple who came to me for pastoral guidance. Whenever I detected that one or both of them was acting selfish, I told them so without mincing words. They needed help to see where their problems resided, so they didn't need their pastor softening his words or sparing their feelings. You don't tell a person with cancer that it's only a boo-boo and then stick a bandage on it. People need to know the truth about their health, whether it is in their body or their marriage.

When Julie and I fell in love and the ink on my divorce was still wet, I didn't try to hide it from the congregation. I was not concerned they would not accept their pastor dating when he had just lost a marriage, nor felt that Julie and I should keep it under wraps for awhile. The first time Julie visited Port Hope, I introduced her and told the folks how we came to know each other and fall in love. They applauded. They accepted us and believed us that we were not having an affair while married to others. I took a big chance with that.

The truth is the truth and I believe in telling it. Certainly, be winsome about it. Don't be rude. Or crass. Or unpleasant. But don't shy away from important things.

And here I was hiding the truth about a tremendously important thing. I was hiding the fact that I am male-sexed and female-gendered, as if this is something for which to be ashamed.

I was not ashamed. While I would rather not be transgender—many times I said to myself, "Let me be male or female, I truly do not care which one, but it just doesn't work being both"—it is nothing more for which to be ashamed than having cancer.

I realized that my being transgender would be news, even big news, but did it have to be so big to fear telling it? Why couldn't it be on the level of "I have cancer," instead of the level it seemed to be: "I am a cannibal serial killer"?

It didn't have to be. What would have happened when I was ten and my grandmother said to me, "Greg, you seem to like to play with the girls rather than the boys," if she had continued, "Does that feel like what you want to do?" rather than what she did say, "How come you don't go out and play with the boys?" Because of how she said it, I recognized that I had better not let it be known I felt a kinship with girls.

I conformed. I hid my feelings. I experienced guilt for feeling them. Ashamed. Embarrassed.

Thankfully, our society is becoming enlightened. Slowly. By 2013, I had read several heartwarming stories of really young children whose parents noted their behavior and listened to them. But I grew up in the 1950s, '60s, and '70s. Sex change was rare—Christine Jorgenson was in the news, and that was about it for a long time—and it most certainly was not family conversation. If a boy felt he were transgender he kept it to himself. He didn't dare let it come out. Coming out would be traumatic, even disastrous.

The few people who now knew of my gender issues and were advising me were insistent that I not tell my congregation. Besides, when would I tell them? I broke the news of my retirement six months before it was to happen. If I had told them I was leaving the parish ministry because of gender dysphoria and that I might transition to live my life as a woman, most of them would have been horrified.

"Our pastor is becoming a woman?! Has he gone crazy?"

A lot of these good people would be hurt. Some of them would hate me, consider me a freak and dismiss me. Plenty would want to understand, but would be confused. Only a small number would decide to learn about the topic and give me a fair hearing.

So, if I could not tell them six months before retiring, when would I tell them? Five months? Four? Three? Two? One? Would I wait until the final sermon of my last worship service? Would I drop the bomb on them at my farewell party? "Folks, I have loved being your pastor. You were so good to Julie and me. I have one last thing to tell you. The real reason I am leaving is because I intend to get a sex change and live the rest of my life as a woman. God bless you! Goodbye!"

Um, no.

How about telling them after I left? How would I do that? They would have a new minister. How would I insert myself back into the congregation to explain I am transgender and am now living full time as a woman?

Would I send a letter to all of the members? Shoot, why not just drop leaflets from a plane?

There was no clear way to do it without the dirt becoming very muddy. Coming out was too big. To the best of my knowledge and research, no LCMS pastor had left the ministry in order to live outwardly as a woman. There was no template to trace. There was no history from which to learn. There was no rite in the hymnal to mark such a revelation.

I return to the question with which I opened this chapter: why is being transgender something for which a person needs to be embarrassed?

I had done nothing immoral or wrong. I had committed no crimes. I didn't choose to be "weird" or desire to be a problem for anyone. I had a situation, a condition in my life with which, to the best of my understanding,

I was born. I am male-sexed and female-gendered. There are a lot of people like me. We are not going away just by our wishing ourselves away. We are not bad people. We are just like everyone else. I sure am just like everyone else.

I have functioned very well in society. I succeeded in business and then as a minister. By all accounts, I was respected and highly regarded by people from every sphere of my life.

Yet, when my "coming out" would come out, I feared that the old saying would be true: "What have you done for me lately?" Everything I was, accomplished, and stood for might be forgotten, as the news of my being transgender would eclipse everything else about me. For way too many people, it would be as if "regular" Greg Eilers never existed, but only "freak" Greg Eilers who must be confused or gone off the deep end.

It might be that I am going too far. Maybe it wouldn't be as bad as I'm suggesting. I've read coming out stories from lots of folks. Plenty have had large numbers of loved ones be accepting, with only a small number in their sphere who could not abide with it. But plenty also have been misunderstood, ridiculed, scorned, and discarded. And rare is the one who is as traditional and conservative as I.

I wish I were not transgender, just as anyone would wish he didn't suffer from being bipolar or have a cancer growing in him. Wishing changes nothing.

Eventually, I would have to "come out." I was determined not to be embarrassed about it. I was not ashamed of it. I worked on a way of telling people that would draw them into the conversation, to learn about gender dysphoria, to appreciate that a person does not desire it any more than he desires any hard thing in life, and, finally, to help them grasp why I might need to transition.

I was not happy coming out had to be such a big deal, but it was. Therefore, I had to figure out how to deal with it. I resolved to give it my best shot for everyone I love.

Before I opened my big mouth, though, I asked: am I absolutely sure about all of this? One does not want to ruin his world unnecessarily.

Could I be sure I am transgender?

20

WPATH standards of care

Is there a test, a way for a person to be sure he suffers gender dysphoria, in order to get a firm grip on whether transitioning might benefit him?

There might be another reason for one hating his gender, body, and life. One man in particular, Walt Heyer, had sex reassignment surgery and lived as a woman for many years before detransitioning and resuming life as a male. Walt was finally able to uncover that his essential diagnosis was not transgender, but dissociative personality disorder, what we once called having multiple personalities.

As a youth, Heyer says he experienced terrible physical, emotional, and sexual abuse. His desire to be a girl came to be seen as his form of escape from his hellish world. When he finally realized the truth about himself, his gender dysphoria resolved. He has successfully lived as a man for a number of years.

Individuals can make mistakes about themselves. Therapists also can make mistakes. First, they have to work with what the patient tells them. If the patient doesn't know the truth, or covers up important information, or just plain lies, the therapist has an uphill battle.

And therapists can sometimes see things that are not there, or not see things that are. When ADHD was making headlines in the 1990s, it seemed that every other young boy was being diagnosed with it. Did they really suffer ADHD, or were folks in the medical community being influenced by the trend?

Longing to be properly diagnosed, I ran Doc ragged as I threw at him every possibility, every question, every last thing I found reasonable to bring up. He had no doubts about my diagnosis. Julie was in full agreement.

In Julie's unceasing digging for information, she located WPATH, the World Professional Association for Transgender Health. WPATH is the professional's go-to for its standards of care. Surely, WPATH's standards would provide me with confidence regarding my diagnosis.

Yup. Nailed it.

Along the way, three words focused me. I put them in the following order so as to create the acronym, PIC. Is a person *persistent* that his gender does not match his sex? Is he *insistent* about it? And is he *consistent* in what he claims about himself?

Use the acronym. Is there a clear PIC of the person?

PIC is especially useful for children. The great debate is whether a child truly has gender dysphoria or is only going through a phase, a period of learning about himself, growing into himself. "I want to be a girl" might be heard for a short period of time and never heard again. Perhaps the young boy's new friend is a girl who receives certain treatment he desires for himself. Unable to rationalize due to his young age, he articulates his feelings as "I want to be a girl."

Wise parents will pay attention.

A good comparison is when your child takes ill. If he has the common cold, there is no need to run to the emergency room. Do what is appropriate for a cold, knowing that colds last a week or so and there likely will be a couple of days when it is pretty severe. If, however, symptoms persist or progress to where you fear he might have the flu or something else, then the wise parent gets in to see a doctor.

All of this transfers nicely to the child who expresses the desire to be the opposite sex or a dislike for his sex. It might be no more than a phase. If, however, the symptoms progress, take a PIC. Is he *persistent* in what he expresses? Is he *insistent* that on the inside he's a girl? Is he *consistent* in how he talks about this? If so, seek professional assistance.

Adults are no different. And let's not assume that we can always express ourselves more specifically than a young person. I know trans people who say, "I had this gnawing agony. I was depressed. I was angry. I couldn't put my finger on it." How would you treat this person? Would he get the common cold treatment, or an MRI, or exploratory surgery?

It was by taking a PIC of myself that I found confidence in my diagnosis. PIC had finally come into focus. I was not suffering from the common cold, but was experiencing a very uncommon dis-ease, and it required specialized treatment.

WPATH's standards of care are used by professionals every step of the way. Therapists especially need to see a clear PIC of their patients before approving what is usually the first step in transitioning, going on hormone replacement therapy (HRT).

Whether a person sees an endocrinologist, who is a specialist in hormones, might depend on who is near or available. Some family doctors now have experience with trans patients, but many do not. HRT is not an exact science. Personal body chemistry affects dosage so the doctor must determine in the male-to-female person how much testosterone needs to be blocked and estrogen introduced, and in the female-to-male person how much testosterone to prescribe.

If a person desires any surgeries, it will necessitate passing a Real Life Test. One must live in the desired sex in every aspect of life, no picking and choosing, say, dressing at home and with friends but not at work, and do so for an extended period of time, typically a year.

For genital surgery, a surgeon who follows WPATH's standards will require endorsements from two therapists. HRT only requires one endorsement, though some doctors will prescribe HRT with a patient's informed consent.

Would I one day encounter each of these steps? Even the first of these steps? As I contemplated my existence in 2013, it sure seemed I would. My sense that I was transgender was cemented, yet nothing felt concrete about what lay ahead.

I was walking in quicksand.

21

I know why people commit suicide

"You hate being a man. You can't be a woman. Just kill yourself."

I would have killed myself if I were prone to do so. It was June, but it could have been May or April or March. The same would be true most of 2013.

I was in terrible anguish over my situation. One day stands out. I dressed up and was so happy, until I was not. I became distressed when it came time to take off my female clothes. I agonized over how temporary was my bliss—only a few hours of feeling right—and then I'd have to go from Gina to Greg, from clothes that made me feel whole to clothes that made me feel lousy, from seeing the face in the mirror which made me smile to the face I hated and could barely look at.

I turned to praying. I asked God to remove from me the desire to be a woman. Then, I told Him how much I want to be a woman. Then, back to please remove the desire. Then, I begged Him to please remove my penis. And back and forth. Crying out to the Lord. Screaming at the top of my lungs. Beating on the bed. Raging until I was red in the face. Huffing and puffing until I nearly blacked out.

Just as the previous time.

And the time before that.

And the time before that.

I lived in Meltdown City.

It was three months after I admitted to Julie that I longed to be a woman. Supposedly, we'd both made the decision for me to transition. She was sure about it. I was not. It was all of the negatives which plagued me: the people I would hurt, the people whom I feared would hate me, the financial strain it would put on us, what it would do to our marriage, the questions people would have about our marriage, who would I be to my grandchildren, and on and on and on.

I was stuck. Dozens of questions and zero answers. I had no hope of getting freed from the noose which was my situation.

Meltdowns were wearing me out. During them, I took to begging Julie, "Commit me to a psych ward. Please. Get me out of here." When she wouldn't, I threatened to go on my own.

She was confident that if I were hospitalized they would have only one way to calm me: heavy medication. Dope me into a stupor. When I asked my therapist his thoughts on it, he agreed with Julie. Even as I knew they were right, in my worst suffering I threatened to hospitalize myself. In those moments, being doped silly sounded great. Get me out of my brain.

What do people do when, in the depths of their despair, they see no hope for their future? Many try to kill themselves. But I couldn't.

I officiated the funeral of a suicide victim. On three other occasions, I ministered to folks whose family member took his or her life. Twice, I called 911 when people told me they were in the process of taking their lives. (Both were rescued in time and lived.) I have personally known people who have shot themselves to death, hung themselves to death, overdosed themselves to death, and jumped off a bridge to death.

When I learned the number "41%," I could not get it out of my mind. Forty-one percent of people who struggle with gender dysphoria or being transgender will attempt suicide.

That's two out of every five.

How does this compare with the general population? In the United States, in any given recent year, fewer than four percent of all Americans attempt suicide.

That's two of fifty compared to two of five of those who struggle with their gender identity.

That is crazy out of whack.

Why is it so high among the transgender? Read my chapter on "coming out." That says a lot of it. Read everything I've written, which pretty much is a manual on why transgender folks feel the need to end their lives. Re-read the opening thoughts of this chapter, and the horrible trap I was in. Keeping reading, because there's a lot more to come.

So, why didn't I do it? Why didn't I put a gun to my head? I could. I own a rifle.

Why didn't I take a bunch of pills and simply go to sleep? I could. We had sufficient medicines in our house.

Why didn't I hang myself? I could. We had rope. We had a garage and rafters.

Why didn't I steer my car into the path of an oncoming truck? I could. In fact, this is the method that came to mind most often. I was on the road a lot. Plenty of trucks came my way. I could very quickly have been done with it.

Or drive into a ditch. While it seemed to me that driving into the path of an oncoming truck would have a higher chance for success, I didn't like the idea of putting another person's life in peril, so the ditch came into play. But, even if I removed my seat belt, it seemed the best launch into the ditch might only leave me injured or, worse, hurt in such a way my brain would still function while my body was left in a wheelchair. Then, I really would be in a fix.

Many days, I wanted death. Most of the time, as I played out each scenario—I will transition and be happy, I can't transition and will remain miserable—this phrase echoed in my head: just kill yourself.

Just kill yourself. When there is no where else to turn, killing myself felt like the only way to turn. But I wouldn't turn there. Why not? Why not at least give it a try?

First, my life is a gift. The Lord created me. He decided when I was to be born. He decides when I die. I remained thankful for my life. I hated myself for hating myself. I wanted to live. I wanted to figure this thing out. I wanted to use it to glorify my Savior by helping others. I couldn't do anyone any good by killing myself.

Next comes Julie, my kids, and everyone who loves me. As I said, I dealt enough with the aftermath of suicide. It breaks the hearts of loved ones. It leaves many angry: "How could he do that to us?" "Why didn't she tell us she was hurting so badly?" "Why didn't we see the signs?" It leaves a huge hole in the lives of spouses and children and friends and others. It harms families economically. It can even give permission to others to do so.

Suicide does nothing good and does loads of bad. It stinks as a solution. It is no solution at all.

Third, I cannot bear to hurt myself. The thought of doing myself bodily harm always bothered me deeply.

I have known cutters, those who carve their arms in frustration over how they feel about themselves. I have known head-bangers, who try to knock themselves into unconsciousness so they can be removed from their pain. I have known burners, who crushed the lit end of a cigarette into their arm. Probably none of these wanted to die. The physical pain masked the emotional hurt.

Self-inflicted pain was of no interest to me.

Fourth, I wanted to live. And I wanted to figure out how to do so.

As 2013's spring grew into summer, suicidal thoughts dissipated as I embraced the decision to transition, vowing not to go back into the which-way-to-turn trap, and to trust the Lord would help us work everything out.

In early September, I was again feeling trapped. After enjoying five relatively peaceful weeks, reality pulled the peace rug out from under me. I felt disingenuous living as a male. Stealing snippets of time for Gina were not enough. I lived a tug of war.

Though I knew I would not hurt myself, every *I am trapped in this life* thought ended with: just kill yourself.

Two weeks of that exhausted me. I knew I had to take action. I picked up the phone and made an appointment with a doctor for beginning hormone replacement therapy.

Beginning my physical transition.

22

HRT and the unexpected

So much of 2013 was not expected. As with getting a disease, one never knows what might come into his life. I certainly was not looking for the insatiable need to transition to female. Nor could I have guessed I would experience meltdown after meltdown, be moved to announce an early retirement from the ministry, or have my every thought end in "just kill yourself."

I never expected that not only would I tell my wife that I needed to be a woman, I would also tell a therapist, several brother pastors, a number of friends and members of my congregation and, furthest from my thoughts, my children.

You might think by the time you get into your fifties, you would learn to expect the unexpected. As a husband and father, and especially as a pastor, I experienced enough twists and turns and tumbles to have my eyes wide open for twists and turns and tumbles. But there are some things for which you can never be prepared.

The first Sunday in September I had announced the decision to retire, but I still faced the daily struggle of trying to maintain my male public life and grappling with suicidal thoughts. After a bit of peace from suicidal thoughts, they soon returned. Julie and I talked about my seeing a doctor so I could begin hormone replacement therapy, or HRT.

In young male adults, HRT works quickly. Subtle changes can be seen in weeks, and dramatic changes in months. For females transitioning to male, they come even more quickly. But for older males, HRT works slowly. Testosterone's impact makes all the more difficult flipping hormones and changing the body.

I could go on HRT months before retiring and, because of my age, there would be no visible signs. The value of going on HRT could be twofold. First, if after retiring I decided to fully transition, I would have a head start. Second, genetic males often report a calming effect from HRT. I was aching for a calming effect.

Julie was encouraging me to start HRT. I kept hesitating. We argued over it.

Thursday, September 19, found me in anguish. I knew I had to do something. I pulled out the two doctor's names given to me by my therapist. I found them online and checked them out. Both were in metro Detroit, nearly two hours away.

I chose one and called his office. I was able to get in, and quickly. My appointment was for the next Thursday with, oh, let's just call him Dr. Smith.

Dr. Smith was a family physician. When Julie and I made our first visit, he told us that more than a decade earlier a patient asked if he could help a transgender friend. Dr. Smith studied transitioning and all that was vital for him to know. He took on the person as a patient. It went well, the trans woman told a friend and, before he knew it, Dr. Smith had a handful a trans patients.

My appointment began with a physical. They took some blood and asked me loads of health questions.

The doctor was very friendly, spent a lot of time with us, and explained everything thoroughly, from how HRT works, to the changes I could expect and those I should not look for, and referencing some of his trans patients for comparisons.

My physical showed me to be in good health, and Dr. Smith said he was willing to put me on HRT. I was elated. Julie was pleased for me.

He prescribed the two medicines. Estradiol, for the female hormone which we commonly refer to as estrogen, and spironolactone, which is a diuretic with a side effect of impotence. For transitioning males, it works as a blocker of testosterone production.

Dr. Smith told me not to expect immediate changes. Give the drugs eight weeks. At that time, I should see the beginnings of their effects: my breasts would become very sensitive and my sex drive would begin to decline.

By the time we got home from the appointment it was too late to go to a pharmacy. The next day I drove to the Walgreens a half hour away in Bad Axe, not wanting to use the local pharmacy where I normally went.

Triumphantly, I returned with my two prescriptions. As I placed them into my hand and prepared to pop them into my mouth, I announced to Julie, "Happy birthday, Gina!" It was September 27, a date to which I would gradually add one after another as landmark days.

A week ahead of Dr. Smith's prediction, in the seventh week I ecstatically informed Julie my breasts hurt. Over the next few days, they became extremely sensitive. Bumping them or hugging someone brought significant pain. Rambunctious grandchildren on Thanksgiving found me constantly putting my hands over my chest to keep from screaming out in pain.

I was elated finally to be starting the real, physical changes I craved so badly.

It was happening. I was in the first stage of growing breasts. Over the next months, I could anticipate my skin getting softer and my body hair becoming more sparse.

I was on my way to becoming Gina. Every item on the checklist to this point had been marked off. Tell your wife—check. See a therapist and get diagnosed—check. See a medical doctor and begin HRT—check. Buy more clothes, work on losing weight, make plans to retire from the ministry, set out on a path to tell all of the important people in your life about your plans—check, check, check.

Every item on the checklist had been marked off.

Except for one.

The one thing that I never expected, that I never could have expected—the ultimate in the unexpected—arrived in week eight.

The craziest thing happened on November 22.

23

Supercalifragilisticexpialidocious

November 22 began on September 27.

On September 27, I started the regimen of daily doses of estradiol and spironolactone—one pill each at 6:00 in the morning and 6:00 in the evening. The doctor told me to look for the first effects around the eighth week. Happily, I saw those effects in the seventh week. I was transitioning hormonally from male to female.

By early November, Julie and I had told my story to a couple of dozen people—pastors, relatives, friends, and co-workers. We were in the process of telling our four children and their spouses. After concluding with that, in mid-November I left for our annual family deer camp, near my home town of Montague.

The first few days of deer camp were okay, even fun. Two brothers and I arrived four days before the season began, and those days were spent relaxing, talking, playing cribbage and Yahtzee, and leaving camp to visit friends and our sister. As the rest of the guys started to arrive—at peak, we numbered eleven guys, five trailers, and one tent—my enjoyment started to leave. When the actual hunting began, I was not having a good time. I didn't want to be there.

I was scheduled to be at camp for nine days, but on the sixth day I could take no more. I decided to leave the next morning. I fed my brother, in whose camper I slept, the line which had been the truth many times: "Hey, I have so much work piling up at home and we aren't seeing any deer, so I'm heading out." He bought it—hook, line, and buckshot.

Since no one in Port Hope was expecting me to be in town until Tuesday night, I had Monday and Tuesday with total privacy—a rare thing for a minister—with a silent phone, no knocks at the door, no expectations of me.

When I got home, I went right into Gina mode. From Sunday afternoon until Tuesday, I dressed as a female the entire time.

Monday was marvelous. I wonderfully anticipated a year from then when I would be living as Gina full time.

Tuesday morning, I was a bit off. I got dressed. I felt so very feminine. I enjoyed being pretty. I loved seeing Gina look back at me in the mirror.

Yet, I wasn't happy. I could not put my finger on it, but it was there. That afternoon, I got into bed and cried.

Wednesday arrived. November 20. Wednesdays were busy days. I taught in our church school, held a chapel service for our school, then an adult Bible class to finish the morning. That Wednesday, I also had a full afternoon and evening. The work kept my mind off of me. I didn't have time to dress before evening, so I only put on my usual nightie for bed.

Thursday arrived. November 21. This was a Thursday filled with another morning class at school, then officiating the funeral of a member who had died while I was on vacation. As on Wednesday, I was busy with work, I didn't have time to dress as Gina or even think about it, and slipped into my nightie at bedtime.

Friday arrived. November 22. Friday was my day off. Mid morning, I thought about what I would do the rest of the day. I asked myself when I would get dressed as Gina, then whether or not I would do so.

The answer came back: "I am comfortable dressed as I am, in Greg's jeans and Greg's T-shirt."

I sat in my office. The house was quiet. Something was happening. I began to get in touch with it.

I thought about the previous two days. Yes, I had been busy, so I had no time to dress and, yes, I had enjoyed my work. Enjoying the work wasn't unusual—even throughout the emotional months of 2013 my job was fulfilling. But something was different. I recognized that I had enjoyed everything about Wednesday and Thursday.

I had not pined to be Gina. It had not bothered me that I didn't have time to dress in the evening. Sure, I slept in the nightie both evenings, but I did that out of habit.

There was more. I felt comfortable. Not only did male jeans and T-shirt feel okay, I felt okay. Greg felt okay.

I was content.

Which made me feel happy.

Thinking about being Greg was perfectly fine with me.

It was a feeling I could not remember ever experiencing, not since my first concrete memories of wanting to be a girl back in 1968, forty-five years earlier when I was eleven.

How could I test this new feeling? Ah, there was a test I could perform on myself! I rose from my office chair and headed for the bathroom.

I looked into the mirror. There was Greg, looking back at me. I looked into his eyes. It had been years since I was able to look into the eyes of Greg. It got to where I simply hated the sight of him. Of that man who kept looking back at me. Whose face was growing old. Whose graying hair was receding from his forehead as quickly as snow melts on a fifty degree Michigan day in March.

But not this day. Not on Friday, November 22, 2013. Now, Greg looked just fine to me.

I looked deeply into my eyes. I smiled. Out loud, I said, "Hi." I smiled wider. I went back to my office.

I asked myself if I were going to dress as Gina that afternoon. No, came the reply in my thoughts, I would not be dressing as Gina. Not that afternoon. Not that evening.

I asked myself if I would ever again dress in female clothes.

How could I ask myself such a question? Since the sixth grade all I ever wanted was to dress as a girl. Dressing as a girl meant that I was trying to be a girl, *was being a girl*, was the only thing I ever wanted.

125

Now, I was on the cusp of making that dream a reality. It was never on my radar that I would transition from male to female, but here I was doing it. My wife supported me and understood me. I had told nearly three dozen people of my gender dysphoria and no one had spit in my face with disgust. I was beginning my ninth week on HRT, expecting the physical transformation for which I longed. I was at peace with this thing happening inside me—which, since spring, I had felt *was happening to me* outside of my own decision-making.

Yet that Friday morning, November 22, I asked myself if I would ever again dress in women's clothes. What an outrageous question! The answer would be even more outrageous, as it came back in the form of a question.

Why would I want to wear women's clothes?

Why would I want to wear women's clothes???

What was going on?

I tried to imagine myself getting dressed up as Gina. I couldn't do it. I tried to imagine myself, a year from then, living as a female full time. The thought felt as foreign to me as any thought could. What was going on?

I thought about the many transgender people whom I have followed on the internet, whose pictures and stories had been my community, my female home away from my male reality. I had no interest in visiting their websites. I had no interest in viewing any of their pictures, of admiring their beauty and femininity.

Nope, not this day. I had no interest in them. What was going on?

I asked myself if I were going to continue to transition from male to female. The answer came back as loud and clear as one would want the answer in such a delicate situation.

No. I am not transitioning. I am a male. I am Greg. And I feel so good!

How good did I feel about myself? I can only think of one word to describe it, and that word is supercalifragilisticexpialidocious.

I decided not to rush to tell Julie. I needed to give it a day. If I still felt good on Saturday, I would tell her.

Feeling great Saturday morning, I went in search of Julie. Locating her upstairs, I said I had something strange to tell her. I laid out the events of the past few days, how good I felt, how I had no desire to be a female.

She was as befuddled and curious and excited as I. She was as cautious as I. And, as I had, she concluded HRT was the likely cause.

We figured my testosterone had lowered enough, and my estrogen raised enough, that my body fell into a place where it was finally rightly ordered. That the typical male hormone levels I had when I began HRT simply didn't work for me. That the DES my mom took when pregnant with me rewired my endocrine system to require a more female-aligned level of hormones.

Could it be this simple? Could a regular course of HRT keep me in this dramatic harmony? Was it possible I might be able to live in this harmony the rest of my life?

Here is how dramatic the harmony was. Now that I was experiencing it, I could finally see how far I had fallen over the previous several years. I recalled the months after my divorce in 2001, that I was not able to listen to music because of how lousy I felt. I had no clue how dreadful I was acting until Julie came into my life, and my boys were kind enough to tell me how sullen a person I had been and how it spilled over into how I treated them. I simply had not seen it.

Back to the present, I had not recognized how dramatically my personality had changed over the previous few years. (Which begs several questions. Did the members of the congregation notice? Did I hide it from them? Was I one person in public and another at home?)

Here is how dramatic the harmony was. I had fallen into the nasty habit of cursing myself. Whenever I would do something dumb—say, drop a glass and break it—or make a mistake—perhaps, forget to save a word file and lose it—I would curse myself. It got so bad that in 2013 I was cursing myself for things as little as forgetting to turn a light off when I left a room.

I had admitted this to my therapist, who pointed out the harm of this habit to my health of mind and body. I had been working on breaking the habit, but it was coming along grudgingly.

Since the harmony, my goodness the change! Not only was I not cursing myself for minor mistakes, I was laughing them off. One day as I was bathing I lost my grip on the soap. It was down to a slim size and hard to grab. I snatched at it. I tried to coax it into a spot to nab it. It just wasn't happening. Old Greg would have cursed and gotten angry. New Greg giggled. New Greg enjoyed the moment.

Here is how dramatic the harmony was. We had three of our four grandchildren at our house over Thanksgiving weekend, and two of them for several days at Christmas. Never once did I do what I was prone to since I've had grandchildren (the oldest was six that year): I never snapped at them when their behavior was bad.

I had fallen into a bad way of biting their heads off, especially the oldest who knew how to push buttons. I always explained to him why he got disciplined—my mom taught me to do that—but it did not excuse the way in which the discipline began.

New Greg remained patient with the kids. Indeed, where I had wondered the previous summer why I even wanted the grandkids to spend extended time with us because I got into a surly mood so easily, now I couldn't wait for them to arrive and was miserable when they left.

This is how wonderfully I was feeling in the new harmony. It was a peace of mind and body I had never before experienced. It was so blessedly terrific that I simply had to drag out that silly word to describe it.

Supercalifragilisticexpialidocious.

24

Investigating the harmony

It was day 22 of supercalifragilisticexpialidocious when I had the next appointment with my therapist. Julie would be with me as she had for all but two up to that point. She suggested I email him a few days before this appointment to inform him of my harmony, to give him a chance to check into it. If he were not familiar with this experience then perhaps a colleague might have a transgender patient who had achieved peace with HRT alone and no longer needed to transition.

Indeed, he was not familiar with this. He did contact some colleagues. None of them had heard of it.

I was not surprised, having never come across it among the hundreds of transgender people whose stories I have read. Even so, I was disappointed. I didn't want to be the first in any of this. I never wanted to be the first LCMS pastor to come out as transgender. I also didn't want to be known as the first male-to-female transgender who stopped transitioning because he believed it was the medicine that got him to this harmony of brain and body. Don't read me wrong; I loved the harmony and the peace, and I hoped that it was in fact the HRT causing it. But it helps to have validation from others' experience.

Below, I will share my testosterone and estrogen levels, and what Dr. Smith said about them. Medicine and chemical levels are tangible, testable things. Black and white, read them on paper, make sense of them. I like

129

that. I have always liked numbers. As a kid, I collected baseball and football cards, and my favorite thing was reading the player statistics on the back.

If the harmony I was experiencing could only be traced to some mental breakthrough—no offense to my therapist—it would be less than tangible and, it seems, would not have given me a sense of stability. Could I retain it easily enough? Would I live in fear of the next meltdown? After nearly a year of meltdowns, I had not suffered one since the harmony began on November 20.

Besides, I did not have a therapeutic breakthrough; this harmony was not a change of mind, logically or behaviorally. There was no "aha" moment coupled with a "I can remain male" change of mind.

The fact is, I didn't change my mind. On November 21, I was transitioning. On November 22, I was no longer transitioning. If it were not the medicine, what was it? There was nothing else to which to point.

My second appointment with my HRT doctor was scheduled for December 20. While I was anxious for the appointment to arrive, it probably was good it was a month into the harmony, so I had a track record.

When the doctor entered and sat down, I told him I had surprising news. I explained about the harmony, when it began, and how I was feeling about no longer transitioning. I longed for him to say, "You know, a few years ago I had a man on HRT who experienced the same thing. He's still a patient because he continues to need the medicine and have his blood tested, but he has remained male and is at peace with himself."

Nice wish. Didn't happen.

Worse, I was a bit miffed when Dr. Smith sounded like my therapist: "The transgender experience is highly individualized." Oh, gravy. Come on, Dr. Smith, I just told you something significant. Don't give me pat answers that feel like advertising slogans.

The direct answer didn't come, but after comparing my testosterone and estrogen levels from before HRT with my current levels, he said something that sounded good.

First, the nitty gritty on testosterone and estrogen amounts. Testosterone levels in men and estrogen levels in women vary widely. Testosterone can be considered in the normal range as low as 350 nanograms per deciliter (ng/dl; a nanogram is one billionth of a gram; a deciliter is one tenth of a liter) all the way up to 1,200 ng/dl. On my first doctor visit, my blood test showed my testosterone at 430. The doctor called that a common level for a fifty-six-year-old male.

Estrogen levels in men should be very low. Men typically have estrogen from ten to sixty picograms per milliliter (pg/ml; a picogram is a millionth of a gram; a milliliter is one-thousandth of a liter). My initial blood test showed me at ten pg/ml.

I had my second blood test at the two-week mark. For the sake of this conversation, that blood test is inconsequential. The doctor used it to ensure my body, especially my liver, was handling the two drugs efficiently.

My third blood test was the one that revealed telling testosterone and estrogen levels. This test was done after twelve weeks on the two medications, one month after my brain and body came into harmony.

My testosterone was 300. My estrogen was 90. The doctor said 300 in testosterone is not yet considered impotent, though I was experiencing very little sexual desire. He said 90 in estrogen is a typical level for a woman my age.

Dr. Smith then said what I was hoping to hear: "If you like how you are feeling about yourself and not wanting to transition, we can work to regulate the drugs to keep you where you are."

There it was! Black and white. Something testable, touchable, readable, identifiable. I said, "That sounds great to me."

We left with a plan. Keep my estradiol where it was—one 2mg pill each morning and evening—and increase my spironolactone fifty percent—one 50mg pill in the morning, when testosterone production is higher, and a half pill in the evening.

The estradiol should have been a low enough dose that I wouldn't experience significant changes to my body. Reducing my testosterone level even more would keep me impotent, a strange thing for a man to desire but I believed it was what I needed.

I had been feeling good long enough that I was having second thoughts about retiring. The first one occurred in early December, the day I officiated a funeral. As the funeral was concluding and folks were being ushered out, I stood at the back of the church. I peered at the pulpit. I could not imagine leaving it, wanting to stay right there in Port Hope.

The feeling persisted. Deepened. On New Year's Eve, it finally left my mouth.

We had an early-evening worship service. Afterward, Julie and I spent a quiet evening by ourselves. We sat in the living room and I explained I had been thinking about not retiring.

She was cautious but intrigued. She had not wanted to leave her job. By then she had nine years in at the H & R Block office in Bad Axe. Julie is as loyal as they come and she didn't want to leave her boss in a lurch.

We loved Port Hope. Even after nearly thirteen years as St. John's pastor, everything felt fresh and good about the ministry, save for my frustrations, which now were melting away. I loved the people as deeply as one loves his family. We enjoyed the village; we had gotten to know many folks and we felt connected. Yes, we remained far from our children and grandchildren, but I felt so good that now seemed manageable. I had been at St. John long enough I thought they would be willing to give me another week of vacation, to four weeks a year, and that would help getting around to see the kids.

We made a decision that New Year's Eve. We would give my harmony another month. If it persisted, I would tell our board of elders the negative things which had led to my decision to retire had greatly eased, and would they be okay if I rescinded my retirement? As I had not lied, but gave a cover story for my retiring, I would do the same now. I would tell them therapy was helping, and I was on some medicine which was working akin to depression medication. I felt like a renewed person.

That was the decision Julie and I made on New Year's Eve. I was feeling so good it was the only thing I could imagine. I even thought, hey, if I lost the harmony a bit Dr. Smith would simply adjust my HRT and surely it would return as clearly as it had arrived.

When you feel as good as I was feeling, you feel like a world beater. I was in fact on top of the world.

I was just plain giddy.

25

Outcast

Thanks to the harmony, I returned to being the optimistic person I had been until crushed by gender dysphoria.

All of the concerns I had—would I transition or wouldn't I? What would the future hold for Julie and me? A thousand concerns surrounding those two questions—all were put away. But a new one arose. It began on Christmas Eve, during our candlelight worship service.

I was preaching on the topic, "Who's afraid of a baby?" I was speaking this paragraph: "Jesus gave help to the helpless, hope to the hopeless, and a smile to those at whom society only frowned. I ask you, who is afraid of a man like this, who is so tender, and caring, and humble?" when I got tripped up.

I got tripped up at "and a smile to those at whom society only frowned." I got tripped up after "and a smile," knowing that "to those at whom society only frowned" was coming next. I couldn't speak. Tears welled up in my eyes.

I thought: I am talking about me.

The day after Christmas, this experience prompted me to write the following.

+ + +

What is the opposite of an outcast? Whatever is the antonym—insider,

134

beloved, favored—I have always been that. I am a white, male, Midwestern American. I am in the middle of the middle class. Married. Kids. Grandchildren.

As an adult, I have been successful. A crowd pleaser. A person who brings life into the room. A card, a cut-up, a guy to whom everyone looks for a quick line, a good laugh, and a fun time.

I had been a respected businessman, supervisor, manager, and co-worker, who became a respected pastor, preacher, and teacher.

Typical. Normal. Regular. In every way imaginable.

I have never been one upon whom society frowned. I've never been homeless, helpless, or hapless. I've not been the black sheep of the family. Never the one nobody wants moving into their neighborhood. Never a person to avoid.

That is, until I open my mouth to the world, declaring I am one who has suffered from gender identity issues all of his life, which erupted into life-threatening gender dysphoria, to the point of undertaking the transition from male to female.

Remaining male, which I now hope to do, will help a lot of people to accept my news. Becoming an advocate for the transgender community will not. Not in my world, the sphere where I am an insider.

I could avoid the mess I am sure I will make. All I need to do is keep my news to the few I've told—who would gladly hold this a secret with me—and continue with life as I've known it. Problem solved. Stay mum and remain an insider.

But I can't. I've come too far to stuff all of this back into its box.

I want—no, I *need* to be the voice of one calling in the wilderness, in the mold of John the Baptist. Trans women and trans men are outcasts to much of American society. Those who are like me—whether or not they transition, if they simply reveal that gender identity is their struggle—are not understood, are not appreciated, are not respected, are disdained by society, are disowned by many family, friends, and acquaintances.

We, the T of LGBT, are years behind the LGB's strides for general acceptance. I usually say we are twenty years behind. It might be thirty or forty.

The fact is, most of us are scared to death to let anyone know we have this disconnect between our bodies and our brains. It's not about the trans person, who has the news to deliver. It's about the people on the receiving end of the news. There is no track record of success among those who have been there, done that. The internet is littered with, and many books have been written by, those who have told their story, who have strived to be stand-up people to their loved ones, and who have been shot down, shit on, and shut out.

At the news they are transgender, trans men and trans women get disposed of as easily as empty french fry cartons, are dismissed as quickly as the latest news about Big Foot, and find themselves shamed and disgraced as if they revealed that they are kiddie porn-producing pedophiles.

We long for smiles from society, but mostly society frowns on us.

Erects walls.

Casts us out.

Treats us as modern day lepers.

We are derided. Mocked. Whispered about as we walk by. Fired from jobs simply because we are trans. (This sort of firing is lawful in many states,) Kicked out of apartments or never given a lease to begin with (again, lawful in many states). And just plain scared to death of a thousand situations in which we will be found out (such as using a public restroom), or have to admit who we are (just try dating as a trans person).

Outcast. Outcast. Outcast.

As soon as I open my mouth in 2014, I fear I am going to become an outcast. If I receive compassion from my highly-traditional, conservative, take-the-Bible-literally church body, I will be shocked. If my congregation allows me to stay on past the date of my informing them of who I am and what my struggle has been, I will be amazed.

But I cannot remain silent. Trans folks have way too few advocates. Families of trans folks need encouragement to love their trans family members. Transgender Americans need laws passed and avenues open so they can live in safety and peace. Most importantly, we need to know the love of God, the smile of Jesus Christ, is for *all people*.

This is the moment for which the Lord has built my life. This is the way I want to serve my Lord Jesus Christ and my fellow man.

The end of the most trying year of my life has arrived; a new beginning is upon me. The end is near of having but a trusted few know who I am; the beginning is near to going public.

Will I continue to be a favored, insider-type of a person, or will I be mocked and blackballed and cast out? I don't know, but I have to find out. I cannot go back into the closet. I have to come out. I have to speak. I have to help.

Remember this number: 41%. Forty-one percent of trans people attempt suicide. That is tragically high.

I cannot remain silent. If I have to become an outcast to be a voice for the outcasts, then so be it. I have two precious promises from the Lord which buoy me, that I can do all things through Christ because He provides my strength (Philippians 4:13), and that the Lord works all things for good in my life as I am one whom He has called according to His good and gracious will (Romans 8:28).

To my Lord, I am not an outcast. I am His beloved child and a favored member of His family, through faith in Christ. I want everyone to know the same love, have the same hope, delight in the same strength, and revel in the same joy.

+ + +

As I reflect on what occurred in the five years since I recorded these thoughts, much proved to be on the mark.

There were many other things to occur which I could never imagine. In 2014, while I told many more about my gender dysphoria, all of it was done in private, insisting they keep it secret.

I did not tell my congregation.

26

Gone

On your mark.
　Get set.
　Gone.

+ + +

I went to bed on the eve of 2014 with the plan to rescind my retirement soon if the harmony of brain and body continued. The plan didn't make it out of New Year's Day.

　January 1, 2014 became numbered with the worst days of my life. Here is what I wrote during the first two weeks of the year.

January 2

It's gone. It lasted six weeks. On New Year's Day, it left. No more harmony. I have no peace inside of myself. I am upset. I am angry.

　I woke up in the middle of the night and I knew it was gone. I woke up and I needed to be Gina as badly as I ever needed to be Gina.

　I can't tell you why. I don't know why. I've never known why. Why I am not content being a male. Craving to be a female. So now I don't know why I am craving to be female when, for six weeks—for forty-two blessed

138

days—I did not.

I don't want to talk about it. I am upset. I am hurting. I am angry.

I am so angry.

I want to scream.

January 9

I don't want to be writing at all. I am only doing it to make sure I get written what is going on.

Each day of the new year, I feel the same, right back where I was on November 19. Well, no, not where I was. On November 19, I had a plan. I was transitioning. Now, I don't know what I am doing.

I am mentally and emotionally shredded.

January 15

Still the same. No, getting worse. I am being ripped in half. When I work, I feel comfortable being Greg and am enjoying my work. I can't imagine anyone would ever guess the hell that I am experiencing. But within minutes after I get done with work my mind spins around and I need to be Gina.

Yesterday provides the perfect example. The local Lutheran pastors meet once a month. We gather around 9:30, hold worship, then spend an hour or so before and after lunch in the Bible and discussing theology and practice.

I love this monthly meeting. I really get into discussing Scripture and applying it to our lives. I enjoyed yesterday as much as ever. I was comfortable being Greg.

Yesterday's meeting was in Caseville, about forty minutes across Michigan's Thumb from Port Hope. As I made my way home early afternoon, with every mile I chipped and chipped. Until I cracked. And then I crumbled. As I drove, I told myself, "If you go home and get into Gina, you know you will feel her so strongly you won't want her to leave, and you will only wind up in bed crying and despairing."

It didn't matter. I had to be Gina. When I arrived home, I almost ran up the stairs to Gina.

I relished every moment but only had a few hours because of a church meeting that evening. And, yes, as my time neared its end, I was destroyed. I bawled. I couldn't believe I had to go back to being Greg all over again.

When I am in those moments, I cannot remember feeling peaceful as Greg when I am working. When I am in those moments, all I can remember is how torn I am over trying to live as two people. When I am in those moments, I just want to run away from it all.

Something has to break or else I am going to break. I promised Julie three things: I won't hurt myself, I won't run away, and I won't destroy things in fits of anger. Fully intending to keep these promises, I told her I might have only one option left. I simply will not leave the house.

I don't know what to do.

I told my kids and almost everyone else who knows that the harmony informed me I can remain male, and even if I lose it I know since I got it the first time I can get it back.

And now I don't want it back. I want her. I want to be Gina, all over again. I want to transition.

I am stuck.

Again.

And I have no idea how much worse it's going to get.

I can't escape myself.

+ + +

During the six weeks of supercalifragilisticexpialidocious, Julie and I talked about what might happen should it leave me. I knew the answer. With every discussion, I concluded, "I will crash, and the crash will be worse than any meltdown I've ever had."

And so it was.

Why did the harmony leave? Did my hormone levels get out of whack? Of course, that was my hope, that a change in my HRT doses would solve it.

As I went on a roller coaster ride with HRT over the next fifteen months, achieving peace and then crashing again would be a theme, and each crash would be worse than the previous.

In January 2014, my low reached a new high. I regularly plotted how I would run away from home, away from my problems. I conceived elaborate plans to where I would drive and what I would do, yet I knew I would never do it. I couldn't hurt Julie that way. I couldn't reconcile wasting money on hotels and eating out.

I always told Julie about my latest scheme. Within a few days, another was in the planning stages.

Greg and Gina became bitter enemies. Each fought for supremacy, desiring the demise of the other. I wondered if I were becoming a split personality. I was not. I never lost sight of who I was even as I found myself needing to referee these two personas. To do that, I created a third, whom I called The Objective G.

As The Objective G, I talked sense to Greg and Gina. Literally. Out loud. That's what it took to get them to listen. If one of them killed the other, they both would be goners. This softened the internal squabble, but the battle continued.

Hurting badly, the thought occurred to me to drink my pain away. Many do; it's a huge problem for gender dysphoric persons. To numb the pain. To forget. To distract.

One weeknight in January, when Julie was working late, I tried it. We had a bottle of wine made by one of our members. I retrieved it. Filling a wine glass, I quickly downed the sweet alcohol. I refilled the glass. I took a couple of gulps.

I felt it, quickly. I never liked the feeling of being influenced by alcohol, so as soon as it arrived I stopped drinking. Despite my determination to get drunk, I didn't like the buzz. Alcohol would not be my salvation from the misery.

I cried. I cried hard, becoming so agitated in my chair I flipped it onto its back. I spilled across it, onto the floor and into a heap. I remained there and bawled.

Some statistics put alcohol abuse above forty percent among those battling gender dysphoria. I, thankfully, would not be one of them.

I was sure I would not turn to suicide or running away or substance abuse. Now, my worst fear was that a Sunday morning would arrive and I would not be able to get out of bed. I would argue with Julie as she tried to coax me. It would get close to church time and I would send her next door to tell them I was sick in bed.

27

"What do you know about gender dysphoria?"

Once. Only once. That's how many times I said, "I am a woman trapped in a man's body."

The third person I ever told about my gender issues was a pastor who had become a close friend. That was a few years before I crashed in 2013. Now, when I sat down with him in March to tell him how I had erupted into crushing self hatred and the need to be a female, I began with, "I am a woman trapped in a man's body."

His response? "No, you're not."

Five months later, in August when I was preparing to tell all to Ken, the pastor who assisted St. John when calling me, I needed a better way to introduce the topic. I longed to draw in my listeners, not shock them with the opening line.

I found a way. I would use it in every one of the three dozen or so conversations I would have with pastors, church folks, family, and friends.

"What do you know about gender dysphoria?"

That's how I began, but never was I able to start out easily. Most of the time, I hemmed and hawed for several minutes, saying, "Once I tell you what is going on, it will change everything. I am afraid you are going to hate me and reject me."

Once I began, it always was with the question. And every time but once—Julie's sister had a coworker who had transitioned—the person replied with, "I don't know what that is."

I would continue, "The word dysphoria means 'ill feelings.' The person with gender dysphoria has ill feelings about himself. How he feels about himself doesn't match who he is. His brain is one thing and his body is another. I've had gender dysphoria for my entire life."

This approach proved to be way better than "I am a woman trapped in a man's body," yet I still feared that my revelation would bring instant indignation.

It never did.

Don't get me wrong. Everyone was surprised. Shocked. Looks on faces and body language gave away what words did not. But no one asked me to stop talking.

For the next hour or two I traced how things progressed since my first memory of my gender mismatch. When I arrived at the Crash of 2013, I provided exacting detail. I was clear that, yes, at this time I longed to be a woman but, no, I did not know what was going to happen but, yes, they needed to be prepared for the possibility I would transition.

That August day with the pastor, he was all parts kind and compassionate and befuddled. He asked good questions. He threw no judgments at me.

A week later I told another Ken, Ken Bush, who was both one of my best friends and the chairman of St. John.

Ken was not a Lutheran when we met, and he and his wife Nancy did not even live in the area. Because they planned to build a house near Port Hope, and St. John was one of only two churches in the village, he and I began an email conversation. He asked every question of doctrine, fell in love with Lutheran theology, and they became Lutherans before moving to Port Hope.

In the process, Julie and I grew close to Ken and Nancy. It was a natch I would next tell Ken because of his dual standing in my life, personally and professionally. The hard thing about broaching the subject with Ken was his being nearly a decade older than me and with a very conservative upbringing. I was convinced he would have to label me a sinner and be done with me.

He listened with fascination. He asked great questions. Finally, he summed things up marvelously: "It's a matter of being, not doing." By that, he meant my brain and body mismatch was a case of who I am, and if I were to transition he could understand it as treating a physical ailment and seeking healing. It was not my doing something sinful.

With Ken's gracious reaction, Julie told Nancy a week later. She, too, was understanding. Ken and Nancy became huge allies.

Next up was my best friend, Tim Todd. Tim was the marketing teacher at our alma mater and lived in our home town. I needed to tell my kids about my retirement before announcing it to the congregation in early September, and my two boys, having returned from Texas, were living in my birth town, Muskegon. I made my way from the thumb of the Michigan mitten to the base of the pinkie. I would give the boys and my daughter-in-law the cover story. Later that evening, at Tim's house, I would tell all to Tim.

Tim and I shared everything. Whether it was our failed marriages, or our Christian faith, or politics, or our love of the Detroit Tigers, or our ongoing shared silliness, there was nothing off the table between us.

Except one thing. The thing I felt like a bum for hiding.

We sat down face to face, close together. It took me longer with him than anyone else to pop my opening question; yes, even longer than with my children. By the time I told them, I had enough talks under my belt it came easier. With Tim, it took twenty minutes of sobbing, of *this will change everything* and *I can't bear to lose you* and *please don't hate me for keeping this secret*.

From my opening question, to my concluding I likely would see if transitioning helped, Tim simply listened. He asked no questions. His face only displayed the deep love we had shared for forty years.

After I finished, he spoke. He requested a dollar. Handing him one, he asked me its value. "One dollar." He crumpled it. Again, he asked me its value. "One dollar." He concluded, "The value doesn't change because it is crumpled."

Message conveyed.

Tim's friendship never wavered in the forty years previous. It would not waver now. Indeed, as I would struggle for the next few years, I often made his house a retreat for a few days.

The next important person to inform was my first wife, Kim. Come November, I would tell our two daughters and two sons, and their spouses. Since I would insist on my kids not yet speaking to anyone about me, it was key they knew I had talked with their mother. They could lean on her and each other. I hoped that would be enough for them as I was sure they would need to share their feelings and, I was convinced, mourn the loss of their dad.

Indeed, over the next two years they all would move through the stages of grief.

Kim and her husband lived in southwest Michigan. Julie and I drove there in mid-October. With Kim, I could skip much of my history. She received my news with surprise, but also with grace and concern. We had long gotten along very well. Since our divorce, for the sake of the family we shared in high school graduations, four weddings, and some Christmases and Thanksgivings. They stayed at our house and we at theirs.

More than getting along, we liked each other. That would be tested now.

Kim's main concern was to be expected. She feared how much the kids would hurt. And if they got hurt, it would impact our relationship. I couldn't argue with her. I agreed with her.

Kim had more to say. She now was able to tell me why she divorced me. Her love for me had grown cold due to my gender issues, because I was not able to be the husband she needed. She spoke gently, no resentment or anger. Everything fell into place for me. I got it. Even more, I realized I should have gotten it before. Finally, it was obvious.

As I write about telling my kids, I've blended things so as not to betray any of them. They would express wildly different reactions. It is not my desire to set any of them apart. And when I speak about my siblings, I do the same for the sake of my brothers. As for my sister Sue I gladly provide details because she immediately supported me and never wavered.

By now, I had told my story a half-dozen times. Thus, despite that it was next my children I was telling, it came much easier. Their every reaction was expected. Surprise. Shock. Sadness for me. But no tears from me, perhaps because I was now immune to my own story.

It turned out all four kids suspected there was more to my retirement than met the eye, which was confirmed when Julie and I insisted we needed to talk in person. One of them wondered if I were planning on becoming a missionary and we were moving to some far off land. Another was concerned I had done something wrong and was being quietly removed from the ministry, or perhaps had a terminal illness.

Julie wanted to be the one to tell her parents and siblings. They were surprised, but supportive. They are a wise and generous and understanding bunch. Naturally, their biggest concern was for their daughter and sister. Because she could honestly demonstrate she was doing well, and was confident in our marriage, they were on board.

Spring of 2014 arrived. I needed to tell my siblings. I informed my out-of-state brother by phone. For the other two, and Sue, I drove to West Michigan.

A dozen revelings now under my belt, I found it curious how some people asked no questions, others had a couple of queries, and others constantly interrupted me with their curiosities. One brother asked more questions than anyone—all excellent, to-be-expected questions mixed with concerns and even some predictions. Sue was the most emotional. She and I are tremendously alike. That she cried a lot, hurt deeply with me, asked many questions, and made lots of observations was no surprise. Indeed, at two-and-a-half hours, completing the conversation took the longest with Sue.

It was with telling the kids that Julie decided we should incorporate a forewarning. She cautioned the kids that it's one thing to hear all of this, but quite another to live with it. Right now, their dad explained things in a methodical manner. They had a lot of information. Logically, it made sense. You feel for your dad and hurt with him. But, in the coming days, as you digest the news, and ponder him actually transitioning, that could be hard to accept, and every affirmation you are giving your dad today might fracture.

I issued the same warning to my siblings.

And it happened just as Julie anticipated.

28

Reactions

By the time I told family members, I had read several books and a host of accounts online in which trans folks detailed how their families reacted. In each one, some of their kids, parents, and siblings were supportive, others struggled, and some outright rejected them.

I could not recall reading where anyone had every single family member on board. If they had at least two children, one would react with extreme negativism. Siblings the same. Parents often were the most problematic. My parents deceased, I didn't have to break this challenging news to them.

I still knew only one trans person. We talked on the phone numerous times over my last months in Port Hope, and she accompanied me to see Doc when I went as Gina. She was nearly my age, never married, no children, with two living parents and two sisters.

That summer, she was ready to tell her immediate family. She opted to do it by letter. I urged her not to because they would not be able to see the emotion in her face and hear it in her voice, and they would not be able to ask their questions or express their reactions. Though my reading informed me that many trans folks inform family, friends, and coworkers by letter, I found it too impersonal, even disrespectful, to these most important people in our lives.

My friend argued I didn't know her family. She delivered her news by letter.

And received full rejection. One sister tried to grasp it. That's the best she got.

I feared I would receive from my family what she got from hers, but I didn't think I would. I did not hear in her the depth of affection in their family as I have in mine. I hoped our close-knit clan, coupled with my preparation and telling them in person, would make a positive difference.

Months before telling my kids and siblings, Julie and I talked about each one. They say that you should not ask a question to which you don't know the answer, so we worked to know how each one would react.

Since this is my family, I remain in protective mode. Without specifying, except for my sister, here are the eight reactions we expected from my siblings and kids.

- Overwhelmingly supportive at the news, but then to have struggles.
- Befuddlement. Generally kind, but will not want to talk about it.
- More concerned about the spiritual aspects. Is transitioning sinning? Will be kind regardless.
- Take it straight to heart. Strive to love and accept me, yet at times find it all so impossible. Ongoing highs and lows.
- Understand and process it logically while emotionally struggling deeply.
- Though love will remain, acceptance likely never will happen should I transition.
- Logical understanding and acceptance. Emotionally hard to digest.
- Shock and sadness, but unwavering support.

Yup, the final one is my sister.

Not only was Sue, who is three years my senior, with me all the way, we grew closer. She became a helpful go-to when I was struggling. Of course, Julie was my number one, but she worked full time. Sue blessedly filled the gap.

I will say only one specific thing about my brothers. I knew this would be hard on them because I am their brother. We were very close, always into stereotypical guy things, and we all grew up in an era, and in an area, and in a family which was largely conservative and immune to things such as transgender.

That's why, after the initial conversation, it was no surprise when none of them would talk with me about this. It was expected.

It still hurt.

I longed to hear, "How are you, Greg?" They simply were not able to go there. Besides, they knew me. I am a gusher. Their quick question surely would not have been answered with a succinct response, but with an outpouring of words and tears. Better to ignore the topic.

I have always defended them to anyone who might ask how they were doing with me, just as I have been fiercely protective of my children.

Some folks, totally on board with my transitioning, failed to understand how my children could not be fully supportive from day one. In a couple instances my kids even got flak for struggling. When I knew about it, I came to their defense.

Of the five stages of grief, anger, depression, and acceptance affected my kids the most. Anger might have played the starring role. So many things were out of their hands, and not having control quickly transforms frustration to anger.

How could their dad be this way? He's so traditional and conservative, and he's a minister. It just doesn't make sense. Why did it happen to my family? To me? How will others treat me? Will they reject me because of my father? Will our whole family be branded as some sort of failure?

If my dad transitions, who will he be—she be? How much change will occur? Everything we know about him, love in him—his wacky sense of humor—will it remain?

Will I even know my dad any more?

The question of sin was right in the middle. We knew so little about what it means to be transgender, and our biblically-traditional Lutheran faith came down on the side of it being sinful to transition, so did this mean I was going to be damned? Can one be a Christian in good standing and be transgender, or is it an eternal death sentence?

My kids asked if the fact I always hid this meant their childhood was a lie. Were their entire lives built on a fabrication? Was everything we Eilers stood for now up for questioning? One asked me why I had kids when I knew I was this way.

All of these questions and concerns often burst into anger. Anger at me in the form of lengthy emails, but more often by avoiding me.

When I told my kids about me that autumn of 2013, I had begun hormone therapy but was still trying to figure out how to remain male. While I didn't lay anything on thick, neither did I slice the truth thin. I told them the possibility was very real I might attempt transitioning to see if it would help me, and that it could begin soon after I left the ministry.

What would I look like? How would I dress? And talk? And act? Or would everything they knew be lost to my new, feminine self?

I would address every question posed in these paragraphs. My kids deserved it; I owed them nothing less than everything.

For my kids especially, but also for my siblings, I had a question of my own: were any of them ever on to me? Had anyone found my boxes of clothes? Had any of them ever seen me through a window and tucked away this knowledge about me?

The answer was a resounding *no*. They never caught me or caught on to me. Not once. Not at all.

I eventually recognized it was everything about me that made my revelation much harder to grasp. As I like to say, I was as straight as a yardstick. Traditional in my dress and theology and way of life. Tremendously conservative in how I spend money, how I vote, how I feel about every hot-button issue.

I got my kicks from jogging and gardening and sports and cutting firewood and reading. I was not a bar hopper. I never got drunk. Never smoked. Never tried illicit drugs. Never got a tattoo. Never went gambling.

Outside of my attention-getting mouth and love for making people laugh, I was perfectly plain and completely apparent. For me to say, "Yet, all these years, I always wanted to be a girl," was as out of the blue as out of the blue could be.

My children would strive and strain for many months. I resolved to remain patient. If they lashed out at me, which I received a few times, I could never fire back. I'm the one who started this trouble in their lives. I could only win their trust and support by being patient one hundred percent of the time.

Indeed, that became my endeavor with every last person, just as I learned from Jackie Robinson, the man who broke the color barrier in major league baseball. He really took it. The name calling. The racial slurs. The vulgarities. The separation from his teammates in restaurants and hotels. He determined he could never complain or retaliate, or he would have lost: "See, he ain't no man. Get rid of him."

And he did it. Jackie Robinson won the day as much by his fine character as by his batting skills and elite fielding and base-running abilities.

That's what I set out to do.

Even when a person sets high and worthy goals in a situation such as mine, it can be impossible to get everyone on board. As 2014 began, since I was still a minister in the LCMS I lived by their rules. My stepping into the waters of telling my story to church leadership would be the challenge that nearly drowned me.

It had me within minutes of being suspended from the ministry.

29

"There is no hospital. There is no therapy."

In 2014, the Lutheran Church—Missouri Synod was the USA's thirteenth-largest church body. Known as Christians who place a high value on education, the LCMS has long operated the second-most Christian day schools, after the Roman Catholics.

The LCMS is biblically traditional and culturally conservative. That it is staunchly pro life points directly to both traditional and conservative. As gay marriage has been embraced in some church bodies, in the LCMS homosexual practice continues to be viewed as sinning, and marriage as between one man and one woman.

Because the T of transgender is linked with the LGB of lesbian, gay, and bisexual, and of late also the Q of queer, doctrine regarding gender identity can be easily blurred with sexual identity. While LCMS theologians are learned and wise, across the board both pastors and laity are largely undereducated regarding gender dysphoria and those who transition. Indeed, I learned that firsthand before I went public. Of the twelve LCMS ministers with whom I spoke one-on-one before I resigned from the LCMS, each of them answered my lead question, "What do you know about gender dysphoria?" with, "What's that?"

What I now write is the second of two areas in which I have special concern in speaking of it. I write without anger or resentment, with sadness but not bitterness. For most of the LCMS, I opened a door which was not only shut, but also for many non-existent. Transgender and LCMS were complete strangers.

The LCMS is broken down into thirty-five districts. I will refer to my district president as DP. Early on, I felt I needed to tell DP. Could I have retired without telling any more people than I needed to? Yes. Some folks advised that. Even urged it.

I couldn't do that. It felt disingenuous to hide it. I believe in facing things. DP and I had formed a good relationship. I liked and admired the man. I had to tell him.

Besides, I knew I would eventually go public, whether or not I transitioned, because gender dysphoria and trans issues must be moved from the dark into the light. My sense had grown quickly that lack of understanding paled in comparison to misunderstanding. I was in a unique position as both transgender and a theologian. I believed it my duty to use for good my skills and experience.

In August of 2013, I called the district office for the purpose of setting up an appointment. A busy man, DP did not have a slot until late in the afternoon of October 25, a Friday. I snatched it.

You can imagine that district presidents suffer a lot of complaining from their pastors. Later, DP admitted he thought I only wanted an exit interview to unload my personal litany of whining. He was as surprised as anyone at my revelation. He did not know much about gender dysphoria. He listened intently, showed concern, asked good questions, and even concluded the ninety minutes with an expression of his love for Julie and me.

He called me soon after with a request. He knew a parish pastor who also was a psychologist, whom I will call Mike. DP wanted to know if he could bring in Mike for assistance. Yes, I replied. I was pleased to have him involved.

Soon, I heard from DP again. He had been contacting doctors, seminary professors, and other theologians in an effort to learn about gender issues and LCMS theology on the topic. The LCMS has a group known as

155

the CTCR, which stands for the Commission on Theology and Church Relations. The CTCR is given topics of concern—new issues, such as when in vitro fertilization was introduced, and thorny questions, such as a Christian understanding of gambling—fleshes them out and then publishes papers on them. They had not yet done so with gender issues, but told DP they received calls every week from ministers and lay people who were looking for information.

Armed with insights, DP wanted to meet again, with Mike along. Mid-morning on Tuesday, December 3, the two arrived at our parsonage in Port Hope. Most of the meeting was Mike's asking us questions. He had known little of gender issues.

He was enraptured. If I had a pizza for every time he reacted to something with "Fascinating," I could treat quite a crowd.

For the first time, I received the question regarding my desiring genital surgery. "How could you mutilate yourself?" My face displayed the hurt I felt. "I am offended at the question," I began softly. "It is not mutilation. It is correction."

The rest of our conversation centered on how things would proceed. DP knew I longed to tell my congregation. I had written my presentation and given him a copy in October. Now, he had me promise I would remain silent. I made my arguments for being able to tell, but still promised my locked lips.

I heard nothing from DP until Mike called early on the morning of Tuesday, January 14. Mike called the house phone, which Julie answered. He did not ask to talk with me. It seemed from Julie's responses that he had been talking with doctors. Finally, he said DP and he would like to meet with us in two days, at one of our congregation's schools in Frankenmuth, a midpoint for all of us.

As Julie filled me in on what he said, my juices quickly flowed. Could it be they found a hospital, a retreat, a therapy, a place where I could go for several weeks to get me on the road to not being torn in two? He gave no clue in the phone call, but it sure felt the door had been cracked open. I was hopeful for a solution to my agonizing struggle.

Longing for something good to happen, I could not stop envisioning the conversation we would have on Thursday. I rehearsed what might take place. I wanted to be hopeful. I didn't want to be let down. I never imagined what would actually occur.

We made the ninety-minute drive, arriving early enough to catch lunch, thoroughly chewing every possible idea we had regarding the meeting, then making our way to the school for the gathering.

DP and Mike arrived. Things were cordial, but the men were tense, and way more serious than in December. The meeting would last almost two hours. The conversation was a complex web of topics. For the sake of brevity and clarity, I have tremendously condensed it and compacted some quotes. Seeking to distort nothing, I have written so as to provide the impact the meeting had on me.

As the conversation ensued, DP informed me of the purpose: "As of this meeting, I am suspending you. I strongly urge that you resign from the ministry. I have a meeting set up for tomorrow in Port Hope to discuss this with your congregation leaders."

If it is possible to think ten things at once, I was doing it. "I'm done in the ministry." "Unbelievable," "Incomprehensible." "I will be a disgrace." Yet, I also felt relief; I was being given a way out.

As he spoke, I broke in. I asked about what Mike had said to Julie on Tuesday regarding talking with doctors. I asked if he found somewhere I could go to get better.

That's when he said it. That's when he spoke the last words I ever wanted to hear.

"There is no hospital. There is no therapy."

He might as well have said, "Terrorists are at this moment entering the homes of your children, killing them and your grandchildren, and burning down their houses."

In those two, four-word sentences, gone was every hope I had for healing, for being pulled from the hell of my gender dysphoria, of rescinding my retirement and remaining a minister. Grabbed away. Snatched as if by some sinister Santa who tells kids on his lap they were too naughty to expect anything in their stockings other than rotting roadkill.

I broke down. Crying. Shaking. Begging for more and better information.

DP called our attention to the pages he had placed in front of us.

The recitation of my sins.

Citing various Scriptures, the first three items accused me, first, of rejecting the Lord's creating me male, second, of effectively causing the divorce of my marriage to Julie and, third, acting as if none of God's laws apply to me. There were a few more items of DP's impression of some things which, after discussing, he understood better and graciously removed, showing the reasonable man whom I respected.

I certainly did not disrespect him for what he was in that moment doing. He was in a tough spot with me. He was trying to do the right thing, not only right by God but also right for the LCMS and, yes, also for me. I told him so.

I debated the points which I was able to get him to remove, but I also wanted to argue the three big remaining ones. Yet, a wave came over me. I knew, as if a strong wind immediately blew through me, that I was not to argue. Now, my own four-word sentence surprised my ears.

"I want to repent."

I don't know if I ever stunned a person more in my life than I did DP with those four words.

The biblical word "repent" means "turn your mind around," that is, to go from thinking one way is correct to recognizing it is not, and to turn to the right way. When I would teach it, I would face one direction, saying, "As I face the sinful thing I am doing, I put the Lord behind me," motioning to my rear. Turning one-hundred-eighty-degrees, I continued, "When I repent, I now am facing the Lord, and the sinful thing is behind me."

My repentance began with item three, working my way up to number one.

I confessed, "I have not intended to act as if God's laws do not apply to me, but I can see how it appears that way. I repent."

I confessed, "I have strived to be Julie's husband, but surely I have failed to be Christ to her as I should. I repent."

I confessed, "I do not want to despise God's gift of how He created me. I'm in a terrible way, and transitioning seemed like the only remedy. I repent."

I concluded, "Please, forgive me."

Exercising the office of the holy ministry of Jesus Christ, DP absolved me of my sins.

They say confession is good for the soul. There's a reason they say that. I was cleansed. Renewed. Invigorated. I had been removed from the valley of the shadow of death and into the green pastures where one feels the warmth of the sun and is nourished.

What moved me to repent? Did I really believe I was guilty of those sins? Before the meeting, I would have argued them until pummeling my opponent into submission, but in that moment there was no spit in me to sputter. I was broken. I had no desire to argue. There was a still small voice in me which to this day still whispers, "This is not you. These sins do not apply to you," but in that moment it was drowned out by the need to humble myself.

I believe it was the Holy Spirit working in me, leading me to humility and confession. If a person were to suggest it was the Spirit's way of keeping me from suspension so I could retire and St. John would not suffer a deep hurt, I would entertain the notion.

I would leave the meeting and strive to live in the repentance. As the weeks and months elapsed, I reflected on it often. I worked to keep it true, to abide by God's commandments, to be Julie's husband, to love the male body into which I was born. I would continue to fall into deep pits of misery, but I would still tell myself I had to do this, I had to acknowledge DP had been right about me, that I could not transition.

Back in the meeting room in Frankenmuth, my repentance shifted the conversation. There was an opening to my not being done in the ministry. After a lot more discussion, I finally asked if I might continue until I retired, even if I had to retire sooner than later.

Fleshing it all out, DP asked Julie and me to give him and Mike an opportunity to speak in private. Sitting in the hall, we returned to the pattern of the previous two days, trying to figure out what might be coming next.

It was at least ten minutes before Mike called us to return. We took our places, the papers still in front of Julie and me. DP reached out his hand to take them, saying, "I am not suspending you."

A second wave of cleansing came over me. I would not be a disgrace. Undue harm would not come to the congregation by its pastor being unceremoniously sacked.

DP instructed me to make use of the three pastors in my circuit whom I had told, calling them on a daily basis if that's what I needed to hang in there. I was to vow I would not tell the entire congregation about my gender dysphoria, and I was to make regular reports to him as to how I was doing.

I was to stop taking hormone replacement therapy, but to consult my doctor as to easing off it. I said I would put my women's clothes away.

I didn't know what to make of ceasing HRT. Since, two weeks earlier, I had crashed from the six weeks of supercalifragilisticexpialidocious, perhaps it would not affect me any worse not to be taking it. I didn't know how quickly my hormones would revert to male levels. I was going to find out.

I was able to agree with his conditions, especially when they would result in this: I could retire as planned.

I cannot grasp how I was feeling so relieved that more than once I said, "For the first time in months, I have hope for the future."

DP looked at me with gentle seriousness, saying, "I hope so." Oh that he would have left it at that. He did not. As he spoke his concerns and counsel, tucked in were his own four words for me.

And in those four words I knew he had no idea what gender dysphoria was all about, that he wasn't grasping my struggle was a physical reality and not merely a sinful proclivity, that as a traditional person and theologian he could not get past the biblical truth that the Lord created males and females, who were supposed to be only males and females.

His four words to me: "Be a man, Greg."

I think I replied, "I want to be," but the moment is fuzzy. He put me into a daze. I wanted to slug him. I wanted to scream four more words: "You don't get anything!"

160

After I retired five months later, I remained on the clergy roster of the LCMS. Thirteen months after that, it was time for me to resign my membership in the church body. Before I did, I needed to talk with DP, to be sure we were in good standing with each other, which is a basic thing all Christians need to do.

We talked on the phone. We discussed the key details of what transpired after I broke my news to him. I expressed my concerns. He explained his thinking. We talked it through. It was a good conversation. Concluding the call, we wished each other the Lord's blessings.

Returning to the closing moment in Frankenmuth, I didn't shout out in frustration. I kept my cool. We all stood. We all hugged. We all said our goodbyes.

Then everything got even worse.

30

Time out

It was early in the evening when Julie and I departed Frankenmuth. We headed not home, but to West Michigan, to our son's place. We'd spend Friday there before returning to Port Hope on Saturday.

It was dark, it was cold, and it was snowing hard, which describes both what was going on outside our car and inside of me.

"Julie, I think I need to take a leave of absence."

This was not a new idea, but one I had trotted out a number of times. It had nearly taken root in the days after we went to Ann Arbor the previous October and revealed all to DP. Three days after that October meeting, we had invited to our house the head elder of St. John and his wife, two people with whom we had a wonderful relationship. We included Ken and Nancy Bush because Ken was the congregation chairman and they were our friends.

The elder and wife received my news with the expected surprise, along with a high level of concern for my health. More than any concern for whether or not I transitioned, they longed for me to do whatever I needed for the sake of my sanity.

It had been a highly emotional evening with them, on the heels of a very challenging meeting with DP three days earlier, with Sunday worship sandwiched in between. The next day, Tuesday, October 29, I had visits scheduled with members in Bad Axe nursing homes. Julie was working in

Bad Axe that day, which she did several days a week outside of tax season.

Making my way south out of Port Hope, I fell apart. I had no vision for how I could go on. Everything was too big, too much, too terrible.

I was bawling. I wanted to end it right then and there. The steep ditch was calling to me. Either side of Ruth Road would make a bowling alley's gutters envious. I could take off my seat belt, get up to speed, jerk my steering wheel to the right, and be done with it.

I couldn't. As with every other time I cursed, "You hate being a man. You can't be a woman. Just kill yourself," there simply was no power in me to pull off and pull it off.

I wailed. I screamed. I shook.

I prayed.

As I arrived at the highway which would take me into Bad Axe, I turned west and formed a new plan. I drove to Julie's office.

Surely, the man was a sight who walked into the office asking the receptionist, "Could you get Julie? I'm her husband." She quickly departed for Julie's cubicle. Just as quickly, Julie emerged. We sat down. Through sobbing, I explained what happened. She went to talk to her boss, in whom she had already confided about my gender dysphoria and who was tremendously understanding. Julie grabbed her things and followed me home.

I told Julie I was done, quitting the ministry that very day. She suggested I call the pastor who assisted St. John in calling me. I reached Ken and laid it all out. He methodically calmed me, encouraged me in the Lord, and then challenged me in a most pastoral way. He was sure I would change my mind about quitting.

By early afternoon, I did. A new idea was born. I would take time off, a sick leave to get my act together.

As Julie and I discussed what that might look like, to her it appeared I would be running away, with little or no therapeutic value. Still, I wanted it. I longed for a time out. But I trusted Julie's wisdom. I am not, by nature, so hardheaded that I don't listen.

That day of reaching a new low, I did not quit. I did not leave. It would stand as the only day I did not work because of my gender dysphoria.

But the seed had been planted. I would water it at times, hoping it would take root. Now, in January as we left the meeting with DP and Mike, fighting the dark and snow on an unfamiliar highway in search of a hotel room, I hauled out the fertilizer.

This time, my idea bore fruit. Julie agreed it was time for me to take a break.

We fleshed it out, discussing everything from where I would go, to how I would spend the time, to how we should go about getting it approved.

We had a nice Friday and Saturday morning with my son, his lovely wife who was pregnant with their daughter, and their young son. Heading back to Port Hope, I called the helpful pastor. He lived on our way to home. He would be able to meet with us. Sitting down with him, he readily agreed that time away was a good idea.

Next, I called the two couples at St. John with whom I had spoken. They came over that evening. They also felt a leave was timely. Desiring to do things correctly, the head elder would call a meeting of the board of elders for their approval and, pending their yes, Ken had a meeting of the church council lined up for Monday evening.

In the Thursday meeting with DP and Mike, there was a promise I was not asked to make, but made on my own. With my female clothes and things in the bedroom, they were too accessible. I decided to pack them into tubs and place them in the basement. Yes, I would know right where they were, but it would not be so convenient to get into them.

Sunday afternoon, I went to the basement and retrieved empty plastic tubs. Early in my packing, Julie came up to see what I was doing. I appeared to her as I was feeling, like a husband finally grabbing the gumption to remove the belongings of his beloved, deceased wife.

I had the twin senses of needing to do this and hating to do this, of being sure this is what I should do, to finding it a ludicrous exercise.

I paused when I got to certain items, holding them, pondering them, cherishing them. Packing my dresses, I arrived at my favorite, a royal blue one. I took it into my arms, then held it to my chest, then broke down. How could I do to this dress what I was about to do? The indignity of folding it up, packing it up, and storing it away made me feel I was a horrible person.

Finishing my task, four full tubs went into the basement. I knew they needed to remain there. It was my job never to wear those things again. I had to go away, get strong, and come back a new man. Hopefully, my leave would be approved.

Despite not knowing the details of my mess, the elders and council backed me. Considering it a sick leave, they graciously gave me a month off at full pay, with the provision that should I, near the end of the month, need more time, they would revisit the terms.

Assuming I would get approval, I spent Monday making arrangements for my being gone so that, come Tuesday, I could head out.

A crazy thing had happened in the days before this all transpired. Our daughter in Indianapolis called, suggesting that I needed time off, inviting me to their place. As Julie and I debated the various places I could go, Indianapolis sounded best. I would be with family—Jackie was married, with our first and third grandchildren. I would have something to do—I would cook meals, pick up kids, and keep the house in order. And I would have plenty of time to relax.

Tuesday morning, January 21, I packed my car and headed south.

I would find Indianapolis in the midst of a very Michigan-like winter. The weekend before I returned home, they would break their all-time record for snowfall in a season.

For four weeks, I would be both physically and emotionally snowed in.

The visit started out well. I missed Port Hope and my work something fierce, even wondering what I was doing in having removed myself, but I soon fell into a routine and experienced the relief for which I longed.

I spent quiet time reading the Bible and in prayer, which was my routine anyway. Now, however, I had another daily task: figuring out how I could return in February and rescind my retirement.

The internet allowed me visual contact with the rest of the world. I made use of it with Doc, having weekly therapy sessions. The first day of the second week, I told him I was still hanging in there, but felt myself cracking.

Doc urged me to get back to penning what I was experiencing. "Write. Just vomit on the page. It doesn't have to be in sentences and paragraphs, just get it out of you and onto the page. It doesn't matter if no one ever reads it, or if it is published. But, perhaps, even if it never gets published it will be read by your grandchildren and will be a good thing for them to know about you."

My return to writing was good medicine. I hoped it would continue to be.

Week three arrived. Writing stopped soothing me. I spent most of my hour with Doc in tears of despair. He did his encouraging thing. It mostly bounced off, making a mess on the floor. I had no interest in mopping it up.

I now was convinced I was losing my mind.

31

Going insane

Suicidal thoughts were not the only words echoing inside me. Concerns of insanity had taken their place alongside the noise in my head.

During my leave, I became convinced that losing my mind was so near it was unavoidable.

Here is what I wrote in my ersatz office, at my computer which I brought with me and set up in my daughter's living room.

+ + +

Going insane is a long, slow, gradual process. After nearly fifty-seven years of life, I believe I am almost there.

I cannot control my mind. I know what I need to do, who I need to be, how I need to order my life, but I can't do it. Because I can't do it, I am being torn in half. The more I tear, the less of me there is left to tear. I'm almost torn all the way through.

It is the end of the third week of my medical leave of absence. It has been nearly two weeks since I wrote about being out of sorts, and writing about it made me feel better. I intend to go home next week, begin my job once more, and not retire.

The first week of my leave, I longed for home and for routine. The second week, I still missed it, but I had a couple of days of longing for my female self. With each day of the third week I got weaker and weaker. By the end of week three, I intended to go home and pull all of my female clothes out of the basement and try to resume being a crossdresser. If I could find a balance, I could still be a man and a pastor, and satisfy enough of my need to be a woman.

I am almost into the fourth and final week of my leave and I am trolling the internet for women's clothes and shoes, wishing I could order some of the cute things I would love to wear. As I click on this and that, I ask myself what I am doing. I know better than to do this, yet I can't stop myself. All I want is to be a woman. My longing is so intense I want to crawl out of my skin.

In my moments of clarity, I know how dumb it is for me to daydream about dressing as Gina and living as a woman, but those moments are getting smaller and shorter. I am potentially only days away from once again deciding to transition to being a woman.

But there is hell to pay for that—family trouble, church trouble and, worst of all, not knowing what the Lord would do with me.

But the only times I feel peace is when I grasp my female self. It is the only time a smile comes to my face, which rises from my spirit. My brain and body sing together in harmony when I let myself completely embrace myself as a woman.

And then reality smacks me in the face. I am watching my young granddaughter, who is napping as I type this. I have to pick up my grandson from the bus stop in a couple of hours. I will be Papa, and Dad, and stuck. I have another week of this sabbatical, and I fear that I am going to leave here in a straight jacket, having fallen off the edge of sanity.

When it gets the worst—as it was, right before I started writing—I cry uncontrollably. I feel completely lost, with no end in sight for my struggling, with no help on the horizon.

"There is no hospital."

"There is no therapy."

"Be a man, Greg."

That's what scares me the most. There is no help for me. No one who says I can't transition has a cure for me. Get therapy, pray, talk, *blah blah blah*. I have done and am doing those things, and yet I keep getting worse. I feel like I have a huge tumor in my brain and all anyone is doing is giving me aspirin. The tumor just laughs and spits the aspirin into my face.

I feel those who know the whole story are thinking I just need to grow a pair and get over myself, stop whining and get on with life.

Funny, but no one calls a person who has cancer a whiner. No one calls a person who has Alzheimer's a whiner. I wonder if they will call me a whiner after I have, in fact, gone insane.

I DON'T WANT TO BE THIS WAY. I HATE MYSELF. WHY CAN'T I JUST BE ONE PERSON?

Right now, I don't see any other ending to this. I won't kill myself, so that option is out. I feel destined to live a long life, and have my life dissolve into being a pathetic person who has to be nursed.

Making matters worse is I am being stifled from speaking about who I am. The church leaders fear my freaking out everyone and creating a storm in my church body, so I have to keep my mouth shut. Yet, on this point—whether or not I transition—is the ONE THING I have felt sure of, that the Lord would use me to help others like me, and their families, and to proclaim the Gospel to these hurting people. But, if I have to keep my mouth shut, then that avenue is a dead end. That dead end makes me feel useless.

It makes me feel there is no point to what I have gone through. If there is no point, then all of my years of crossdressing, which put a great strain on my first wife's ability to love me, will have just been a great big stain on me. If there is no point, then the dysphoria's having gotten to where I find the need to transition will simply have been a terrible wear on Julie and our kids—a very expensive one in time consumed, emotions pushed and pulled, and money spent.

So, this is how a person goes crazy. It percolates in him for decades, then it finally comes to a boil. It can only boil so long without going over the sides. It can only go over the sides so long before it finally makes a complete mess of things, dries out the pot, and the pot melts on top of the heat.

I am almost dried out. I am preparing myself to melt on top of the heat.

+ + +

I did not go insane. There would be more occasions when I thought all of the water had boiled out of the pot of me. I would always be able to refill the pot.

At the end of four weeks at my daughter's, I was in no better shape than when I arrived, but I was ready to get back to work, to be home, to try to normalize my life, even to rescind my retirement.

The church season of Lent was near, which would require an extra sermon each week for the Wednesday services. I would be tremendously busy for seven weeks, until the day after Easter, and the Sunday after Easter would be the confirming of our eighth-graders. A busy schedule looked good to me; the more I worked, the fewer times I would have to be alone with my thoughts.

On Tuesday, February 18, I departed for home.

32

Back to work

I arrived in Port Hope mid-afternoon. Julie was at work. I unpacked my car, put everything away, and headed to the basement. I retrieved the four tubs, hauled them to our bedroom, and put everything where it had been.

No one in town knew which day I was returning, so I had privacy until at least Saturday. I made good use of it. I painted my fingernails, with the rare opportunity to leave them polished for a few days. I dressed as Gina. I felt like Gina.

And yet I still did not want to retire.

And somehow I still thought I had a fighting chance to remain a male, remain a minister, remain in Port Hope.

Writing my sermon for my first Sunday back, I knew I needed to address my absence. The people deserved to hear from me. I knew there had been heavy chatter about why I left so abruptly, even though Julie had spoken to them after church the first Sunday I was gone.

Here is the middle portion of that sermon.

After a whole page of my first sermon back from my leave, that brings me to talking a bit about it. I begin with this question: what is your purpose in life?

Ultimately, that is what my struggle has been about. What would the Lord have me do? I thought, last summer, that He answered my prayer by leading me to announce my pending retirement, that it was okay for me to leave Port Hope, that

He had plenty for me to do in service to Him and His people, even if I did not know what that ministry would be.

I thought I knew. I was at peace with the decision. Julie and I were forming a plan for our future. Then, a funny thing happened on the way to retirement. Just before Thanksgiving, I felt at peace with myself in such a way I no longer wanted to leave Port Hope. I was loving my work and comfortable with myself in a way that I had not been in so long that I can't even remember.

The peace continued. In early December, after officiating a funeral, as I stood in the back of the church I looked at the pulpit and felt like I could never leave it. I told Julie I was having pangs to stay.

The peace lasted through Christmas. Didn't you notice what a good mood I was in? At Wednesday Bible class, they accused me of having too much caffeine, or that I was high on the pain pills from my foot surgery. But it wasn't either of those things. I simply was at peace with myself and it was bubbling over.

After church on New Year's Eve, Julie and I talked about staying here. I would say that we were 95% certain I would not retire and we would stay.

I can't explain to you what happened to me on New Year's Day—if I understood it myself it sure would be nice—but the peace was gone. The old struggle, which has been brewing in me especially hard for the last year, which has been percolating for years, came back with a vengeance.

And it was worse. When you heard that I left town, you probably were scratching your heads because I looked like my old self whenever I was with you. I spoke of it in the letter that Ken Bush read the first Sunday I was gone, and Julie also referred to it as she eloquently spoke of how badly I was hurting and assured you that, despite the rumors, we were not getting a divorce.

This has nothing to do with you, or my work with you. I am confident I would be having this struggle wherever I lived, whatever job I had. This is something that has been in me long before I ever heard of Port Hope.

The struggle was worse because my work life and my personal life grew even farther apart. I was loving my work, and feeling good about myself when I was working. But within minutes after Sunday worship, or driving home from making shut-in calls, or coming home after an evening meeting, I would fall so far and hard I wondered if I would even be able to leave the house the next morning.

That's what was happening the first weeks of January. I wanted to tell you my last Sunday with you, that I was going to take a leave of absence—I wanted to tell you myself, not have Ken and Julie tell you—but that weekend the plan was only in the works. So, at this point, I need to thank a lot of people. Thank you, first and always, to Julie. She is my Jesus in the flesh. When she told me she wanted to speak to you, I was so proud of her. She made the three most important points, that this is not about you, that we think St. John is the best congregation on the planet, and that she and I remain crazy about each other.

Thank you to Ken and Nancy Bush, and to our head elder and his wife, for being so supportive. These four have been there for me, for many months. And Ken is always ready and willing to lead worship, so I pray you are thankful to him, too.

Thank you to the elders and the church leaders who approved my leave, and who were prepared for me to be gone however long I needed to be gone. I have thanked the pastors who filled in for me. I pray that you have been served in my absence.

Many of you are concerned I am coming back too soon, while a couple of oddballs have shown concern that I wouldn't come back at all. I feel that a month was enough time. I learned I really would love to remain as your pastor, but I also learned my struggle has a long way to go before I might be healed. What I am saying is, if I still retire this year it won't be because of you, or because I don't want to be your pastor. It will be because I simply am not able.

Now, to tie this in with the sermon and the question: what is your purpose in life? That question came to me because that is what I am trying to figure out about myself. But, you know what? I already know my purpose. So do you. Indeed, I have spoken of it, so many times. Your purpose and mine is to live the two greatest commandments, to love the Lord our God with all our heart and soul and strength, and to love our neighbor as we love ourselves. Or, as I like to say it, we show that we love the Lord by serving our neighbor.

After I had been back for a few days, I learned the most widely held idea about me was I suffered from bipolar disorder. My highs and lows made that a good stab at my condition.

The next Sunday was three days shy of the thirteenth anniversary of my installation as pastor of St. John. I had achieved the rank of St. John's third-longest serving minister. I would have to remain until my late eighties to take over the lead, but second place was easily doable and I so wanted to achieve such a tenure. Loyalty is important to me, and the long term with them would be indicative of how much I loved serving them and living in Port Hope.

When I initially announced my retirement the previous September, the first Sunday in March was to be my retirement date. Immediately, the board of elders asked if I would stay on through the busy Lenten season and Easter, and since confirmation was the Sunday after Easter could I please be here for that, too? So, my retirement would have been the first Sunday in May.

Now, this first Sunday in March, I told them I was going to try to stay. I would give myself the month to decide, hopefully enough time to get a good read on things. I didn't want to leave them hanging too long.

They graciously poured out their "I sure hope you stay" kindnesses. That felt mighty good. But could it ever be enough to uphold me?

The answer came quickly.

33

"I have dysphoria"

I had no business introducing the possibility of my rescinding my retirement. It was dumb. I was naive. It was strictly because I hate letting anyone down.

The news of my retirement had shocked the folks of St. John and Port Hope. While some were able to say, "Good for you, for knowing what you need to do," way more said, "Oh, I do hope you change your mind."

In 2008, I had received a call to be a minister at another church. In the couple of weeks after I announced this, I received phone calls, emails, letters in the mail, and visits from members, all expressing their hope I would stay put, that after seven years I still had plenty of work to do at St. John. The same had happened when I was in Iowa, contemplating the call to Port Hope.

Talk about a no-win situation when you hate letting folks down. Stay where you are and the folks there are happy, while the ones at the other church are disappointed. Take the call and make the new church happy, and crush the spirits of those who long for you to stick around.

That's where my pending retirement had me. The hardest reaction for me to process was the one I heard the most: "You're too young to retire." Some generous folks padded it: "You're too good at what you do." And some made it even worse: "The LCMS is losing an excellent minister."

I wanted to cry out, "Okay! Okay! I'll stay! I don't know what I was thinking!"

I never did that. I would remind them I didn't want to retire, but I needed to for my emotional well-being. I would stress I knew the Lord still had work for me to do, that I might be leaving the pulpit but I had no intention of retiring permanently.

It now was the end of March. I had returned from sick leave, opened the *I might change my mind about retiring* door, and promised a timely answer. In a section of my sermon, I set the table for my answer, which I would provide after worship, not wanting to completely lose their attention during worship.

I used the sermon to do for them at least a bit of what I had been itching to do. While I promised not to divulge my gender dysphoria and possible transitioning, there was much more I could say to help them grasp my struggle.

They deserved to know way more. This all being so mysterious was completely unfair to them. They knew by then, especially because I took a month's sick leave, that my troubles were way deeper than I originally revealed six months earlier.

Without seeking anyone's opinion, and not even running it by Julie, I decided what I would say that Sunday. Here is that section of my sermon.

When I returned from my leave of absence, I told you I didn't want to retire, but I still might have to. In February, I informed our elders it would be my goal to tell them, at our March meeting, what my plans were. I started a new medication about that time and hoped to see positive results by this time. Last week, at our meeting, I told the elders where things stand with me. After worship, I'll fill you in on that.

I want to explain more about my struggle. I am your pastor, and I don't like keeping things from you that significantly affect you, which my health situation most certainly does. Some of you picked up on the fact that, during my first sermon back from my leave of absence, I didn't really tell you what my condition is, only how it affects me. Today, I will tell you what my condition is.

There is a very difficult thing about my condition that must be confusing to you. I look just fine. I act just fine. Nothing seems wrong with me. Last Sunday, after church, I had so many people tell me that the old me was back, that my zeal had returned, and so forth. This is the problem: when I am with you, when my focus is on leading worship, or teaching, I usually am fine. Not always. Sometimes, I have to paste on a happy face.

My condition is this: I have dysphoria. Dysphoria is an uncommon word with a straightforward definition. Dysphoria means ill feelings. You know the word euphoria, which means you have good feelings. Dysphoria is exactly the opposite.

I know some of you have wondered if I have bipolar disorder. I don't, but it can look like it. Ordinarily, I am not depressed. My doctor feels that, under the extreme stress of the last year, I am suffering some form of depression, at least at this time. I am on medication, hoping to ease that.

I have had dysphoria for my entire life. I was diagnosed with it only last year. As Julie and I have learned about it, it is very possible it is more than a mental, psychological condition, but originates as a physical, biological condition. I really believe I was born with it.

It began to affect me when I was very young. At first, it was fairly minor. I didn't feel right about myself. As I have learned more about it and myself, I think I might have become a person who has a great need to be liked, and an even greater need to entertain people, because I was covering for the ill feelings I had about myself.

The ill feelings grew over the years, slowly and gradually, like a snowball rolling down a mountain. In recent years, they intensified. Last year, the snowball became an avalanche that crushed me. As with any illness left untreated, it is not going to get better, it is going to get worse and, finally, it is going to get really bad.

Since I already had dysphoria, I suspect I was even more greatly affected by many of the events of my life, especially since my divorce. I was severely depressed in those months. I felt like I had disgraced you. Remember, I offered to resign. Thankfully, you supported me so wonderfully, but I still carried tremendous guilt.

Then, as your pastor, I have been under severe stress from all of our tragedies. You know I wear my heart on my sleeve. Well, I bear your burdens inside of me with great intensity.

When I had my heart stents put in, I experienced anxiety for the first time in my life. I received the stents around the time the last of the kids moved away. I don't want to sound like a whiner, but honestly tell you how profoundly things impact me, and the kids leaving, and all moving so far away, devastated me, just as I told you when I announced my retirement.

I put my finger on something about that, only a few weeks ago. When I grew up, I was the middle of five children. When I left home, it was when I got married, and there were still two kids at home. I didn't move far from home, and we started a family right away. All of my extended family lived within a few miles, and we were very active together. I never knew anything but family, as many of you have much of your families living around here.

I think what happened to me, when Julie and I became empty-nesters, is I lost a huge part of my personal identity. This is one of my reasons for wanting to be closer to my kids and grandkids. Julie and I are so isolated from family, and having a job where you work weekends only makes it worse. And I was dealing with this as a person who always struggled with how he felt about himself.

As my ill feelings about myself took a serious hold of me a few years ago, I noticed I could not even look at myself in the mirror. I couldn't stand the sight of myself. When my dysphoria exploded last year, I just plain hated myself. And then I hated myself for hating myself, because the Lord is so good to me.

Here it is, in a nutshell: I feel completely at odds with myself—with my body, and my brain, and my life.

I have been seeing an excellent therapist for almost a year. Julie has attended many of the sessions with me, which has been a blessing. My therapist has helped me to understand myself, but, sadly, my dysphoria keeps getting worse.

After using the word *dysphoria*, I feared two things would happen. First, I thought I was going to hear from the church leaders who were in the know. I had given Julie the heads up after I wrote the sermon, and she was on board, but I thought the others were going to hang me, that I revealed too much. Second, I thought for sure members would go home, do an internet search, and find that *dysphoria* is always attached to *gender*, and the jig would be up.

Neither happened. The church leaders found I had explained things well. As for the members' curiosity, later, after I went public, I told some of them

I was sure they were going to figure it out when I was still their pastor. One replied perfectly: "We were so concerned about you. I don't think it occurred to anyone to question more than what you said."

During the after-worship announcements, surely everyone in church knew I now was going to tell them I was retiring. Even so, some faces still looked as though I had punched them in the gut.

I would retire on June 30. My final Sunday would be June 29.

Since this now was my third retirement date, on the way out of church one of the venerable members, a known cut-up, quipped, "We'll work on getting you to stay through the end of the summer, and then we'll work on longer than that."

Finally, I had set a date which would stick. We had exactly three more months in Port Hope, and a million things to do.

34

Retirement

To where would we move? How would we forge an income? What would happen with me?

We got busy.

While it seemed inevitable I would proceed with transitioning, I still was in *remain male as hard as I can* mode.

We had in mind moving to Indianapolis. We grew to like the city from the numerous times we visited our daughter. The weather is warmer than Michigan, which was a big draw for me. Should I transition, it would offer at least some of the services I would require. Our Indy daughter is the only one of our kids, all whom by now had their own children, who did not have any grandparents in the area, so we would provide that. And, perhaps best of all the reasons, Indy is fairly centrally located to where all of our kids were living at the time, with our older daughter in Georgia, older son in West Michigan, and younger son in West Virginia.

But, Indianapolis is in the heart of a state which, as much as any, represents a bygone American era.

Julie posed the idea that we move to Portland. The one in Oregon. A tremendously LGBTQ-friendly city. She was convinced I would transition. That transitioning was what I needed. That it would stick. And so she was concerned for my safety in Indiana.

But, wow, is Oregon ever far from our kids. Even if relationships were currently on the strained side because of my revelation, and fearing they would worsen before they got better should I switch to Gina full time, a great distance would be as bad as living on the moon.

Soon, Indianapolis was it. Soon, Julie found a house for us to rent the first year, in the same neighborhood as our daughter, with our plan to purchase a house early in 2015. Soon, we were sorting through the huge parsonage, which we had crammed extra full for having joined our two households, needing to greatly reduce our possessions.

Burnable trash went to our backyard campfire spot. No-longer-wanted-but-still-useful items were offered to members or given to the thrift store. Every Sunday, the day before the church's Dumpster was emptied, we filled whatever space was left. We retrieved boxes from the convenience store, stuffing the garage with our crammed cartons.

For me, the pastor, Lent gave way to Easter, which gave way to Confirmation Sunday, which led to the final month of the school year. I loved all of the big church events, preaching my heart out. And, once again, I was falling apart.

On the way home from the final youngster's confirmation party, I crumbled. Arriving home, I wound up on the kitchen floor, screaming out my pain and tears. It was another of the many *I want to be a pastor and remain a male and I can't possibly transition but I don't see how I'm going to survive unless I become a woman* meltdowns.

I restarted HRT. After the January meeting, when I came close to being suspended, I had promised to stop HRT and not take it as long as I was still a minister. I now found myself desperately needing it for calming my brain.

And it did. In a couple of weeks, I was feeling really good. And then I was thinking really dumb. My brain was so colored by the desire to remain male I convinced myself the reason I was feeling good was because retirement was finally near, that leaving the stress of the pastorate was my solution, that leaving the ministry would enable me to hang in there as a male.

It was a slightly less profound second coming of the supercalifragilisticexpialidocious I had experienced to close out 2013.

After a month on HRT, I stopped again. Feeling so strongly it was the coming retirement that provided my elation, and not wanting the outward physical effects of long-term HRT usage, I stopped taking it the end of May.

June was as busy as a month could be, with my final Vacation Bible School—all morning, Monday through Friday—our two Indianapolis grandkids coming up for that and remaining until they rode home with us when we moved—it was their yearly stay at what Julie had dubbed Camp NaPa, a play on our grandparent names, Nana and Papa—and the never-ending packing.

June 29 arrived. I didn't think the early service would be overly full, with most folks coming to the later service, then heading straight to the retirement party at Port Hope's AmVets hall. And so it happened. A nice group gathered at 8:00; then the pews were packed at 10:30. My sermon felt like the final episode of so many beloved TV shows; it could never live up to the moment, no matter how much time I spent writing it. The same would be true for my speech at the party.

Oh, the party! The committee outdid themselves in every way. From my favorite meal—turkey and all the trimmings—to the reminiscences—pictures shown on the wall and a poem written for the occasion, with speeches by some folks with whom I was close—to the humor—one son of the funeral home owners played emcee, and his dad and brother properly roasted me—to Julie's speech, in which she was far too generous in her assessment of me as a husband and pastor and person, and for which she rightly received the sole standing ovation of the day—to the crowd—the place was even more packed than the church, more than three hundred to see us off. We were tremendously gratified the hall was populated not only by St. John members, but by many from the community and from the nearby church I had served when they were without a pastor.

It was a day I wished would not come to an end. I wanted to stand before them and speak until I had no more breath in me.

On Monday, I finished my work as pastor by making three calls to shut-in members. More goodbyes. More "I can't believe you are leaving us." More longing to stay.

Wednesday saw me heading to Bad Axe to pick up a U-Haul truck. First thing on Thursday, volunteers from the church would flood our place to help us pack it. We had so much help some folks mostly stood around and chatted.

It was soon evident we needed more space. Someone headed out to rent a trailer, to haul behind the truck. As that filled, there would still be enough left we would have to rent another truck, return the next week, and garner another bunch to help us pack it.

Emptying the parsonage was hard enough. Returning the next week was downright torture. All I could do was walk into each room, picture it as when we lived in it, and long for the good years. It was, hands down, the best house, with a lovely yard, ideal garden spot, beautiful woods on one side and the church with its expansive grass to its rear, in which I have ever lived.

Early in the afternoon of Thursday, July 3, I climbed into the truck, while Julie and the grandkids piled into the car, their parents having taken our other car back with them when they came up for my retirement party. We set off for Indianapolis.

Our Fourth of July would find Julie and me, with our daughter and her husband, emptying the trailer and truck and filling the house. The next few days were an almost frantic time of putting things where they needed to be, because we had another load to bring.

The next week, I rented another of U-Haul's largest trucks. Thankfully, we didn't have to cram things in to finish the job. Even more thankfully, I am married to a woman who is an artist at planning and storing. Going from a five-bedroom to two-bedroom house, from a two-car garage to one, we succeeded in arranging things to serve our needs before we would buy a house and pack it all up again.

Independence Day was a Friday. The weekend's hours had us moving so quickly, turning this way with a box and into that room with a piece of furniture and then down to the basement or into the garage with a storage item, that the Tasmanian Devil of cartoon fame would have looked as if he were standing still.

Monday arrived. I finally sat down and breathed. I fell apart.

I had been off HRT for a month. My hope, that retiring was the big thing I needed, proved to be a pipedream. Surely, my hormone levels having reverted to levels appropriate to a male—but not appropriate to me—is what did it.

I resumed sessions via the internet with Doc. Soon, we learned our insurance would not cover them being held in that fashion. We now had almost no income—my pension would barely pay half a month's rent—and had to watch our bucks. I ceased therapy.

I was determined to exhaust every avenue, so I looked for a pastor. Not only did I desire to feel better and remain male, I needed to do everything possible so that, should I transition and people asked, "Did you try this? And this?" I could say, "Yes. I tried that. And that. And everything I could think of."

I eventually sought help from at least a half dozen pastors. None of them knew what to do with me, other than to lead me to trust the Lord. When I pleaded with them, "I am losing my mind," I asked, "What am I supposed to do?" Every one of them gave me the same answer: "I don't know." I was at a dead end.

My post-retirement crash was a new low, a new worst, a new level of self hatred. And hatred for everything around me. I hated our house. I hated Indianapolis. I hated every last thing about my life. The saving grace was how near the kids were. I watched the grandkids a lot. I made supper many evenings of the week for all of us. These were the lone bright spots of my days.

A month of the terrible suffering was enough. August 1, I restarted HRT. Before retiring, I got every available refill, so I had two months of pills. In a couple of weeks, I was feeling good again. I was feeling so good I made the dumbest decision, and then compounded it by telling my kids.

"I decided I can no longer entertain the notion of transitioning."

I had always allowed for transitioning to be a possibility. Now, however, I figured that as long as it was an option, it would continue to tempt me. To have a mindset it was not available would help keep me focused on the only answer: remain male, and perhaps even find some contentment in being a guy.

Once again, not wanting the long-term effects of HRT, I stopped taking it the end of August. I could have predicted what was to happen. I could have, within a few days plus or minus, set the date it would happen. And it happened right on schedule.

It arrived on Monday, October 6. This crash seemed, as each one had, worse than the one before. Everything I hated in July, I now hated more. I had no way out. Despite my fantasizing about it, I could not return to Port Hope and be the pastor at St. John. When out jogging, I was constantly pestered with the thought of throwing myself in front of a truck. Daydreaming about running away was my constant companion.

In August I had once again packed my female belongings into tubs and put them in the basement. I resisted going to get them.

November arrived. Deer camp was on my mind. My older brother, having been retired for two years, would be setting up his trailer a week before November fifteenth's Opening Day. I would once again head up early to enjoy the peace, the beauty of the woods, and hopefully have a good dose of the fun which deer camp used to bring since I began hunting in 1982.

Saturday, November 8, I was pulling my camping stuff from the basement and preparing the food I would take. While in the process, I found myself utterly at odds with my male self. This was a unique sensation, a new way in which I found myself falling apart. I told Julie, "If I don't go downstairs, get some clothes and put them on, I will have no strength to stand and will collapse in a heap."

Down the stairs I headed. Once dressed, I relaxed.

On Monday, I headed out on the five-hour drive north to Michigan. The first few days of camp went well. It was just the two of us, then one more brother arrived, then the rest of the guys piled in. That was too much for me. I felt like a girl who needed some other girls around to balance out the overtly male behavior.

Back to Indianapolis, I emptied the tubs and refilled my closet. December arrived, bringing with it a few storms which dumped a Michigan-like amount of snow. My heart was chilled to the bone in utter distress.

We thought we had finally found a church which we wanted to join after having visited seven LCMS congregations. It was a tiny group of folks. We found in them a lovely heart. The pastor preached good sermons and was very likeable.

Christmas morning, we were in attendance with about fifteen others. I dressed as I often did for worship, in dress pants and a polo shirt under a sweater. The clothes were stuck to me as if they were foreign objects. I needed out of them.

That afternoon, as Julie and I settled into naps, I could not sleep. One thing was on my mind. It was time to attempt living full time as Gina. I had to know if I could do it. I had to see if it would help. I would start in one week. New year, new life.

This was no run-away-from-home daydream. I formed my plan, a realistic one. When Julie awoke, I laid it out. I did not know what to expect. She easily could have argued I was not ready.

She did not. She said, "It's time."

I began the process of phoning my kids and emailing other key folks who were in the know.

35

Real Life Test

The clock was ticking. I had one week to prepare to live full time as a female. A key step in the WPATH guidelines toward fully transitioning, this process is called the Real Life Test.

It's one thing to think you can go into the world as the opposite sex, to desire it, to plan it; it is an ascending-of-Mount-Everest feat to actually do it. It is common among trans folks to give great care to how they present. They risk losing their job should they present in the opposite sex, so they might continue to go to work as they are known. Family and friends, church and social groups, and true concern for safety in any number of places play into the decisions one makes.

There are folks who are okay with being gender fluid, who find their identity is neither strictly male nor female and so they go with the flow of how they feel at the time. That wasn't me. I needed a clear definition. Either I was going to succeed at living as a male, or I was going to do so as a female.

All of my closest family and friends knew of the possibility of my reaching this point, but it is one thing to be warned and quite another to be told the day has arrived. This one reacted with sad acknowledgment, that one responded with a strong "don't do it," and some let silence speak for them.

There was more to it than my attempting to live full time as Gina. I was going to go public. I always knew, whether or not I transitioned, that I was going to use this as a teachable moment. From the many with whom

I had spoken, and from countless things I had read, worse than not being understood was that transgender folks are misunderstood. TV and movies did not help. For decades, if there were a trans character—always male to female—she was the maniacal killer, the fun-loving prostitute, the drug-abusing sad sack.

I knew better than the caricature. I resolved to educate. It was no stretch to know I would offend many by transitioning, so I desired to teach the truth about being transgender.

I also had my name to defend, and equally important was demonstrating one can be a Christian and transgender, and continue to take seriously everything he believed.

I was going to make videos to post online. I would start a blog and write essays. I would cover this topic from every possible angle, both regarding me and the transgender topic in general.

Everything I had been contemplating for two years was coming to a head. What more can make one do something radical than the feeling he is jammed up against a wall and pressed into a corner, with the ceiling coming down on his head. I was cracking.

I had written scripts for a few videos. These would be made as Greg. Each video would be part of a series, beginning with the question with which I had begun every conversation, "What do you know about gender dysphoria?"

I struggled so badly with sitting in front of the camera and making these real that I put off the job until New Year's Eve.

One of my best friends in the ministry was pushing me hard not to go public. He could only envision a mess. He suggested if I had to live full time as Gina I do so quietly. I argued I might be able to begin the process quietly, but in this internet-connected, social media-saturated age, it would be impossible to keep it quiet. It was better to be out in front and use it to instruct and inform. If I lost the moment, I could lose everything. People would think, "He was too chicken to tell us," and, "He wasn't who we thought he was." I could envision nothing but these reactions and total rejection.

New Year's Eve morning, I was one day from Full Time Day. Julie was at work, having found a good job in October. She had determined only to apply at places which are trans-friendly, with health insurance which covers transitioning. There are not many of them. She narrowed the list to two, then chose one she thought would be a good fit for her experience. She applied and was hired.

No matter my ups and downs, my continually trying to be a male, Julie never wavered in her conviction I would transition, and that it would prove to be what I needed. Now, if I did progress and proceed with surgeries, with her job we would have insurance to help with the cost.

In our dining room, I readied my camera on the makeshift tripod Julie had created to hold my phone. I had practiced my scripts. I began recording.

Before I got the first one completed, I stopped. It was too much, too big, too terrible for me to imagine posting these videos online.

Already cracked, I fractured all the way. I now was bawling. I walked around the house, pleading with the Lord for help, for direction, for peace.

I screamed. At the top of my lungs, I screamed. Pacing from living room, to dining room, to bedroom, to dining room, and back to living room, I screamed out my petitions to the Lord to rescue me.

I thought about killing myself, then replaced it with a plan to run away. Now, today, I thought running away was a real possibility. But what of my promise to Julie that I would never do that?

I had an idea, a way that I could run away and not break my promise. I would run home to Montague, either to stay with my best friend, Tim, or with my son and his family. On the way, I would text Julie exactly what I was doing. This way, I would not be running away, but getting away, something I had done several times in the preceding months, always to Montague. To home.

I chatted online with sister Sue most mornings, so I now connected with her. She thought a getaway was a good idea. I packed a bag.

Halfway to Montague, I sent the text to Julie. Soon, she phoned. She agreed the getaway was a good idea.

Arriving in Montague, I stopped at Tim's, talked for awhile, then headed to my son's, where I spent the night. I calmed down. The next day, New Year's Day 2015, soon after I awoke I no longer wanted to be away from home. Staying away would get me nowhere. I would have to face things eventually, so what was I waiting for? I headed back to Indy.

At home, I immediately changed into female clothes and painted my fingernails. I told Julie if I were going to succeed at the Real Life Test, I needed to do something challenging. I resolved to go grocery shopping the next day. As a woman.

In December I'd ventured out twice in female attire, but both were to safe spaces. We were aware of a trans social group and decided for the first outing to attend the group's annual Christmas party.

Stepping out our back door to leave for the party, I felt every neighbor's eye was on me. Even so, it was exhilarating. I felt good in my festive top and skirt and heels.

The party was a blast. We met many nice folks, and were happy to see a number of supportive spouses. We learned of an LGBTQ-friendly restaurant in town. The next Saturday, Julie and Gina went there for dinner. All went smoothly. Though we already knew it to be a safe place, I received a boost to my self-confidence. The acts of leaving the house, traveling to the place, walking from car to door on a public street, then dining in public, were all vital experiences in preparation for a bigger step.

There is a lot to consider when a trans person takes the plunge to go out in public. I was wearing a wig in those days. I had a receding hairline, and had thinned so much I could not imagine making use of my own hair. Nonetheless, I started growing it out, but it was far from being a length I felt was comfortably feminine.

Though I always kept myself clean-shaven, I had a typical five o'clock shadow. At Julie's urging, I began electrolysis four months earlier. Her argument was even if I remained male I might as well get rid of my facial hair since I hated having it.

Julie and I had felt I should not attempt the Real Life Test until I got enough mustache and chin whiskers removed so I did not need to wear loads of makeup. Even with makeup, my stubble was visible. Electrolysis is a terribly slow process. In an hour, a few hundred hairs are zapped and yanked, never again to appear. Divide that by the thousands on a typical male face and you learn it can take as many as two hundred hours of electrolysis to clear one's face.

Laser treatment is quicker, but only works on dark pigment. Most of my beard had grown gray. I still had some dark hair above my lips and on my chin. Eventually, six laser treatments would clear those, eliminate my five o'clock shadow, and reduce by dozens the number of hours of electrolysis. But that would not take place until later in 2015.

For now, early in 2015, I was stuck with the stubble shadow. Even worse, I was stuck with myself and desperately needing to move forward. Thus, Julie and I eased our standard. I simply had to step into the world as a woman.

I made my grocery list. I dressed simply, as any woman my age would dress for this task. I was in jeans, a simple top, flats, and light makeup. It was cold, so I had on my women's purple winter coat.

Whether or not a genetic male is able to pass in public as a female, the key is to blend in, to act natural. The more you stand out, the easier it is to get clocked. That's the term for when others spot you are trans—they clock you. Thus, you want to dress appropriately and act naturally. Like you belong there. Like you're just another person. Like no one is looking at you. Even if you think all eyes are staring you down.

Here is where my self-confident disposition paid off. I was able to walk up and down the aisles with ease. It was not my preference to encounter other shoppers up close, passing them in an aisle or reaching around them for an item, but when those situations presented themselves I did not shy from them.

The big step was to check out. I am a chatty person. I love making small talk with everyone who serves me, from wait staff in a restaurant, to receptionists, to healthcare providers. Now, however, my male voice, which I would attempt to soften and raise, would seal the deal on my being clocked.

I made small talk with the woman cashier, who was around my age. I received no chat back. I got one look from her. It was neither friendly nor disdainful. I read it as "Let's just get you checked out and on your way."

I headed to my car. It was still early enough in the morning that the parking lot was quiet. As I loaded bags into the trunk, I noticed a woman a few spaces away, who was looking at me too long. My gaze meeting hers, she quickly turned away.

I made it the three miles to home without incident. Back in the house, I was equal parts relieved and ebullient.

Home was my safety zone. Sadly, for too many trans persons, it is not. For us to work through the internal inferno of our conflicting identity and body and life, the externals rage against us, often out of control. Home can be the most challenging place for us.

When a trans person with a mate comes out, more often than not it means the end of the relationship. Trans young people still in their parents' house can find themselves no longer welcome. For those looking for a place to live, if they don't blend in and are easily clocked, too often they are denied apartments.

We would be buying a house in 2015. How would it go for us, with my being transgender?

Having retired, I didn't have a job at which I had to come out. In many states, transgender folks are not protected as are the classes of race, religion, and age. Trans folks can, and regularly are, dismissed for being trans.

Another primary concern for trans folks is personal safety. One never knows when someone will take exception to the person whom they see as a freak, a person who needs to be taught that their kind are not wanted. Transphobia is, perhaps, worse than homophobia. Gays and lesbians have been making inroads toward acceptance for decades; trans folks are way behind. While we can ride the coattails of much of the work done by the LGB, the TQ is separate in vital ways, often in the one that gets immediate recognition: how we look.

All of these concerns were in my head in my early days of the Real Life Test. None of them were going to stop me. Fear long ago ceased to have power over me, a personal attribute which never was more of a blessing than now.

I went to my next therapist appointment as Gina. I'd begun seeing Kathy in mid December, after a thorough search to find a therapist experienced with trans folks. My first appointment was as Greg, a crying mess and on my last legs hanging in there as a male. This time, witnessing a cheery and upbeat Gina, Kathy marveled at the difference in me.

I didn't go out a lot, but everywhere I went was as Gina. So far, none of the places involved the experience that is an especially unnerving one for trans folks—using a bathroom. That hurdle was yet to come.

Julie and I could not go to the LCMS church we had chosen. The end of December, I invited the pastor over to tell him everything. The poor guy was at a loss. Not only had he no experience with all of this, here I was, a former pastor, telling him I was going to attempt transitioning. He took seriously everything I told him, but after speaking with his board of elders he let me know the verdict. No, we could not worship there with me as Gina. He added, "We are struggling to come back from years of decline. We don't need the trouble."

I now was trouble.

The outcast.

I found a congregation which is part of the Evangelical Lutheran Church in America. The ELCA is a larger Lutheran denomination than the LCMS and more modernistic. The ELCA has women pastors, where the LCMS only allows males to be ministers. The ELCA now accepts practicing gays and lesbians as pastors and, recently, trans women and trans men. I met with the pastor, and she was very encouraging. Our first Sunday at the church, several members warmly welcomed us.

I resumed HRT, again wanting to lower my testosterone and raise my estrogen. Cutting the dosage, I had enough of the two prescriptions to last me into late February. I was hopeful Kathy would write me an approval letter to officially resume, so I could see a doctor and get new prescriptions.

The Real Life Test was going well. I was feeling good, feeling way better about myself. In late January, I mentioned to Julie I could be pursuing getting my name legally changed before the year was out. That conversation was both daunting and exhilarating.

The second week of February, I was set to see Kathy late one morning. I pondered getting dressed. The thought of going as Gina, up until then a delightful exercise, sounded awful.

36

Going public

I dressed in casual but feminine attire. I was not happy. I left the house and stopped to pump gas. I felt conspicuous. I sat down with Kathy and started blabbering. I lost it.

I told her I felt the harmony of brain and body was arriving. I was certain the next day I would feel completely male. This was now the fourth time I started HRT. The pattern was predictable.

Sure enough, the next day I felt completely male. I felt great. And I hated it. I wanted it so badly, but the longest it had ever lasted was six weeks. The second time was shorter. The third about the same as the second. I feared the coming crash. I was certain it was on its way.

It arrived the very next day. I enjoyed one day of peace and then it was gone.

I wanted to rip myself apart. That evening, right before Julie went to bed, I told her I was going out. To get ice cream. Mint chocolate chip. My go-to flavor. She didn't try to talk me out of it.

I ate nearly the entire half gallon. It served its comfort-food purpose. I calmed down enough to sleep.

But I was right back at January and July and October of 2014. Because I was now at turn number four, the crash felt worse than ever. How could I continue to live this way? I resumed my lament: I don't care which one I am, Greg or Gina, just let me be only one person.

I halted the Real Life Test. Well, I broke my streak of living as Gina every single day. Now, how I presented myself depended on how I was feeling. Julie and I went to the ELCA church through Easter. They only saw Gina.

On Thursday, April 23, I sat in Kathy's office. As Greg. As Greg at the end of his rope.

I raged.

I was angry at everything and everyone. I screamed out the conflict between male and female in me. I cried out the constant battle with the Lord and the Church and how I could not possibly transition without being condemned by the LCMS. I wailed at how my kids were having nothing to do with me since I told them I was going to live as Gina. If there were records kept of decibels reached and tears shed in one therapy appointment, I surely set new marks.

Driving home, a thought dawned on me. It was almost exactly two years to the day since I began seeing Doc. Two years of therapy. Two years of trying to figure it out, to straighten me out. I became livid with myself. *Failure! Eilers, you are a failure! You are a no-good-for-nothing piece of work, that's what you are!*

Three months earlier, I thought I would be going public with my gender dysphoria. I was praying like crazy for the Lord to direct me in this. I was always praying: Lord Jesus, please show me your good and gracious will, and then help me to follow it.

I arrived home and prayed. And then it happened. As vividly as the moment when I realized I would go to seminary and everything was going to work out just fine, giving me a peace which was previously incomprehensible, it happened again. In an instant I knew now was the time for me to go public. That therapy session would be my launching pad.

I had initiated a blog and only recently begun populating it, writing fun family stories from my youth. I would now use it for its intended purpose, telling my story, *telling my transgender story*, to the world.

On Friday, April 24, 2015, I posted the following, which I titled, "Therapy."

+ + +

I just marked a noteworthy anniversary. In late April 2013, after spending nearly three months completely falling apart to the point where suicidal thoughts reared their ugly head every day, I sat across from a therapist for the first time in my life.

Yesterday, as I sat across from my second therapist, I spent the entire hour letting go of the intense anger which has once again built up in me.

For those, to whom I have told every detail of my condition, know these things:

- I am essentially back to where I began.
- I hate myself.
- I don't know what to do with myself or what to do about myself.
- I am fighting so I can be the person you want me to be.
- Things have changed since last December, when I gave you that news you never wanted to hear.
- There are so many of you that I beg your forgiveness for not staying current with all of you. I pray you will find how I write about this to be helpful—helpful to you, to everyone, and to me—to inform the rest of my world of my situation.

While I am not suicidal, I would be lying if I said the thoughts don't find themselves seeking entrance. The noise in my head is deafening. I can't concentrate. I don't enjoy life. I wake up every night and can't go back to sleep. I constantly form plans to run away from home, as if by hitting the road I could run away from my problems. Every time I walk to the kitchen with an empty cup or dish, I want to throw it at the wall.

Two years ago, I promised Julie—who has been a little Christ to me—that I will not hurt myself, or run away, or destroy things. I have kept my promise and intend to do so.

I am finally prompted to become public about this for a number of reasons. With the lovely encouragement of many, I tried to be my old self on Facebook, began a blog, and undertook writing what amounts to my memoirs. I feel like a liar, a fraud. I suspect that some are thinking, "It looks like Greg is finally feeling better." No. Greg is not feeling better. Greg is feeling worse.

My anger has reached the boiling point. I need to harness it for good. That is why I am publishing this.

A large slice of my anger is that I have been stifled from being public with my condition. While some have felt I could and should go public, the number has been few. Most have thought that my situation is too sensitive, that many simply won't understand or comprehend, that by talking I will do way more harm than good. I never agreed with that. I wanted to stand in front of people and show them I am a person of integrity, not one who runs away and hides. I remained silent out of respect for them.

I have told nine brother pastors, and none of them knew enough about my condition to fill the bottom of a teaspoon. They all were very understanding, kind, and helpful. Ultimately, I have been counseled that I should remain under the care of my pastor-friends, repent and bear my cross in Christ's strength, and keep my mouth shut.

I have sought the Lord, and sought the Lord, and sought the Lord. Please know this: my trust in Jesus Christ has never been stronger. I know and believe in Him in a way I wish all people did. I constantly pour out my heart to Him, seeking His good and gracious will, repeating His promises back to Him. So, have no concern that I have lost or altered my faith.

I suspect I will be hearing from some of the folks who think I need to be quiet. I pray they agree this actually is the best time for me to explain everything, when I am smack in the middle of struggling. So people can encourage me. So I can educate people. Because this all will be public someday and I don't want it spread like gossip in which the truth gets twisted and my good name gets smeared and my family gets hurt.

To my kids, my siblings, all of the other several dozen friends and church people I have told: I promise to strive to write in a way which is God-pleasing, which shines the light of Christ, and which seeks to serve my fellow man.

All I have wanted since this began to crush me two years ago is to fulfill the two greatest commandments: love the Lord my God and love my neighbor as myself. I might never again be a pastor, but I know the Lord wants me to serve my fellow man by showing how a person can hurt so badly and still trust the love and mercy of Christ. I know the Lord is working to fulfill His Romans 8:28 promise in me, that He works all things for good in the lives of those who love Him, whom He has called according to His purpose.

It will take several days to roll this out. My next post will likely be on Monday.

Finally, I feel like I am doing something which will be therapeutic.

+ + +

I received an outpouring of concern and affection from those who had previously known nothing. From the vocal ones who had opposed my going public I received more opposition. For the first time, I stood my ground. My trust did not waver that the Lord had answered my prayer.

That didn't mean I wasn't scared. In the five days before I would tell my story on April 29, I posted a number of items to further pave the way. I expressed my concern that once I told my story some would reject me. I was assured by many there was no problem I had which could lead them to reject me.

After writing "Who am I?" I surely edited it twenty times. Before hitting Enter, I stepped away from my computer and prayed. My confidence remained. It was time to let the world know. I returned to my computer, sat down, looked at the screen and then at the button.

I pressed Enter.

+ + +

I have gender identity disorder. The clinical name is gender dysphoria. Dysphoria = ill feelings. Because it feels like my gender (brain) and sex (body) do not match, I have ill feelings about myself and my entire life.

There is great diversity in how this condition is experienced. I will normally refer to it as a condition, never as a disease, but my favorite term is dis-ease, which perfectly highlights the ill feelings.

A typical life with this condition and the dis-ease of it:

- As a young child, he is told he should be outside playing with the boys. He grasps that his behavior is wrong. He learns to comply so he doesn't get into trouble.
- In middle school begin the thoughts that will be with him every day of his life, dreaming about being a girl.
- During the teenage years, he takes action. Clothes are the obvious way to look and feel female, so he sneaks them whenever he has a chance.
- Growing up, getting married, he had hoped that love would be the cure but his feelings overcome him. As crossdressing intensifies, so does guilt and shame. Over the years, he will purchase and toss out a small box of items, over and over and over.
- In later middle-age, everything intensifies. He hates the sight of the man in the mirror. His body feels wrong on him. Getting dressed for work, he curses his male clothes.

In these five points, I have briefly described my experience.

In 2013, this finally crushed me. I began therapy. During my many meltdowns, I begged Julie to commit me to a psych ward. I cried more that year than the first fifty-five years of my life combined.

Trying to calm my brain, I began hormone replacement therapy. Raising estrogen and lowering testosterone often makes guys like me more at ease. I entertained the possibility I would transition, often thinking that was the only way I would survive. Of course, that flew in the face of everything in my life—faith and family—and, as by summer 2013 I began telling pastors and family and closest friends, "shocked" does not begin to describe their reactions.

I hope you appreciate this is why it was so hard to get to this day. People like me can't be transgender! *Wake up, Eilers!* There is nothing in my life which fits the profile—as if this chooses whom it afflicts (which begs the question: how did I get this?).

I am small-town middle class, lifelong committed Christian, husband and father and grandfather, traditional and conservative in every way from how I live to how I dress to how I spend my money to how I vote, and as a Lutheran minister I am one who holds a very by-the-book biblical doctrine. I am as straight as a yardstick.

In my post, "Therapy," I spoke of my suicidal thoughts. Among gender dysphoric people, 41% will attempt suicide. In the general population, the number is under 4%. Why is it so much higher for gender dysphoric and trans people? Because we fear coming out. We fear the reaction, the rejection. We can't deal with our internal struggle. We cannot see a good answer for ourselves.

"Greg, you cannot possibly transition"—a logical statement based on my resume. Yet, how much can a person take, even one who is strongly supported with these two pillars—faith and family?

There is no prescription, as for high blood pressure. There is no fix, as when I had two stents to heal my heart. With therapy, some can abide. I wish I could find the magic therapist. We all do, which brings me to the many folks who sent me private messages since Friday. I don't think any of us suffer from the same condition, with symptoms of frustration and despair and anger and sadness and so forth, yet each one listed the same problems which often seem insurmountable.

I will advocate no position on the topics of transitioning or anything else. I seek no permission or sympathy. I am opening up for two reasons, because the people who make up my world are largely in the dark about gender dysphoria and what it means to be transgender: for us to be understood and for others to be educated that this is a condition as real and horrible as the worst disease.

I am inviting you into my world because I have exhausted every avenue to live with myself. I want you to know the gravity of this condition. It is not the stuff of TV sitcoms. It goes to the core of one's being. It forced me out of the job I so loved, for which I was perfectly suited. I held it together in public and fell apart in private. It sent me to extremes I never imagined, even to the brink of death. It is a condition to be reckoned with, with humility. The world needs to learn about it in a calm, measured, non-sensationalistic way. I am here to do just that.

This post barely scratched the surface, but the surface has been scratched. I welcome every respectful comment and question. I suspect there will be so many questions that I will assemble them into Q & A posts, as early as Friday.

I conclude with this. The last several days, I have been male-brained. That, along with the two-year anniversary of having started therapy and finally grasping the answer to my ongoing prayer, is why I am speaking now—now, when I have renewed vigor to fight to remain male.

When I am male-brained, I am able to fight. When I am female-brained, I cannot imagine living as a man. When both brains present together, which happens more often, I can't do anything. I hate everything. I cry and writhe in pain. I remember my promises to Julie: I will not hurt myself, I will not run away, I will not destroy things. I pray like crazy, asking the Lord Jesus to show me His good and gracious will, reminding Him that I only want to do good with my life.

+ + +

I sat back and waited for comments. I didn't sit back for long. I barely sat back at all for the next several days.

37

Feedback and fallout

Everyone was fall-all-over-themselves kind.

The likes to my Facebook post collected as quickly as the comments underneath. The shock of the news was minimally heard, taking a back seat to the concern for my well-being and the generous assessment that I was brave to go public.

When I posted, my thought was I would allow folks to comment without my replying, not intending to get into conversation at the time but only to see their reactions. Within minutes, I found I needed to get in there, to thank each one, to give them answers to questions they posed.

By noon, I was worn out. I needed food and a break. I grabbed a quick lunch. I tried to close my eyes for a short nap. Unable to rest, I was soon back at my computer and catching up.

Because I was still Greg and proclaimed I was striving to remain male, I was seen as a champion for all things traditional and Christian. That morning, a pastor asked me to write an article for a church magazine that is geared toward teens. The article I submitted was largely my "Who am I?"

Published in June, it was received with mixed reviews. Loads of fellow LCMS Lutherans—pastors, adults, and teens—were pleased the magazine took the leap in discussing a topic which is timely and relevant. Others were not. They flayed the magazine's editors.

Some of my feedback was unfavorable. Some agreed with those who did not want me to go public. They argued that this was not conversation for public consumption. I replied that real people, in their real churches, are suffering from real gender dysphoria, and it is wiser to bring it into the light than pretend it doesn't exist.

Despite that I was striving to remain male, I immediately lost some friends. I gained others, significantly increasing my voice. I initially signed onto Facebook to see pictures of my grandchildren; now, it was my new pulpit.

I was invigorated to remain male. I wanted to be the hero, the man who beat gender dysphoria. I wanted to be in the LCMS and not an outsider. I was still on the LCMS roster and wanted to preach and lead worship in my retirement. Should I transition, I would have to resign from the LCMS, and surely many would reject me. Thoughts of rejection were a strong motivator.

Correspondence continued flowing in and I kept current with it. I was also writing my next blog post, and my next, and my next. I would post almost every weekday for months, longing to cover as many angles as I could.

The first few days, my sense of being male was strong, then I completely lost it. I felt my brain switch as surely as the wind shifts when a cold front moves in. Online, I kept up a good front. I was fighting the good fight.

We now were in the process of buying a house. Since Julie had a full-time job, it was mine to work with the real estate agent, to line up visits to houses which interested us. The agent was my age and very engaging. I opened up to her. She would have been my advocate had I chosen to present as female throughout the process. Because I was so back-and-forth at the time, I opted not to put into jeopardy someone not wanting to sell to us. I did everything as Greg.

In April, we found our house. We negotiated the price. Our bid was accepted. The home inspection uncovered issues with the foundation. We could not agree with the owner's repair proposal. We got out of the deal.

In early May, we really found our house. The home inspection went well and the closing went efficiently. We began moving things via our cars, making many trips on the six-mile, fifteen-minute, ten-stoplight drive. The end of May, I rented a moving van, filling and emptying it on my own, twice in one day. The first of June, I rented another, made one truckload on my own and then rounded up my son-in-law to help me with the two-person large items.

June 3, we moved into Merrymoss, which I had dubbed our house as a tribute to its last owner, Mary Moss, who had been an Indianapolis-area jazz singer.

Many things have always made me feel male. Jogging, mowing the lawn, and working in my vegetable garden these days still did that. The movements and flexing of my muscles brought me the sense of my familiar self, the boy who spent hours playing baseball and football, the man who pounded the pavement and worked the soil. Now, moving did this. Everything about my lifting and carrying heavy items made me feel like the Greg of old. When I felt that way, I so wanted to retain it.

The job of moving completed, the hours of feeling male no longer predominated. The two-person struggle returned. Even as I thought I needed to resume the Real Life Test, I fought it. A new reason existed. I already met the neighbors on either side of us and across the street. They met Greg. They had seen Greg mowing the lawn, getting the mail, leaving and returning by car.

By late June, I was back at the point of despair. I had remained on HRT since resuming three months earlier. Now, I had so much experience with all of this—the hormones, the internal battle, the external concerns—that I saw only one way to remain male without losing my mind. I would have to be heavily medicated on psychotropic drugs.

I had witnessed a few folks who had been heavily medicated, who required such powerful drugs it left them dopey. Shaky. Emotionless. Listless. I had not yet undertaken this path, so I could not know for sure, but my fear was real that emotionless and listless would be my lot.

That list Julie and I had made in the spring of 2013, the one where we listed the pros and cons of my remaining male or transitioning? The list had not changed. Greg's pro list still was eight items long. Gina's had but the one item.

When your very life is at stake, one beats eight. I resolved to restart the Real Life Test. Based on the things I wanted to do and people with whom I wanted to talk before resuming, the date would be July 2.

Restarting in person did not mean going public about it. I needed to see how it went, see if it might stick, before I could see myself letting the world know, before changing my online profile from Greg to Gina.

My poor kids. They didn't know what to make of their dad. One said, "I wish you could just settle on male or female, and then we could breathe." I got it. Transitioning is a family-wide event. Uncertainty is hard on everyone.

In August, I went to Montague as Gina. I stayed at Tim's house, as I usually did. I talked with my daughter-in-law. I wanted to visit. My son and family lived five minutes from Tim's, across the lake in Whitehall. She talked with my son. Yes, she got back to me, I could come over.

The thing about switching from male to female is one cannot know how dramatic the change will be. In January, Julie and I had begun attending a trans support group in Indy. Getting to know many trans folks, and some just beginning their transitions, I learned transitioning isn't as dramatic as one might suspect or fear.

Our personalities are integral to us. We don't ditch them and assume new ones. Sure, one attempts to take on the more visible cues of her or his new sex—I was mindful about how I used my hands and how I walked—and one might work to raise or lower the pitch of her or his voice. In most cases, those changes are subtle.

We want to fit in, so we strive to dress the way most people in our age group dress. We don't want to stand out, so adopting outlandish, overly feminine or masculine behaviors is not wise. And we have these personalities, which we have honed our entire lives, which, well, they are who we are.

My daughter-in-law prepared their two kids, who were two-and-a-half and six months old. The older one reacted with a giggling, "Papa's not a girl!"

I arrived, knowing my son was still at work. My daughter-in-law, who had been a wonderful ally, received me without a flinch. So did the kids. I had dressed casually, the most feminine things about me being my glasses, necklace, and painted fingernails. I wore no makeup.

We had chosen Gigi as my new grandparent name. Julie arrived at it, saying, "It's a combination of Greg and Gina." I loved it. The grandchildren struggled at first making the switch, but it did not take long for me to hear only Gigi coming from them.

I was playing on the floor with the kids when my son phoned. He and my daughter-in-law talked his entire drive home from work. This child of mine is emotional like his dad. He got pretty worked up with anticipation. My daughter-in-law continually reassured him.

He arrived, blew through the front door, spied me in the dining room, and rushed to me. I arose, fell into my son's arms, and we cried as hard as we hugged.

"I love you, Dad." "I love you, son."

It was early evening. We kept things light until the kids went to bed. Finally settling in to a good chat, I sat close, right across from him. We talked. We laughed. Everything felt as every other conversation we ever had.

That's when I stopped him from talking. "Have you noticed anything?" I began. "This is how we always talk."

"Yeah. You're right."

"But I'm wearing my chick glasses, and necklace, and my nails are painted, and I have on a woman's top."

"I don't see those things."

"Why not?"

"You're still you."

It was as wonderful as the moment I saw him enter the world.

This one had told me he was afraid that female Dad would no longer joke around the way male Dad always did. If that would be the case, he would lose so much. This epitomizes what goes through the minds of loved ones as they ponder the transition. How could he know if female Dad would still enjoy big laughs at the goofiest things? How feminine would Dad be? How different? Would Dad even be recognizable, or would Gina be an entirely new person?

This was a watershed moment. He would be able to assure his three siblings the change was not so big, so strange, so hard to take.

This would not be the case for many, especially a large number of my fellow Christians, when I knew I was ready to tell the world I was living as a female, that the Real Life Test was going well, allowing me to live with myself.

And changing my online profile picture and name from Greg to Gina.

38

Presenting Gina

August 17–20—a Monday through Thursday—were packed with activity.

I had been contacted by a Lutheran layman, with whom I became friends after meeting at a convention, about being interviewed on a podcast he and his pastor had. I was about to go public about the Real Life Test.

On August 17, I published "Not in My Wildest Dreams," in which I outlined the course of my life and my desire to be female. The next day, I followed with "Real Life Test," in which I admitted I was in my seventh week living as a female. Then, the next day, with as much excitement and trepidation as I have ever experienced, I changed my profile and picture to Gina.

The morning of the eighteenth, I had a pre-interview conversation with the pastor and layman podcast duo. I told them I was going public the very next day. They still wanted to interview me; indeed, they were very objective in their assessment of gender dysphoria and my transitioning. On Thursday, we conducted the interview. The first part was my answering basic questions regarding gender dysphoria. The second part began with the pastor's question, "How is it you know so much about this?" The podcast would not be put online until Sunday, after I had gone public, so I spoke of all that had been happening.

I needed to take one more big step this week: the time had come for me to resign from the clergy roster of the Lutheran Church—Missouri Synod. The LCMS has neither female nor transgender pastors, so in good conscience I had to resign. It did not matter to me whether I would succeed at living as a female; because I was going public, it was time for me to leave the roster.

I'd put in a call to the office of my former district president, DP. He returned my call on Thursday, before the interview. As we covered my areas of concern, so we could part as brothers in Christ I let him know I was resigning because I was living as a female. He was gracious toward me.

The resignation papers arrived in a few days. Though I never imagined the day, thinking I would die a minister of the LCMS while hoping in retirement to remain active, I had no hesitation signing my name and placing the envelope in the mail.

"Real Life Test" prompted a lot of response. Most was encouraging and kind. Some was harsh and unfair.

I received several emails from Christians, both pastors and lay folks, who took me to task, called me to repentance, and letting me know they unfriended me from Facebook. I was told: "You are letting the devil drag you by the nose." It was assumed: "You are following the way of the world." I was convicted: "Your offense is scandalous."

I composed gentle replies to every person. My explanations made no difference.

I was curious what the reaction would be when I changed my name and profile picture. People love new and different and controversial, so I should have expected many to jump on it. They did.

Surely, because the first ones were all positive—"Nice to meet you, Gina!"—no one, who was against my transitioning, was going to be the sore thumb amongst so many giving me a glad hand. I was grateful. Tremendously grateful. They affirmed me. I was accepted by many who have known me as friend and as pastor, and by many relatives who are online. I was especially appreciative how many from St. John, Port Hope, Michigan, where I last was pastor, were able to accept my transitioning. I eventually would learn many did not, but for all the fear I had in the months before retiring, when I wanted to tell them everything before I left, so many more were able to be accepting than I could have imagined.

The online hurdle jumped, I was still navigating my physical environment. Prior to the Real Life Test, I'd gone, as Greg, to a new eye doctor. In July I was due for a second visit. This would be the first time I had gone somewhere in Indy as Greg and now needed to tell them I was transgender.

How does one handle such a thing? I decided to call before my appointment, not wanting to surprise them by arriving as Gina and giving them the opportunity to tell me their position on having trans patients.

A few days before my appointment, I phoned. I explained about my gender dysphoria, that I was transitioning to see if it would help me feel better, and then asked if they would be okay with my being transgender. The receptionist's reply was quick and lovely. "We have trans patients. No worries. We will be glad to see you, Gina."

I could hear the smile in her voice. That she called me by my new name was gratifying. I went to the appointment with confidence. There would be plenty of other places where I would have to go through the same Greg-to-Gina process, so I relished this first experience.

I was still legally Greg, so my records had to remain that way. I asked at the eye doctor if they had a way of recording my preferred name. They did. Some offices have this spot on their forms, and some do not. Regardless, I hoped it would not be long before I made Gina legal.

This is how right I was feeling. Though I wished I could remain male, to make the hard stuff go away for me and my loved ones, when I let myself relax I felt good. I felt right. The two-person struggle melted into finding solace as one female person.

One September Saturday, I returned from jogging to find our next door neighbor in his back yard. This was the man with whom we had enjoyed a nice, long chat soon after we moved in. He and I waved, and I proceeded to our patio, where I sat and began cooling off. I knew I needed to seize the opportunity, so I arose and called to him.

I sure did not want to tell him his brand new neighbor is transgender. I ripped the bandage off quickly and awaited his reply. The man already had given the impression he is good-natured and easygoing; he now proved it. "You'll find the people in our neighborhood are pretty accepting." He assured me I was okay with him. I went into the house, eagerly searching for Julie and excitedly telling her of my achievement.

Every challenge I faced in the first months went well. All concerns fell by the wayside that Indianapolis might be too conservative for my transitioning. I feared going nowhere, but I could not yet go everywhere.

We did not have an LCMS church where we could attend. I had bared my soul to five local LCMS pastors. They all were kind and concerned, but none would welcome Gina and Julie to their churches.

Jogging in our new neighborhood, I ran by an ELCA church, only half a mile from Merrymoss. We found their website. This was a tiny congregation and multi-cultural.

The second Sunday in July, we headed there for worship. We were greeted by the church secretary, a gregarious woman with a lovely name—Gina—who was very welcoming. Soon approached a man who happened to be the congregation's president. He, too, was very friendly.

Though it would take getting to know us for some of the elderly folks to accept me, they received us with open arms. We were encouraged to attend their post-worship fellowship lunch that first Sunday, and gladly did so. After an hour of good food and better conversation, we made the short drive home with grins plastered on our faces. Entering Merrymoss, we almost fell all over each other to be the first to exclaim, "I think we found a church home."

We had theological concerns, the differences in belief which keep the LCMS and ELCA separate from each other, yet no LCMS church would welcome us. We breathed out and plunged in. In October, we joined the congregation.

I still had not taken one big step—the step into a women's restroom. That would come in September, when Julie and I made the ten-hour drive to Iowa, to spend a week with her parents.

Making our first stop for gas, I asked Julie to wait for me, before going inside, until I was finished filling the tank. We entered the store together, then the women's room. She finished quickly and departed, leaving me. A woman entered, with a young child. They took the stall next to me.

My heartbeat increased. By their conversation, it was clear this was a grandmother and grandchild. Oh, gravy. I wanted out. No way, my first time in a women's restroom, did I want to encounter an older woman with her granddaughter.

I hurriedly finished, exited the stall, washed my hands, and got out. Spying Julie in the store, I felt better, but I still longed to get out and into the car.

We would need one more stop on the way there, and two on the way home. Each went just fine. Thankfully, "smooth" describes every one of my experiences these first potentially harrowing months.

A big occasion was on the horizon, and I was fearing how I would react. November always brought deer hunting season and our family camp. This year, I would not be welcome. Julie and I talked about it in October. She feared how it might affect me. We soon were to find out.

39

Family rejection

When I moved from Montague to attend seminary, I changed a significant part of my life. Until then, my siblings and I all lived within five miles of the house in which we grew up. Moving away, and knowing I'd selected a vocation in which I would work weekends, I would be cut off from the everyday occurrences I enjoyed—cutting and splitting wood with Dad on winter Saturdays, seeing a sibling in town and catching up, getting together for an impromptu evening of cards—and from the special occasions—weddings, high school graduations, birthday parties.

I was sad about this aspect of chasing my dream, but I accepted it. I attended as many events as I could. I drove from Iowa to Michigan for the funerals of two aunts, one of whom was my Godmother. My ability to travel home was too rare. Still, this geographic disconnect was of my making; it was not thrust upon me, but caused by me.

Some might argue that my transitioning was similar to moving away: I put myself in a position of not being able to attend family events. The argument falls short though when it is not distance and work circumstances that kept me apart, but instead because my presence would be uncomfortable for, or rejected by, some in attendance.

That is where I found myself with family deer camp. I knew Gina was not welcome. This was not my assumption. Things had been said.

I had no intention of forcing my way in. I would not point out how I was a valuable member of camp, the one who cooked breakfast, the one who built the huge campfire to celebrate Opening Day Eve festivities, the one who had for years written the camp poem, which was a fun way of poking hilariously at our foibles, and the one who was the camp clown, always providing dumb stuff to provoke big laughs. It didn't matter that I would, except for a bit longer hair, resemble Greg in every way, from the clothes I wear at camp, to the way I talk and act and look.

It is not my personality to force myself on others. Or to make a scene. Or to put others on the spot. I knew that even if I went to camp dressed in my usual garb, most likely tucking my hair in my hat, the others would see me as the guy who now identified as a woman, and they would be uncomfortable.

Was this on me, because I chose to transition? Or was this on them, not dealing with me, not working to understand me, not giving me a chance to show them—as my son learned three months earlier when we saw each other—that I was the same person they always knew?

Certainly, it's both. When you are the one in my spot, it hurts that your loved ones … reject you. That's what it is. Rejection.

From the people with whom I am the closest in this world, I was being rejected. Even though I knew it was coming if I transitioned. Even though I understood why it was hard for them. All of the understanding in the world I could muster could not remove the fact I was being rejected.

For the first time in my life, I was an outsider with my own family.

As deer camp time neared, the smart approach would have been to keep my mind completely off it. However, one of my brothers and I were emailing. He was the one who had given birth to the camp poem, exhausted ways to write it so passed it on to me, and then took it back for 2015. I asked him to email it to me.

It was really good. He recaptured his glory from his first go-round with the poem. I laughed a lot and emailed him my praise.

And then I fell apart.

I wanted my old life back.

I bet you know the feeling, when something has happened and you want a time machine to get back to before everything went wrong. Before your spouse left you. Before you lost your job. Before the doctor's pronouncement of cancer. Before a loved one's death.

From my reading and getting to know trans folks, I believe one hundred percent of us experience rejections by family. Sometimes, it is stark: "You're no longer my child." Often, it is blunt: "I'll never use your new name." Regularly, they persist in using the pronouns of our birth sex, no matter how much we appeal to them to correct it. Many times, they set ground rules: "You can attend family functions as you, but not as this person you are pretending to be." And, in that decree, they show their attitude regarding our transitioning. That they have not truly heard us. Have not grasped our struggle. Our pain. How badly we have been torn apart for so many years. How much we need to figure this out so we can finally experience peace. Wholeness of being.

We suffer the worst rejection from the ones we need the most. We are not respected in the place we most deeply long to be understood, to be valued, to be beloved.

Yes, there are allies. Perhaps one of the two parents will be understanding, even wonderfully so. A sibling or two will hear us and rally to our side. Grandparents often surprise us with their love, their ability to accept our revelation, when we fear their being two generations removed will make that impossible.

We are deeply grateful for the ones who accept us. We rely on them. We cling to their affection. They often go to bat for us. They try to pave inroads with other family members. They are the ones who might be heard when we are no longer given an opportunity to speak.

Sadly, though, we rarely achieve a full round of acceptance. Without the complete support of family, there remain gatherings to which we are quietly not invited, or blatantly unwelcome: "You will in no way go to the funeral."

These are the stories I have heard firsthand from trans folks. These are the accounts I have read on social media and blogs and in books, and in emails I've received. These are the situations of my own experience. These are the matters which plumb the depths of our hearts and the pain we suffer, the aching for love, the longing to be understood. To be included.

When we come out, we often are not allowed in.

We suffer similar hurts from friends but, in the end, they are replaceable. Some friends are lifelong, but many come and go depending on where we live and work and the groups we join. We can fill in with new friends the hole created by friends who reject us.

But we only have one set of parents. And children. And siblings. And grandparents. When we lose them, we lose way more than home and acceptance. We lose the first identity we knew in life. The identity we carry in our last name. In our history. In our legacy.

This is what visited me that day I emailed about deer camp with my brother, when the realization hit home I was not welcome. That I was rejected. That I was an outcast.

That I was an outsider in my own family.

I spent the morning weeping. I did what I always do in these times: I lay on my bed and called out to the Lord. I begged Him for help, for mercy, for direction, for everything I had been begging Him for three years.

How could I be in this spot? How could I get out of it? How could I bear up under it?

I grew angry. Angry with the guys of deer camp. Angry with myself. Angry with everything about my life.

I had a big, deep, long meltdown.

This would not be like other meltdowns, where Julie would pick me up and talk me through it so I could move on. Julie wasn't home. She was at work. I wouldn't see her for six more hours.

That evening, she saw it. She asked me how I was doing. I fought not to tell her. Logically, I knew I needed to get it out of my system. Emotionally, it seemed too much.

Julie waited me out. I broke. Out it came, in a flood of tears and a landslide of words and an earthquake of emotion.

This was a meltdown that couldn't be cured by talking it out. This one sat on the calendar. I would not be able to ignore it, as every day deer camp moved closer and every day another stab to the heart knowing I couldn't be there.

I needed a diversion.
In a blink, I had two.

40

Two diversions

Jackie was our first child to marry. That was in 2006. In 2007, she announced she would have our first grandchild. He arrived in October.

Jackie moved to Indianapolis to get her Masters degree. At that time, her mom lived west of town. Indy had a school with a program she liked. A dear friend from high school just happened to have landed in Indy. All of these made the area a good choice. After a few years, she and her husband bought a house in town. In 2011, they welcomed a daughter.

On Halloween of 2015, Julie and I accompanied Jackie and her kids to Jackie's friend's house. Kayla had three little ones of her own. We had a fun day watching the kids play, filling the gaps with lovely conversation.

I had forgotten Kayla's husband was an editor with the magazine Indianapolis Monthly (IM). Each month, IM includes a number of features, highlights local events, provides a restaurant guide—everything one needs in a slick glossy about the happening town of Indianapolis.

Kayla had read my blog. She complimented my writing and the importance of the subject matter. She suggested I contact her husband about writing an article for IM.

I pitched him the idea. He replied, yes, they were interested. My chances were not hurt by their having not yet printed an article on the topic of transgender, or one by a trans author. It also happened that early in 2016 the Indiana legislature would be considering a bill regarding transgender rights.

We had to move quickly. They wanted it for the March issue. The suggested outline was for me to write about my struggles with gender identity, provide general information on the topic, and then bring it around to the hot topic of transgender rights. They wanted three thousand words.

As I went into the mega meltdown of missing family deer camp, I was trying to concentrate on writing. I wanted to be ahead of every deadline, so I had no time to mope. Thankfully, ideas came and words flew out of my fingers. I envisioned every section of the article. I set my keyboard ablaze.

On the heels of this serendipitous development, Monday, November 16, brought sad news. Jackie texted me that her husband informed her he was going to divorce her. After work, she came to our house. She fell into my arms.

The divorce was underway quickly. As things unfolded, it worked better for him to remain in their house and for Jackie to move in with us. That meant an addition of three: she would have her kids half of the time.

When Julie and I were house shopping, we looked at both two- and three bedroom places, at those with one bath and one-and-a-half baths, at those with and without basements. Thankfully, our first effort whiffed; the place we decided against had only two bedrooms. We now were tremendously happy we'd chosen a house with three bedrooms, one-and-a-half baths, and a full basement. We would make use of every square inch.

Julie is as crafty a planner as you will find. Previously, we were spread out, with her using one bedroom for an office. She came up with a design for cramming more stuff into our bedroom so we both could have our computer desks in it. We purchased a bunk bed for the kids, who were eight and four at the time, turning the corner bedroom into the kids' room. Jackie moved some of her favorite pieces from her house and properly appointed the small bedroom, giving her a space all her own.

As for me, I had people to look after! People who needed me! The best diversion of all!

A challenge for folks who retire is the loss of identity their job provides. My retirement ripped from me a large part of who I had become, especially since the "dad" role lessened when my kids grew up and moved out. Though I now was a year-and-a-half into retirement, the wound often opened and bled as to how my condition forced me out of the work I loved.

I had my writing. The blog was doing what I wanted, educating regarding all things transgender and how one can still be a Christian along with being trans. And now I had the IM article. But, too often, writing was not enough.

With Julie working, I had become "house spouse." The lawn and garden were always my responsibility, but I'd added to my tasks cleaning, grocery shopping, laundry and—a newfound love—cooking.

Now, concerned about the upheaval in the lives of my daughter and grandchildren, I longed to make them feel welcomed and loved. It was my joy to plan meals, and I relished taking care of my expanded household. We readily became a three-generation home for the next nine months.

Settling into our new arrangement, I once again settled into my new self. As 2015 came to a close, I was feeling good again, working on edits of my IM article, posting essays to my blog, and pondering my future.

I now had the wrong name. Legally, that is.

I was living as a female. I was going by Gina Joy Eilers. My drivers license was for a male named Gregory John Eilers. My credit cards were for this man.

In October, I took a leap that was ridiculously hard for me. I got my ears pierced. This is something Greg would never do, despite his two sons having pierced their ears in their early twenties. No, Greg was way too old-fashioned. Way too straight-laced.

I wanted them pierced, though, and the time was ripe. It's crazy how big a deal it is to get one's ears pierced. I had to show my ID. This would be the first time I did so since transitioning.

It wasn't as if I were giving anything away at the piercing parlor, with the woman who requested my ID. I never hide that I am trans, mostly because I know my physical appearance doesn't fool anyone that I'm not a genetic male. The woman gave no reason for concern; she was as kind and easy going as can be.

So, while it wasn't hard to present my male ID, it simply was the first time

Gina used Greg's credentials, and it was a stark reminder of a huge step that had to be seriously considered.

That's what I was doing as 2016 arrived, contemplating petitioning the court to become Gina Joy Eilers, a female person.

41

Making Gina legal

Changing one's name and gender marker are big items on the platter of transitioning. Every state has different laws for such changes, and varying burdens of proof for requesting a change. In some states, a trans person can simply file a form to change the gender marker on the driver's licence, a practical adjustment that makes going about life much easier. Other states require significant costly and time-consuming hoops to make gender marker changes.

I knew in Indiana I needed a letter of endorsement from my doctor, demonstrating I was successfully living full time in my desired gender. She agreed and wrote the letter.

There are websites dedicated to helping trans folks learn the ropes and know the rules of their state. At our trans group meetings, the topic was regular conversation—and conflicting information.

I am a person who needs to know the rules. Instead, I was hearing a medley of this person did it that way, and that person did it this way, and perhaps you should try this or that. This name-change business reminded me of what I heard Julie say during her many years as a tax preparer, how if ten people called the IRS with a question they'd get ten different answers.

I learned as much as I could, read up on what Indiana required, and downloaded the forms. When I was ready to file them, it was February. At the city/county building, I learned the forms had to be notarized, though there was no spot which indicated such. (This is the sort of thing which drives me bananas. Do you require forms to be notarized? Then clearly note it. Put it in a nice box, where it is easy to recognize!)

There are bail bond offices across the street, where one can get forms notarized. I made my way to one, and greeted the woman at the counter. She had, to her knowledge, never before met a trans person. Before we knew it, she was asking one question upon another: "I hope you don't mind. I don't mean to pry." "No," I replied. "I love the questions. I appreciate everyone who asks with respect and wants to learn." Fifteen minutes later, she did her notary thing. As I asked how much for the service she waived it off, glad for my willingness to entertain her questions.

I returned to the city/county building, finished the processing, received my court date—May 2, mere days after my fifty-ninth birthday—and left for home feeling victorious.

Two months before that, my article would be published in Indianapolis Monthly. IM had me get the works for a photo shoot—professional hair styling and makeup. Did they ever make me look good! Even so, I joked that I hoped IM did not have in mind doing a full page spread with my picture, because no one on earth should have to flip the page to the likes of me.

Sure enough, the left side of the spread included a full page, from-the-waist-up photo of me, in all my smiling glory. The right side was dedicated to the title: "The Real Me: What it Feels Like to be Transgender."

On March 10, IM put my article on their website. I now could link it, online.

Statistics junkie that I am, I began watching the shares of my article, mostly through Facebook but also some Tweets and Pins and emails, curious how it might be received. I saw most IM posts had a few shares, some a few dozen. Occasionally, an article got into the hundreds. One, a patriotic piece about the flag, had a couple thousand.

Writers write for at least two reasons. Inspiration motivates us. So does the desire to be read, to have what we pen appreciated and found useful. If my article would not be shared much, I believed it would indicate it was not well-received.

By the end of March, it broke the one thousand mark for shares. Eventually, it would pass 1,700. I was as pleased as can be.

March brought another big event. The previous year, Indianapolis got a surgeon who performs sex reassignment surgery, now commonly called gender confirmation surgery. In February, I secured my therapist's endorsement letter that I was passing the Real Life Test. While I would need a second therapist's endorsement to have the surgery, the first was enough to get an appointment with the doctor.

Julie took off work to attend with me. The doctor was very helpful in explaining everything. Though I had read plenty, seen pictures, and watched videos of trans women who had undergone the surgery, it was daunting to hear her walk through each step, with diagrams and pictures to explain the procedure.

For over a year I'd been having electrolysis to remove my beard, at once-a-week appointments with a lovely woman, Barb, whom I dubbed "Barb the Impaler" for her constant stabbing. I now would have to shift the work from my face to my genitals. Since the flesh of the penis shaft and genitals are used to form the vagina and labia, all hair had to be removed. One painful jab and yank at a time. I hoped to have the hair cleared by autumn, to have the surgery before 2016 expired. I also hoped in 2016 to have facial feminization surgery (FFS) for the purpose of softening the masculine features of my face.

Male facial structure is far different from female. Brow bones jut out, eyebrows are lower on the forehead, noses are larger, chins are more prominent, cheeks are less round, lips are thinner. I saw a plastic surgeon in town who had done a lot of FFS. Sitting in his waiting room one spring day, a woman looked at me and asked, "Do I know you?" I didn't recognize her. "No, I don't think so. Where do you work?" Ruling out possible ways we knew each other, she finally exclaimed, "You have an article in Indianapolis Monthly!" I felt like a celebrity.

This plastic surgeon was not in our insurance network. Though my FFS would be approved by our insurance, being out of network meant we would be responsible for significant costs. We simply could not afford it. I had to drop it for the time being.

Despite the FFS setback, my transition finally was cruising. Internally, HRT had my hormones at levels for a female in my age group and I felt right about myself. Socially, I was succeeding at going everywhere as a woman. Emotionally, everything was fitting. Relationships with my children had returned from nearly two rocky years.

Though the deer camp snub stung bad, I had my first return to my extended family. In February, my father's youngest brother died. Four sisters remained. The funeral would be near my hometown of Montague. I wanted to go, finally having the time to attend family functions.

Would Gina be welcomed? I resolved I would go, but as Greg, and it would be a chance to reintroduce myself to the Eilers clan. Yes, this was a good plan.

Until it wasn't.

Within two days, the thought of putting on Greg's clothes and trying to play the male sounded just awful. I asked sister Sue what she thought. She said, "You're Gina. You should go, and go as Gina."

I told Julie. She echoed Sue.

I then contacted two cousins online. They did not hesitate. You're Gina, they said. Come as Gina. I called one of my aunts. She could not have been nicer. The assumption that older folks just can't grasp or accept transgender is an unfair notion. My aunt was in her eighties and, though she admitted all of this really surprised her, she was on board.

The service would be at a funeral home. I decided I would find a seat in the rear corner. After the service, rather than approach folks I would let them come to me, not wanting to put anyone in a spot should they be uncomfortable. It worked out well. All four aunts, and many cousins and friends, came over to me, hugged me, worked hard to use my new name, and graciously accepted me. I drove back to Indianapolis positively ebullient.

April brought spring and the opportunity to begin a vegetable garden at Merrymoss. I only had time to plant tomatoes the year before. Now, as I had done at every place I've set down roots, I fired up the rototiller, worked the lawn, and created a space for onions and broccoli and zucchini and corn and tomatoes and more.

May 2 neared. I continued to look forward to my court date and the changing of my name. It felt good. It felt right. I was ready,

A crack in my resolve arrived in early April. I was able to shore it up. The cracks kept coming, increasing almost daily. By mid April, I was fighting myself something fierce. As had become the case with every step in transitioning, I was fighting to remain male.

Logically, I had no reason to believe I could stop transitioning, go off HRT, return to living as a male, and succeed. Emotionally, I was trying to convince myself being a male was the only path for me. I had to do it. I had to stop this transitioning nonsense. What the hell was I doing, anyway? Transitioning was the stupidest thing on the face of the earth for who I was.

Eight days before my court date, my surliness showed through and Julie called me on it. I admitted all to her. For a change, she did not commiserate with me. She got just plain angry with me. "You always do this," she accused, and left the room.

We got back together and talked it through. Nothing changed. She knew I was hurting, but she also had a realistic view on things, a view which I was not able to see for the fog I was in.

Regardless, the next day, a Monday, as she went off to work I phoned the county clerk to inquire how one might cancel a court date. This would require writing a letter stating why. I immediately did that. I didn't print it. I decided to give it a day before proceeding.

Within an hour, I knew it was a fool's game I was playing. I deleted the letter. I knew one week from that day I would be going to court. Resigned as I was, I suffered as badly as ever. I wanted to get out of this. I wanted to run away. I wanted to escape everything about my life.

I did escape for a few days, to Montague. A few days with my son, his wife and two young kids, and sleeping at best friend Tim's was the unwinding I needed.

I returned home, and I returned to stewing. The next day, May 1, I was an emotional wreck. Monday morning, needing to leave for court by 8:00, I quickly wrote the following and posted it to my blog.

+ + +

"I wish I didn't have to do this." I wiped the tears from my eyes and resumed looking at Julie. "It will be okay."

This was last night, as Julie was kissing me goodnight. She sat on my lap, facing me. I peered into her eyes. Mine welled up with tears. I spoke of the big day finally upon me, the legalizing of my female name. "I wish I didn't have to do this."

A tear slid down my cheek and landed on my shirt. I removed my glasses and with a tissue soaked up the pools in my eyes. Replacing my glasses, I calmly continued, "It will be okay."

A strange thing happened on the way to my court date, when my name will be legally changed from Gregory John to Gina Joy: Gina has no joy at the arriving of this landmark day.

As I think back to December 2014, to the first trans person with whom I spoke about this topic, I recall the triumphant tone in her voice, the unbridled joy in her words: "I left the courthouse and was barely touching the ground as I walked to my car. I finally had my name to go with my authentic self, and I was so happy."

Two weeks ago, a trans friend got her name changed. With that, and the receiving of her corrected Social Security card and drivers license, she was just plain giddy. Her reaction is the expected one. This is one of the top steps in the long ladder of transitioning, and the sense of accomplishment is strong.

I am writing this two hours before my court appearance. I have no sense of my authentic self being acknowledged. I know I am a male, and would be if not for the endocrine disruption which left me feeling female. Thus, this is not a "Yay, the day is finally here!" moment for me. I just want to get it over with.

What is going on with me? Do I feel I am making a mistake? As the ten weeks have elapsed since filing my paperwork, this has weighed on me. The past two weeks have just plain been painful. A week ago, I found myself at the crucial point, asking whether I should do this.

I imagined cancelling today. I remembered what happened to me every time I stopped transitioning, each time I took a step back and tried to resume living as a male. I recalled that not only did I wind up crashing after a matter of days, each crash was worse than the one before.

There simply is nothing in me that can imagine being a male. It's not in my brain. Why do I keep struggling over it?

I continue to desire it because Greg can move through the world without a care in the world. The recent bathroom debate exemplifies this. Friday evening, I was in a women's restroom, in a stall, when numerous young women came in. One was showing a new employee how to change the towel dispenser, another took the stall next to me. While I have been in similar situations, with emotions running high over bathrooms I was not eager to approach the sink on this day. Thankfully, the coast cleared for me to wash up and get out.

Greg never has this concern. Greg never has people misgender him because his phone voice doesn't match his gender. Greg doesn't have his own people-group—traditional Christians who are politically conservative—as the vocal opponents of trans folks in the bathroom debate. Greg doesn't cost his family a lot of money for doctors, hair removal, and prescriptions. And none of this is to discuss the impact on my family and my Christian family.

Greg had it made, and so I continue to long for his return, and it happens every time I reach a milestone in my transition.

The problem is I cannot find myself in a spot in which I have any realistic hope of resuming living as a male and not having it work to destroy me.

Despite things like public restrooms, I, Gina, go about my business in the world with relative ease. I am self-confident. I don't look over my shoulder. When, as Friday evening at the brewery where my son's band played and I watched with joy, I see the stares of people, I don't wince.

I feel right as Gina. I am happy to see a way-more-female-looking person in the mirror. I find that man on my current drivers license to be a handsome guy, but I don't identify as him. He doesn't feel like me. He has become a foreigner to me. I ponder his life as if looking through a family photo album.

There is no course of action but to continue to transition and I have practical needs, none more practical than having a drivers license which is appropriate to me. And then credit cards which match me. And on down the line so that mail no longer comes to a person who does not reside at this address.

Julie and I will be heading downtown minutes after I post this. I am not nervous. I am neither excited nor upset. I am neither happy nor sad. I am simply resigned. I will be glad when it is done.

Maybe, just maybe, I will even be pleased about it. I suspect I finally will be pleased about it. I certainly want to be. But I can't shake that mourning feeling.

As much as Gina needs this, Greg didn't deserve it.

+ + +

As the online crowd vigorously reacted to this post, Julie and I headed downtown. I had a date with a judge.

42

Self-identity

Almost immediately after I changed my online profile to Gina, I was asked, "Are you a lesbian?" Early in 2013, in the first weeks of our discussing my possibly transitioning, Julie and I talked about our sexuality. I was only attracted to females. Julie was only attracted to males. Regardless of what happened with me, we both sensed we would continue to be attracted to each other.

Now that I was transitioning, did our thinking prove correct? Yes, it did. I was not surprised to still be attracted to Julie, but it was a crazy notion she might remain attracted to me, now with long hair, and wearing everything that identifies me as a woman.

Julie remained attracted to me because she fell in love with me, this person who did not change, and the outward things did not impact how she saw me. Indeed, when I got dressed up nice she was kind enough to compliment me on how I looked.

Many spouses and partners are not able to make the leap. The change is too dramatic. Some, such as Julie, are able to see past the aesthetics and maintain attraction. Sometimes both parties realize their sexuality is more fluid than they'd realized. Some transitioned folks also transition regarding whom they find attractive. For example, a trans woman previously dating exclusively women while living as a male might find, as a woman, she is now attracted to men. There simply is no box into which we all fit.

Of the trans women I have met, many of them insist they have always been female. From their youth, they so identified with the other sex from which they were assigned at birth that their having a male body meant nothing to them in how they identify. Others are more like me, recognizing though they had a tremendous desire to be female they did not always hate being male and they previously did not have a need to transition.

How much one transitions is a many-faceted thing. Not all trans folks want or need to surgically alter their bodies. Even when a person does desire one or more surgeries, costs can be prohibitive. Few have health insurance which covers the cost. Many trans folks are not financially healthy; money is a significant issue.

Our name is tremendously important to us. Some so despise their birth name, so rue the fact they had to battle through life to finally live authentically—a word and idea which is common among trans folks, because we feel like liars and fakes living a gender with which we do not identify—that they completely reject their birth name. It becomes a dead name. They will not even tell it to people. And when those who know it use it, they will likely say, "He dead-named me," with resentment, even anger.

Does a person change her or his or their (more and more, a pronoun of choice) birth certificate? Even when one desires this, it can be impossible. States vary in their rules, and some make it extremely difficult to change a birth certificate. For example, some states require proof of genital surgery, which is not an option for many trans folks. Some want both a legal name change and birth certificate correction, for practical reasons as well as personal. Should a woman need to present her birth certificate, and it shows her gender as male, problems arise.

A few go one step further, seeking a court order to seal all personal records from their past. In some cases, they simply do not want others to delve into the years before they transitioned. Other times, they are transitioning stealth—not revealing they are trans—and it could be disastrous for anyone to learn their history.

Trans parents have a variety of feelings as to their identity with their children. In the most absolute cases, they switch their identity from dad to mom, or mom to dad. Children will adopt the new name for them. Other times, a compromise name will be selected. The author and trans advocate, Jennifer Finney Boylan, who remained married to her wife with whom she had two sons, ended up being "Maddy" to the boys, a mashing of mom and daddy.

It is important among trans folks that each person has the right to identify herself, or himself, or theirself. What is my sex? What is my gender? What is my sexuality? How do I feel about my name? What pronouns do I prefer? How much do I transition? How do I present myself? Each question is answered exclusively by the trans person, and never should anyone—including other trans folks—decide for another the answers to these most personal questions.

Answering these questions was a long process for me. Often, I did not pin down the answer until I reached the next step in transitioning. Sometimes, it took being put on the spot—as when on Facebook that woman wrote for all to see, "Are you a lesbian?"—to finally put the question to bed.

By the time I went to court on May 2, 2016, I had finished the process. I knew who I was, what I wanted, how I would answer every question.

My answers define me—and only me. The trans experience is highly individualized. How I feel about and see myself applies only to me, and is not to define any other trans person.

+ + +

Who am I? I am a male. My genetics informs me of this. That I fathered children confirms it.

Who am I? I am a heterosexual male. Regardless of how far I transition, since I am genetically male and attracted to females, I am a heterosexual male.

Who am I? I am Julie's husband. I am my children's father. I am my parents' son. I am my siblings' brother. For practical reasons, Julie refers to me as her spouse, but I still refer to her as my wife and I her husband. Biblically, this informs who I am to her, to be Christ-like, to take care of her. As for my children, I wanted them to continue to call me Dad. I love that I am their father. In public, I told them they may call me Gina if they prefer, or my new name by the grandchildren, Gigi, but if they used Dad around other folks that was fine with me if it were fine with them. Sue easily switched to calling me her sister, and bless her heart for doing that, but I am okay with my siblings continuing to refer to me as their brother. My parents are not alive, but I suspect they would still view me as their son.

Transitioning later in life, with a long history of my male roles preceding me, I am comfortable with my family using male titles for me.

Who am I? I believe I am intersex. Due to a disruption of my endocrine system, I was left with hormones which inform me I should be a female. Hormone replacement therapy, which gave me sex hormone levels of that of a female, and made me feel right about myself, further informed me that I am intersex.

Who am I? I am transgender. Because I am intersex, I suffered from gender dysphoria, which finally prompted my transitioning to female. I am a trans woman.

Who am I? I am a male, who is heterosexual, who is intersex, who is transgender, who is a trans woman.

Who am I? I am Gregory John Eilers. I do not despise my birth name. I was given a good first name and blessed with an honorable family name. I built a good life as Greg Eilers. Because I was Greg to the world for fifty-eight years, even if desired it would be impossible to expunge it. I don't desire to. Unless laws are enacted to make it necessary to change my birth certificate, I will not be doing so.

Who am I? I am Gina Joy Eilers. Living full time as a female, I desired and needed a female name. I loved the name I chose for myself, and I loved the sound of it being used by others. I needed to make Gina legal for practical reasons, because I was not living as Greg. It's as simple as that. Not a rejection of Greg, but an embracing of Gina.

Who am I? Ultimately, I am a Christian—one who belongs to Christ. I am confident that in the resurrection of the dead I will be raised to live forever as Greg. And I will be content.

+ + +

The morning of May 2, Julie and I headed to downtown Indy for my day in court. There were a number of people waiting to do the same thing—a young woman who desired the last name of her foster parents, an older woman who recently learned her birth history and wanted to claim her rightful name, a man who learned the name he was using was not his actual name. While I was pleased to be selected for the first group ushered into the courtroom, I was glad I was not chosen to go first. It was an enlightening morning.

I was the final one to be called for the first group. Julie and I entered and took the last two seats. There were no officials in the room and it was deadly quiet. Settling into our seats, I said to no one in particular, "If I ever do this again, someone please take me out into the woods and leave me." Everyone laughed and the tension was broken. Friendly chatter ensued. Soon, the judge entered.

When you go to court, have the necessary documents! Two women were forced into second court dates because they did not bring their birth certificates. I was antsy—did I have everything I needed?—and though I was not nervous I was anxious to get through this.

More than an hour later, it was my turn. I took my new seat and was sworn in. Everything was perfunctory; certainly, for the judge it was, even if it were my first time. She checked my paperwork. She asked if I had any felonies on my record. Quickly, she granted my request.

Um, that was for my name, but what of my gender marker? I asked. She examined the paperwork and my doctor's endorsement. She mulled a bit then came back with, "Your doctor's letter contains all of the information it needs, but it is not notarized." Again, with the notarizing when nowhere was it indicated!

As with the missing birth certificate women, I, too, would have to come back to court for the purpose of changing my gender marker. In August. In the mean time, I pestered my doctor for a new letter—flabbergasted, she said, "I've written that letter for many people, and never had one rejected. That judge must have it in for trans people"—informed my trans friends—one said, "My judge didn't require my letter to be notarized"—and wondered if this would slow down changing my drivers license and other documents.

Leaving the courthouse, I was more relieved than happy. I experienced no second thoughts. But to say I was like the trans woman who told me she was floating on air as she left the courthouse? Nope. I took a couple of selfies, and my expression was positive, but I wasn't ecstatic.

It occurred to me why I was not over the moon. I was only mid-flight. I would not arrive until I first went to the Social Security office, then the Bureau of Motor Vehicles. Everything after that would be gravy—credit cards and the like—but the drivers license stood before me as my moon landing, my Sea of Tranquility where I could finally set down and breath easy, arrived safely as Gina.

After lunch, I went to the Social Security office. That went as smoothly and quickly as one could ask. On Wednesday, I headed to the nearest BMV office.

I presented my documents. The gal wasn't sure about the gender marker change. The BMV website showed three ways a person could qualify for this, and I had the doctor's letter which was one of the options. Still uncertain, she called on the branch manager. The manager declined me, just like the judge.

That evening, I barely had this out of my mouth when Julie interrupted with, "They're wrong." She brought up the web page and printed out the list. The next day, I returned to the BMV. As soon as they opened. Before it got busy. So I could secure the same woman and not have to start over with my story.

I made my case and she once again called on the manager. I made my case with her. She checked the web page. She scratched her head. "I need to call downtown." Fifteen minutes felt like two hours, but it proved worth it when she returned. To me: "You're right." To the clerk: "Process this for Gina." Back to me: "Gender markers can only be changed downtown, so you will have to wait as they process that." In the mean time, I got my picture taken and took a seat in the gallery. Another fifteen minutes felt like another hour, and then I was called back to the clerk. All done! I left with my driver's license declaring Gina Joy Eilers, gender F.

Onto the busywork of changing credit cards and every other thing where Greg needed to become Gina.

There was one change for which I had concern. My pension with the LCMS, the church body in which I was pastor. A male pastor. Where they only have male pastors. Would they give me trouble? Would they have a rule where I lost my pension? Julie had done her homework and was confident legality was on my side, but would someone make it an issue?

In a few days, an envelope arrived from them. Name changed. No problem. No question. No issue. Indeed, it was addressed to Gina. They even wrote, "Let us know if we can do anything else for you." I smiled. I laughed. I gleefully waved it at Julie when she got home from work.

2016 was proving to be a red-letter year and a continuing roller coaster. I survived my second mega meltdown in five months. I came out of that dip to ride the rocky rails to one of the peaks of transitioning, crested its crown, and came gliding down with my hands held high and gleefully screaming at the top of my lungs.

Back at the BMV, as I walked out I stopped by the state insignia on the door and took a selfie. This photo showed way more than relief. I was exuberant. I replaced my phone in my purse, made my way to my car with a skip in my step and a smile I could not contain. I got in and shut the door. "Woo hoo!" I shouted at the top of my lungs, my hands flying above my head in triumph.

Finally, I had my joy-filled moment.

43

Controversies

In my new world, controversy came calling.

Transgender Christians? Not in the Lutheran Church—Missouri Synod!

Transgender folks using the public restroom of their choice? Not in my state!

I was not to blame for 2016's USA-wide arguing over bathrooms, but I directly created a firestorm in my former church body. Returning to March, contention arose between my pastor and me, at the ELCA congregation we had joined in 2015. I had already been restless over being in the ELCA. I longed for the LCMS both for its doctrine, with which I remained in full agreement, and also to be a voice to educate regarding transgender.

In a sermon, my ELCA pastor said something with which I took strong disagreement. I met with him a few days later, made my theological case, and got nowhere. I told him I already was pining for a return to the LCMS, and now I could no longer reconcile being a member of an ELCA congregation where I have strong disagreement with the doctrine being taught.

We attended worship one more time—Easter Sunday—and said our goodbyes. We once again became Christians without a congregation, with no reason to believe an LCMS church in town would have us.

Julie and I talked about the possibilities, the congregations we had not previously visited. A small, multi-cultural LCMS congregation was not too far of a drive. I called the pastor. He read some of the things I suggested.

We talked again. He was kind and understanding, and then said he did not want to take a chance of creating a problem in his parish.

There it is, again. I am a problem. An outcast.

We missed one Sunday of worship when Julie made a suggestion. "Let's go to the big LCMS church in town. Let's just go. Don't call the pastor. Let's just go and see what happens."

We had not previously considered that place for a number of reasons. One, because it is so large, with over three thousand members. Two, because we knew it to be progressive, and though Julie and I are hardly sticks in the mud we are traditional in the practice of our faith. Three, it was twenty-five minutes away.

But we were out of options. I took Julie's bait. We attended the late traditional service. In the large sanctuary, there were over three hundred in attendance. We entered, worshiped, and left, with no incident. Introducing ourselves to one of the pastors on the way out, I assumed he could tell I was transgender. Because he was the one I met, I chose him as the pastor I called the next day.

I wasted no time, informing him exactly who I was, a former LCMS pastor. We met that week. He was kind and understanding—there's that theme—but, as the meeting ended, his tune was a new one: "Keep worshiping with us. Don't rush into joining. Get to know us." Bless his heart!

Soon, I met with three of the four pastors, then with all four, then Julie and I with all four. In each meeting, we discussed every theological angle, every question and concern. They were thorough. I answered every question they had regarding theology and all things transgender. When Julie joined us, she astutely addressed their concerns about herself and our marriage.

While they continually told us they did not know what to make of these things, they did not pronounce me guilty of sin. They continued to welcome us. By mid-summer, they invited us to take the new member class. On September eleven, we stood before the altar with twenty others and confessed our faith, becoming members.

Over the five months we had been attending, Sunday after Sunday we had entered and worshiped and left without incident. The pastors kept telling me only a few folks had asked about us, and none of those members were critical about our presence. All of that would now change, immediately and dramatically.

All of the new members had pictures and bios published in the bulletin. In mine, I included my blog address.

What did the members see in the bulletin, when looking at Gina and Julie Eilers? We appeared to be a couple, two females, and married. The LCMS does not sanction gay marriage.

My blog provides thorough statistics; how many visitors, what they view, and where they found me, as in from Facebook, an internet search, or from other websites. I had written a long piece about our joining this congregation, rejoicing at being back in my beloved LCMS. Blog traffic saw a bump beginning on the eleventh. On Saturday, the seventeenth, it turned into a veritable traffic jam.

I expected twenty or thirty page views per hour. I found the previous hour to have had over three hundred. What on earth?

Within minutes, a friend informed me my blog post had been linked by a pastor to a Facebook group for confessional Lutherans. When we Lutherans use this word, confessional, it is generally synonymous with all things traditional and conservative. Too often, though—and in a manner typical of our polarizing culture—"confessional" has been co-opted by those who seek an insulated worldview, where they are unable to even entertain a conversation outside their established opinion.

I found the Facebook page—I'd joined the group several years ago—read what the pastor wrote about me, then checked some of the comments. I want to be charitable, so let's just say the people commenting in the group found me galaxies outside their worldview.

Soon, another Lutheran website linked to me. Then, another. Then, a newspaper, famous in the LCMS for finding and publishing dirt on folks, found and published the dirt on me. All together, five (that I knew of) prominent groups had made me known to the LCMS. None of them were charitable toward me.

Four days before this blew up, I was called before our pastors because members were now asking about us. They assured me our church membership was safe, but some members were threatening to leave if we were allowed to stay, and so the pastors wanted to meet and go over the key things we had previously covered. I satisfied them that, while I was as aware as they that my being transgender was dicey in the LCMS, I was striving to treat my condition as any Christian would a malady, disease, or illness. I reaffirmed my confession of faith. They never pointed out any error in my theology; quite the opposite, I continually spoke as confessionally as the very pastors and lay folks who were condemning me.

We worshiped on September 18. All went well. On Wednesday, my phone was ringing again, my being summoned to another meeting with the pastors.

In this phone call, the pastor told me I had been the topic of conversation among the leaders of the LCMS. The cry from across the church body had gone out to the presidents of the thirty-five districts which cover the country. Our new congregation had already been on the radar of a subset of confessional pastors for their being progressive—for example, they hold a contemporary worship service concurrent with their traditional service, in a separate worship center. Our becoming members was, for many, the last straw. For the complainers, this congregation either needed to shape up or be shipped out.

My experience with the LCMS allowed me to figure things out with few details provided. When Julie got home from work Wednesday evening, I told her of the next day's meeting, and what I suspected would be the crux.

It was either them or us. Either we resign our membership or the congregation and pastors would be kicked out of the LCMS.

Are you wondering if there are any LCMS congregations with any transgender members? Well, of course, there are. I had known of some. I might have been the first former pastor to announce being transgender, but I was hardly the first trans person to be a member of an LCMS church. Even more, our new congregation was hardly the only progressive LCMS parish; there are loads of them across the nation.

No matter. I and our church were now the poster child for everything that needed to be expunged from the LCMS, and the opportunity was seized by a group of outspoken critics.

I told Julie if it came down to the congregation or us, we would have to resign our membership. We were the ones who created the problem for the congregation. If they might have to suffer, and if our resigning could keep that from happening, we had to resign. She agreed as quickly as Sunday School kids grab donuts doled out by their teacher.

Julie joined me for this meeting. When we arrived, not only were our four pastors in attendance, so was a synod official of the LCMS, whom I will call SO. SO had been in the meeting of the LCMS leaders and was there as their official representative.

He opened by explaining a few things that had happened, the same news our pastors had delivered the previous week. He summed it up, "It's not theological. It's political."

He was right. If this were being handled theologically, our pastors would have told us where we were sinning and called us to repent, as DP had done. In the Gospel of Matthew, the eighteenth chapter gives us the process as laid out by the Lord Jesus. As regards our pastors, it also appeared they were not told where they were sinning, that they might repent. No, this was not being done in the manner of the church, but in the way of the world.

I had not met SO before this. I appreciated him calling it what it was. But, not wanting him to get too far, I asked if I could make a short speech before he opened the entire onion. I did not want him to say what I knew was coming. I wanted to show them the honorable people whom Julie and I are.

I laid out some of the key things that had transpired. My words were measured. My demeanor was calm. I only showed respect. And then I said, "When Pastor called me, yesterday, I suspected the congregation was on the hot seat over us. I am sorry about that. All they did was seek to do the right thing the entire time we've been here. They did not presume to have the answers on trans matters, but they heard our confession of faith, and the Gospel won the day. Because they did not invite this trouble on themselves, Julie and I cannot let them take a hit for it. If what is needed to save them trouble is for us to resign our membership, then that is what we will do."

The pastor with whom I initially met said, "We knew that is what you would do."

Julie wanted to speak. Calmly, respectfully, with fortitude, she eloquently depicted our marriage and our faith, of the terrible challenges for transgender folks, of our concern for the Lutherans who were hiding in the pews of our LCMS churches who might be left thinking God could never love them. A few days later, when the senior pastor called to catch me up on things, he commended Julie and me for how we handled ourselves in the meeting. He then singled out Julie: "She was amazing."

Yes, Pastor; yes, she was.

Now, in the meeting, the four pastors all had something to say. They were gracious. They showed concern for our spiritual welfare. They invited us to continue to worship with them—Christian churches never want to keep anyone from hearing the Word of God—but, since we could not be members, we lost all rights and privileges of membership. We could not attend Holy Communion.

Since we had nowhere else to go, we were thankful for their extended hand of welcome. We decided we would remain faithful in our worship. We were determined to win over the members.

The Sunday after we resigned our membership, the pastors held a congregation-wide meeting regarding all that had taken place. Over three hundred attended. We did not. In the weeks that followed, a number of folks approached us to introduce themselves and tell us they were glad we were in their church. If anyone who saw us in worship did not want us there, they never spoke with us. A small number of folks left for other churches.

It hurt terribly to sit through the Lord's Supper, watching the pews empty as the others went to the altar. The first few months, Julie and I came to tears as we sang the Communion hymns. I now was an outsider in two families, Eilers and LCMS. And, across the country, many highly vocal Americans made it clear they wished I and my sister and brother trans folks were outsiders to the USA.

In the same year I triggered a firestorm in my church body, another controversy was brewing across the nation. The Bathroom Debate, as the flurry of activity in the summer of 2016 would come to be called, was ignited by states and localities and schools which were either implementing, or trying to implement, laws and rules about which bathrooms trans persons could or could not use. For those in opposition to our using the one of the sex with which we identify, it always came down to our birth certificate. What that says, male or female, is what you are and is where you will pee. End of debate.

Except, it hardly was. If you had a pulse in 2016—I hope you did, as that was the election between Hillary Clinton and Donald Trump!—then I don't have to rehearse the national headlines. I experienced most of what occurred nationwide.

Some women were kind: "I have no problem with trans women in the women's restroom." Some women dug in their heels: "I don't care how you live, but I don't want you peeing in my bathroom." Some inflamed the situation as in the media: "This just allows perverts easier access to hurt us." Some asked sincere questions: "Gina, what do you think about all of this?"

I wrote a number of essays about it. I answered the mother of young children, who was concerned for her kids, commiserating with her for her deep desire to protect them. I used the occasion to explain that trans folks are not perverts. I regularly sought to douse the flames by shedding light, especially in my conviction that perverts are not going to dress up as women and go into public restrooms to take advantage of women.

Besides, you can write every law you want. If a man intends to abuse a woman or child, no law is going to stop him.

After my inaugural women's restroom visit the previous September, I now had used them a number of times, always without incident. There were a couple of times I feared the situation might get awkward, as in the time I stood in line for a toilet with four young women. I sighed relief when none of them even batted an eye at my presence.

June of 2016 brought the massacre at The Pulse, a gay nightclub in Orlando, Florida. This set my trans friends aback. At our next group session, some spoke of their fears of going out in public, even to the grocery store, and of their heightened concern with using bathrooms with the debate raging.

I am not a person who scares easily, but here's the thing. Just as those innocent victims at The Pulse thought they were safe that June evening, with no idea of the evil about to descend upon them, neither does any of us know when someone is going to mete their hatred upon us.

Our fears are real. We are left thinking that many fellow Americans have judged us to be troublemakers and perverts, yet we are like most everyone else. We want only to live in peace, go about our business, prosper in our families and jobs and neighborhoods, and not call attention to ourselves. As for bathrooms, we tend to be the most behaving of any people group. These are our red zones. We feel the bullseye on our backs every time we push open the door to the restroom which fits our gender identity. The last thing we intend is to create a stir, to make waves, to bring trouble upon ourselves. As one Indianapolis trans woman entertainer came to belt out in the satirical song she penned, "I just wanna pee!"

Controversy is the last thing we want but, at this point in American history, we are walking, talking controversy causers. Yet, we just want to pee.

And live in peace.

44

Meanwhile ...

The spring and summer controversies of 2016 were kept in perspective by plenty of good things filling my days.

In March, Julie and I visited the surgeon who would perform what formerly was called sex reassignment surgery, now often referred to as gender confirmation surgery, and more recently simply as bottom surgery.

The surgeon is in Indianapolis. When we moved here in 2014, she was not. I was certain that, if I transitioned and wanted this surgery, I would have to drive a ways, at the very least to Ann Arbor's University of Michigan hospital, or to Pennsylvania, or further. After Julie found a job, I found U of M to be in our insurance network, so I began communicating with them. Mere days after I received their first email reply, I heard the news that Dr. Sidhbh (pronounced "sive") Gallagher would be joining IU Health, arriving in October 2015. IU Health is in our insurance network; indeed, my endocrinologist worked at IU Health. So, win/win for me.

How did I come to decide on bottom surgery? I always thought if I transitioned I would want the surgery. It's not that I would not feel authentic living as a woman while still having a penis. *Authentic* is a huge issue for trans folks. Our brain/gender and body/sex not matching can be distressing. For some, getting as much in line as possible is vital. For others, it makes no difference.

The saying applies: when you've met one trans person, you've met one trans person.

In my case I found my penis to be the wrong genitals. It's as simple as that. My brain informed me I was a female, even if, logically, I remained able to continue to say I was a genetic male. Practically speaking, I now was living as a female. I had long hair—it grew more quickly than I could have imagined and, since I could style it to minimize my receding hairline, I went wigless. I had breasts—though they still were on the smaller side, considering my age my breast growth was more than I could have expected. Every stitch of my clothing was female.

My penis felt wrong on me. I did not like to see it. I did not like to touch it. I stopped standing to pee even before my first attempt at the Real Life Test. When I pondered myself with a vagina, the thought was marvelous. For me to have a vagina seemed as natural as my arms and eyes.

I had my endorsement letter from Kathy, my therapist, which got me my initial appointment with Dr. Gallagher. Julie and I found her to be a friendly and professional woman. Yes, her first name is Irish and, yes, she hails from Ireland. What an accent she has!

One cannot jump right into bottom surgery. Dr. Gallagher follows WPATH standards, which call for two therapist endorsements, and which our insurance would also require before approving the surgery. The second therapist would not require many sessions, but would rely on my already having been endorsed by Kathy. He would ask pertinent questions to affirm the first therapist's observations about me.

Secondly, as earlier noted and way more severely, since the skin of the penis shaft and scrotum are used to form the vagina and labia, all of the hair must be permanently removed. Since my hair is gray, it meant electrolysis. Hours and hours of electrolysis. Because of the sensitive area, extremely painful electrolysis. Painful, even with numbing cream liberally applied.

It would take thirty hours for Barb the Impaler to prep the area for surgery. Thirty root canals would have been more pleasant.

If nothing else were to scare off a person from bottom surgery—cost, lengthy recovery, risks during and after surgery, the fear of regretting an irreversible surgery—electrolysis could do it. I had Barb stop working on my face, to concentrate on my genitals. I would apply lidocaine to numb the pain. It helped. But not enough. Some areas, and particular hairs, were super sensitive. I would cry out, every session, numerous times, from the zapping pain.

For eight months. For thirty excruciating one-hour sessions.

The previous August, around the time I was interviewed for the podcast, a trans friend informed me she was getting involved with Indiana University, to participate in Q & A panel discussions on gender dysphoria and transgender. I went with Jen to Bloomington, home of IU, to meet with the coordinator, who brought us on board.

Over the course of the 2015/16 school year, I drove to Bloomington for fourteen panels. Most had three or four of us trans folks—trans women, trans men, gender fluid, gender queer, and a-gender—but two I handled solo. Some of the classes were for future educators, and others were for workplace diversity, sex and gender, and psychology.

As I became known, I was asked to sit on an LGBTQ panel, and that opened up an opportunity to go to a local Walmart headquarters to do the same with their managers. In December 2016, I began participating in an LGBTQ panel at the school of dentistry in Indianapolis, one each for their first- and second-year students.

All of these panels were outstanding opportunities to educate about who trans people are, how we tick, and what concerns we have. The questions often are those which I would not have guessed—"Do you ever get over having gender dysphoria?" "How do you think your life would be different if you were a child today?" "Do you feel free?" For the students, panels such as these are a valuable resource to prepare them for the diverse world in which they live, study, and work.

They helped round out my education, too. My long-range goal had become more than blogging and magazine articles. I love public speaking and educating. In these post-pastor years, I still longed to work for the Lord and my fellow Christians, and I especially wanted to educate inside the LCMS. Despite how I was currently viewed by many in the LCMS, I hoped I could one day break through and be given the opportunity to educate what it means to suffer gender dysphoria, and show that one can be transgender and remain faithful to God's Word.

The more Q & A panels I experienced, the better my answers. I continued to study, now focusing on endocrine disruption and intersex conditions, striving to learn what might be behind one's suffering gender dysphoria. Many trans folks do not display a concern for why their sex and gender don't match. One trans woman told me it didn't matter to her why she was trans, that it likely never would be pinned down, and that she is the way she is and didn't care to dwell on it. I found her attitude to be shared widely.

Not me. I continued to hate this condition. I longed for answers. I wanted concrete reasons toward which to point, shunning conjecture and dismissal.

I was antsy to move forward. I found plenty on which to write and post to my blog. I made a number of videos and had a YouTube channel.

I found that my panel experience, my depth of knowledge, and my ability to speak made me ready for a larger audience. As 2016 began, I thought that audience might be on Indiana's political landscape. Our state legislature was considering a law to protect transgender citizens. We are a conservative state, with Republicans in the majority. The initial legislation language was being whacked to bits and edited to nonsense.

Freedom Indiana is a political advocate for LGBTQ Hoosiers. They sought trans folks to prepare them to speak before our legislature. I signed up. Sadly, after one legislative session in which two of our trans folks spoke at committee, the issue was tabled.

Both politically and in everyday issues, I often found myself at odds with my new trans friends and acquaintances. As a theologian, I was forced to weigh every issue first as a Christian and second as an American. In the LGBTQ arena, liberal thought—both politically and in religion—holds sway.

At one meeting, where only trans folks were invited, I finally tired of the constant bashing of conservatives and Christians. I got the floor and asked, "Who here practices a traditional Christianity and is politically conservative?" No one moved. I stood. "I am both of these. Yet, I am with you all the way on everything you want for us in the USA. Not all Christians and conservatives are the jerks you paint us to be."

It had no impact. My differences with these folks only grew. By the end of 2016, I felt some of them did not desire my presence. Save for a few folks with whom I grew close, I wanted to stay away. As I had feared, I felt like an outcast among outcasts.

As this was developing early in the year, I was in contact with two men, Jeff and Dan, who were professors at an LCMS university and who host a podcast called Virtue in the Wasteland.

Virtue in the Wasteland goes for the long form in order to dive deeply into a subject. The time had come for them to broach the transgender topic, and I was the logical guest.

For the podcast, they would for the first time create a two-part show and, also for the first time, make a road trip. Julie took the day off work, and the four of us talked in our living-room-turned-recording-studio.

Julie's involvement was integral to providing the fullest picture we could paint in every facet of our lives. We talked more than two hours. Jeff and Dan edited out nary a word. The show attracted a huge audience and a lot of feedback. They took many jabs for doing this topic. Though I answered their every question in a way which espouses LCMS doctrine, and Julie and I spoke as a couple who continues to identify as husband and wife, and I stressed the medical aspect of my transitioning, the conservative bent of the LCMS largely was not swayed by the interview.

Many in the LCMS appreciated the podcast, though, and they spoke as loudly as the others. Soon, I heard from Dan and Jeff that many in the LCMS—including some leadership—truly heard us. My spirits were buoyed.

The next month, one of my seminary classmates, who remained a good friend in our ministry years and had been empathetic since I went public, connected me with his district president. In October, I met with him, my friend, and two other pastors.

We had a friendly, open conversation for a couple of hours. For my part, I outlined my history, explained about intersex conditions and gender dysphoria, stressed my theology had not changed and that I was transitioning as medical intervention. For his part, he went to the meaning of male and female as God's Word teaches, providing deep, theological understanding. It was excellent stuff. I told him I was in full agreement.

Along with the sanctity of being created male and female, a passage always cited is Deuteronomy 22:5, where God says that men and women are not to wear each other's clothes. Again, I do not disagree with God's Word, I only want to properly understand it. My reply is that if a man disguises himself for sinful pleasure, to deceive anyone, or to take advantage of another for selfish gain then, yes, God forbids it. As God called Old Testament Israel not to mimic the unrighteous behavior of other nations, in the same way He directs New Testament Christians.

However, the person suffering gender dysphoria does not take on the clothes of the opposite sex for sinful pleasure, in order to deceive anyone, or to take advantage for selfish gain. For the gender dysphoric, clothes are treatment; they are akin to medicine.

I stressed my point, that mine is not a theological problem. He disagreed, insisting my only cure was the Word of God, through repentance and absolution.

My problem, he declared, is that of my frail, sinful nature. He had done little or no studying of the topic, yet found himself able to judge it. In the end, I realized he did not hear me, that his mind was made up.

This is what I have found with many of my former brother pastors in the LCMS. They were not hearing me as to what is behind gender dysphoria. LCMS theology is so steeped in God's Word and its truthfulness—and I remain in doctrinal agreement with the LCMS—that it can be hard for them to grasp real life matters that fall outside the comfortable black-and-white.

Well, my dear LCMS, a lot of things are hard. And a lot of things are not black and white. It is a Christian's job to listen and learn and not judge things unfairly. When a pastor tells me he has done little or no studying on gender dysphoria and transitioning, and then he casts a judgment on me, and I point out to him his lack of knowledge, and he still doesn't recognize the situation for what it is ...

Ugh. Even the best theologians can be blind.

I couldn't dwell on these things, as much as they crept into my mind and gnawed at me. I kept busy with my work of educating. I continued to pray, "Lord Jesus, show me your good and gracious will, and then help me to follow it. What do you want me to do? Please, give me direction. Help me!"

45

Surgery time

By the autumn of 2016, I had transitioned in every practical way. I still had not undergone any surgery, though, and there were two I intended to have—bottom surgery and facial feminization. I was prepping for bottom surgery, which I hoped to have before the end of the year, but that pesky hair was such that I was not ready in time. The delay worked to our advantage insurance-wise, as I ended up having both surgeries in 2017, and even added a third.

I knew there was vocal cord surgery, but did not know it had been dramatically improved. The last I was aware, it was a dicey proposition, having one's vocal cords cut and sutured to create a smaller opening, allowing for a higher pitch. In September, I heard a trans woman speak, who had the surgery. She had a lovely, feminine voice. I had been trying to raise my pitch on my own, but with little success. After a short time, the stress on my throat would cause my pitch to go down. I did not persevere with it.

Now, I learned there was a surgery which works, and I found a clinic in Indy that offered it. I scheduled an appointment.

In the meantime, I found a plastic surgeon in our insurance network, Dr. Barry Eppley, for my FFS, facial feminization surgery. I had a consultation with him. It went well. The insurance approval process began.

In early December, I met with Dr. Gallagher. She pronounced my genitals clear enough of hair, and any live hairs she found she would scrape from the back side during surgery. We set the date for my surgery—Valentine's Day!—and I was floating on air.

I then had my consult at the voice clinic, with Dr. Noah Parker. Julie came with, as she loves to do with my first appointments. Dr. Parker checked the pitch of my voice. I registered at 115 vibrations per second, which he said is perfectly average for a genetic male. For fun, he checked Julie. She was at the top of the 180-250 female range, at 246.

Next, he wanted to run a scope through my mouth, to my throat. I could not keep from gagging. Selecting a different scope, he went through the nose. Goodness, that is a funny feeling.

He found my vocal cords to be healthy, and I to be a candidate for surgery. I asked all of my questions. He answered them well. They went to work submitting the paperwork for our insurance to approve it. I was shocked when, only two weeks later, I received a call informing me approval had been secured. I eagerly took the January 19 opening for surgery.

I remained elated for a few days. I then returned to the angst-filled days before I changed my name. By the day after Christmas, I was plotting how I might go back to living as Greg. Julie and I would mark our fifteenth wedding anniversary on December 30; I was longing to be her husband, to be the husband I always wanted to be, without the interference of my female-inclined brain.

I thought maybe I could go back to living as a male, but this time remaining on HRT. I kept getting tripped up over my name change, my Gina Eilers/female drivers license, and the changes that had been made to credit cards and all.

I knew I was playing a fool's game, but I allowed myself to sink into the familiar pit of hating being transgender. "This is happening *to* me, and I cannot stop it" smacked me upside the head, again and again.

I confessed to Julie all I was feeling and thinking but, unlike when I told her this a week before my name change, I was able to tell her I knew all was going to be okay, that going backward never helped, that moving forward was the only option.

As usual, talking it out got me over the hump. Surgery day was twenty-four days off. From December 26 onward, I did not waver for a second. I anticipated the surgery with joy.

Even as I now was in a good way, I continued to ponder it seriously. As I posted about it online, some folks commented how one's voice is so personal to who that person is, and they could not imagine mine sounding different. These landed right square in my heart. I certainly did not despise my voice. It was only that it was working against me, the single-greatest reason I was misgendered. I longed to consistently hear feminine pronouns used for me.

Serious thoughts continued. I am not a worrier, but I certainly had honest concern that Dr. Parker would do his job well and there would be no complications for me.

A few days before surgery, I had a physical. I passed every test and we proceeded.

The January 19 date had put my vocal cord operation and bottom surgery not quite four weeks apart. Mentioning this to Dr. Parker right before surgery, he asked whether I would be intubated for the bottom surgery. Rats, a potential snag.

During surgery, Julie called Dr. Gallagher's office. Yes, because bottom surgery is a very serious, long surgery, my breathing would be assisted by a tube down my throat. Dr. Parker had told us I would need at least two months for healing. My new bottom surgery date became April 11. Rats, again. I had been counting down the days.

The vocal cord surgery went perfectly. As I was awaking from it, the nurse immediately said, "Gina, don't speak. Don't speak." Groggily opening my eyes, she said, "Here's paper and a pen. Don't talk. Write what you need to say."

I would be on total vocal silence for the next twelve days, providing the best situation for my vocal cords to heal. When I needed to cough, I had to work hard to stifle it, practicing what's called the silent cough: at the first sign of an impending cough, breath in deeply, breath out quickly, and swallow.

I made it work about two thirds of the time. With each cough, and the

255

occasional sneeze, and a handful of times I instinctively began speaking when caught off guard, I feared I was ripping sutures apart. With a cut on an arm, one can observe it; with the throat, you're left in the dark.

I was pensive when Julie and I returned to the voice clinic twelve days after surgery. Being ushered into the exam room, the nurse asked me a question. I pointed to the pin they had given me, which announced I was on total voice rest. She said, "It's okay. You can talk now."

I opened my mouth to say, "You know I had surgery, right?" That's what I meant to say. That's what I eventually said. But, on the first try, only silence and air escaped my mouth.

Give it another try, Gina. Ah, here it came … a croaking of two words. Why didn't anyone warn me how hard it would be to speak and how terrible I would sound twelve days after surgery? The trans woman, whose voice I heard a few months earlier, never mentioned the recovery period.

Dr. Parker entered. First, he checked my pitch. My *eeeee* came in at 240 vibrations per second, right near Julie's pitch. Wow, was I happy about that! So fearing the surgery might not work, I cried tears of joy.

Next, he scoped me, commenting everything looked great. Removing the scope, he showed us the pictures. The wound was white, occupying the lower third of the cords. He said the stitches were holding. My biggest concern was allayed. I now melted into tears. He said, "The emotions are no surprise," and smiled at me.

I was to return in five weeks. At that time, another scope showed almost complete healing. He said every stitch had held and the webbing was forming perfectly. The voice therapist joined us for this check-up, then whisked me to her office for my first voice lesson.

She gave me a series of exercises to strengthen my vocal folds. The hoarseness that remained in my otherwise now-feminine voice was due to the folds not completely closing. "You have new anatomy," she noted, "You need to learn how to use it." With training, I would be able to close the folds, making my voice come out nice and clear. This turned out to be a rigorous process.

After more than a month of dutifully doing my vocal drills, I reached a standstill. Worse than that, my voice was just plain rough sounding. Returning to the voice clinic, down went the scope. Ugh. A granuloma had formed. Granular tissue sometimes grows at the spot of a wound, and I grew a good-sized granuloma which was keeping my vocal folds from closing. I would need to use a steroid inhaler for two months, in order to shrink it.

But I was now only a week from bottom surgery. Dr. Gallagher did not want me to begin the steroid until two weeks after her surgery. Indeed, I was off all my medications in preparation for this serious surgery.

When I received pre-surgery instructions for my bottom surgery, there was an item which shocked me. "They want me to do what? They want to take away my lifeline?" A month before surgery, I was to stop taking HRT. Estrogen makes one prone to blood clots. This surgery, in the middle of the body, is notorious for causing blood clots. By having me go off HRT, in three to four weeks my estrogen would be back to a genetic male level. Of course, my testosterone also would return to near its typical male level.

For the terrible crashes I had experienced the previous times I went off HRT, I was scared at the thought of what might happen to me in the final days before surgery. Julie sought to soothe me, encouraging me not to dwell on it. I calmed myself by envisioning the surgery and the result, for which I so longed.

In mid-March, I went in for a pre-surgery physical. As with the January physical, all went well. I left the hospital happy and hopeful and counting down the days.

It was under two weeks to surgery when I felt the impact on my hormones. To my relief, I experienced no crash. I proceeded smoothly to surgery day.

The morning of the surgery, I remained at peace. I did not even have the kind of nerves one gets when highly excited about something. I was as calm and collected as can be. My blood pressure even reflected it, sitting right on what is normal for me. You could have knocked me over with an IV bag.

The operation took more than six hours, with no complications. I awoke in the room where I would be for three days, with Julie by my side.

The next day, I had to remain in bed. On Thursday, I was allowed to walk. And did I walk! The staff told Julie I was walking way more often and farther than they typically see. Well, I wanted to go home on Friday, so I was motivated. And, on Friday, we went home.

Julie had taken the week off and was to go back to work on Monday. I was in rough shape, not only unable to walk far but restricted from driving, which had me apprehensive at being left alone, daughter Jackie having moved out nine months earlier. When Julie went out, Saturday evening, to get us supper, I nearly had a panic attack she would get in an accident.

On Sunday my confidence returned, and on Monday Julie returned to work. More than my beloved wife, she now was my nurse. As with every task she faces, Julie readily took on the job of changing my dressing. I was so swollen and black and blue I couldn't bear to look down there, yet she didn't flinch.

On Thursday, we returned to Dr. Gallagher. It was time for the removal of two things, the catheter through which I had been peeing and the packing in my neo vagina.

Doctors don't wish to be alarmists, but I sometimes find they play things down too much. "Will it hurt?" I asked. "Just a bit of a pinch," came the lie.

White hot, searing pain is the only way I can describe the second it took for that tiny tube to be pulled out of my urethra. I broke out in a sweat and was panting. After a cup of water, it was time to unpack my neo vagina.

More white hot, searing pain …

I suppose, if we were warned about these things beforehand, no one would ever have surgery.

Dr. Gallagher presented me a set of four dilators, from small to large. Since my vagina was human-made, it did not have the muscles to stay open. I would have to dilate five times a day for several weeks, then three times a day, then once. At the one-year mark, I would be down to three times a week, then, eventually, to once a week.

Dr. Gallagher described the process as she inserted the smallest dilator. Removing it, she held a mirror to help me guide it in. Getting the angle right was the trick. I soon had it.

My healing went perfectly, despite how I was regularly uncomfortable.

Two weeks post-op, when I tried to ease myself off the pain pills, I found out how much they were doing for me. A week later, I began to reduce the dose, and was able to stop them completely a few weeks later.

For the surgery, my feet had been in stirrups for six hours. My left foot suffered significant neuropathy. The area was numb, yet hyper-sensitive. When it began to heal, the nerves awoke like fireworks shooting off in my foot.

At the same time, the nerve-awaking fireworks happened in my bottom. Often, I got zapped with jolting pain from both areas at the same time. The jabs caused me to jerk and call out, "*Ow!*" The evening of my birthday was the worst. I was on the couch, writhing in pain. Julie longed to help me. She dashed to the store for some analgesic cream for my foot. I would use it for days, but I could never tell whether it helped.

Since the age of twenty-three, I've been a jogger. Dr. Gallagher did not want me jogging for six weeks, but I could walk as much as felt comfortable. I wasted no time. My goal was to be walking five miles by the end of the six weeks. I quickly went from walking the street in front of our house, to the end of the block, to a half mile, making regular progression to my five-mile goal, which I hit five days before I could begin running.

Walking was one thing; running seemed quite another. I had the sense that if I ran my bottom would fall off. May 22 was the six week mark, and I intended to run. I walked a half mile before accelerating to a run. I felt great! That day, I mixed in several dashes of a few blocks. Each day, I increased the jogging and decreased the walking.

I would see Dr. Gallagher on June 10. I wanted to announce I was back to running five miles. I plugged away at it. On June 7, I was so giddy to have achieved my goal I made a video as soon as I arrived home. Three days later, the first thing I did when seeing Dr. Gallagher was to triumphantly show her the video.

I now was pain-free all over. Dr. Gallagher was pleased with the work she did. When I saw her for my final, one-year appointment, she beamed. Indeed, her skill provided me with perfectly functioning vagina and clitoris, which look as natural as on a genetic female.

By July, I had completed two months of steroids for the reducing of the granuloma which had grown on my surgically-altered vocal cords. I returned to Dr. Parker. One last time, down went the scope. Thankfully, we saw that not only was the granuloma gone but the surgery was completely healed, and perfectly so.

So why was my voice rough sounding, and why was I not automatically speaking in a higher pitch? What felt natural was higher than pre-surgery, but it was still in the range of a male. I was able to speak in a higher, female-range pitch, which came out nice and clear, but it didn't come naturally. The rest of 2017, I found myself speaking in the lower pitch. It seemed more comfortable, by which I mean that my being female was easier on others if I still sounded closer to how everyone was accustomed.

Julie encouraged me toward adapting to my new voice. My kids said it was okay. Yet, I dragged my feet. Returning to the voice coach in December, her counsel and pep talk launched me toward working on it. As 2017 moved into 2018, I finally was making progress on consistently speaking in a higher pitch.

I had one more surgery to complete my transition, which would be comprised of two procedures. I would have my face feminized and receive breast implants.

I should not be surprised, when I bring up how male and female heads are shaped differently, that most people are not aware of it, because I had not known this either before pursuing transitioning. Indeed, the differences are striking. Generally, the male forehead protrudes toward the brow, while it does not on females. Also, female eyebrows are higher. Women's noses are smaller, their cheekbones more prominent, and their jaws less square.

Examining me, I clearly had a protruding forehead and low eyebrows. My cheeks and nose could be modified, but Dr. Eppley, Julie, and I decided I could forego work on those. I was especially leery about making my nose too feminine, fearing it would too dramatically alter my appearance. I would wind up being happy I left it alone.

My lips were very skinny. Dr. Eppley said, "They're almost non-existent." He explained that vermillion—the pink part—is very stretchy. He would cut the skin from around my lips and reattach the vermillion, doubling the size.

Being sixty years old, I could use a face lift, which would do wonders all by itself. My hairline had receded a lot, so he would give me a scalp advancement, even if he could only gain a quarter of an inch.

I was to have surgery in mid-September. Once again, a snafu caused a delay. I was rescheduled for November 22, the day before Thanksgiving.

I told the office gal I was struggling whether to have this surgery, unsure I wanted to alter my face. I had until early November before I would need to cancel it.

Besides talking with Julie, I ran this by several of my closest allies. Everyone said, "You've gone this far. Finish the job." I finally gained confidence about it, and headed to surgery day in good shape. On November 22, I had scalp advancement, forehead shave, eyebrow raising, lip enhancement, face lift, and breast implants.

The next day was Thanksgiving. I sucked egg nog through a straw.

If coffee through a straw is an act of desperation, then color me desperate. I did it each morning for almost a week, when I finally regained a bit of feeling in my lips.

Feeling was returning but, mostly, everything from my neck up was numb … except for my nose. For that reason, and a reason I could not see coming, I was glad I had left it untouched.

Sparing you the volumes I could write about the miseries of this recovery, I will share only the removing of the stitches from my lips. I hoped against hope that the lip stitches were dissolvable. I had never experienced stitch removal. I longed for someone to tell me it was only a little tug.

Perhaps it's only a little tug when the stitches are on your arm. On the lips? A few were a little tug. Some were an uncomfortable pinch. Others were, well, remember how I described the removing of the catheter? Yeah, like that. About one third of the three dozen.

By Christmas, I was healed enough to have Julie take photos of the fully transitioned me. I had done everything possible to position myself as a female in my body and to live in the world. I still looked like me, yet I was nicely a female version of me.

I set my sights on 2018. Now that I was done transitioning, I needed to find meaningful employment. That, and finishing this book, were my goals for the year. I was ready to move on in life as a female.

Before I could begin to put my plan into motion, a change occurred I never saw coming and never imagined, the timing of which was about as preposterous as could possibly be.

Though I would finally embrace it, when it happened it was as jarring as when my gender dysphoria grabbed hold of me five years earlier.

The second week of January 2018, I ceased to feel female.

46

The return to Greg

In the weeks which followed my face surgery, I was positively exuberant. I was experiencing that top-of-the-world sense of having accomplished a huge thing. More than being pleased for being done, I was feeling good about all of it.

When I looked in the mirror, I liked the woman I saw. When I got dressed, the clothes felt correct, and I found myself to be a respectable more-than-a-bit-past-middle-aged female. Going out in the world—shopping, dining, church—I was comfortable and confident, even though I still didn't blend in as a genetic female.

2018 was to be the year of the restart. Settle in living as a female.

What I experienced the second week of January was as unexpected as everything else which hit me over the course of the past five years. I stopped having any sense at all that I was a female.

I recognized it the same way I had in November 2013. I was sitting at my computer, pondering myself. As I reflected, I recognized something had been occurring in me the past couple of days. When I put my finger on it, I was shocked.

I felt like a guy. Through and through.

I was supposed to be a transgender woman, and I now felt like a man. Grasping how I surgically changed myself, I saw that I was a man who now had a transgender body.

This drove me into a deep depression.

Every day, I found myself yearning to live as a male. With this, I found myself pining to be Julie's husband, and I wanted the world to see me as her husband.

But I had gone and surgically altered myself, and had legally changed my name. How could I possibly resume living as a man? How could I hide my breasts?

At times, I felt like the biggest idiot on earth.

I was angry. Why did this happen now?

I was happy. For decades, I wanted to feel like a guy with no desire to be a female. This was as profound as 2013's six weeks of supercalifragilisticexpialidocious.

I was confused. What on earth was I to do?

Every day, I prayed the Lord would comfort me. I prayed what I had continually prayed throughout my transition, that the Lord would show me what He wanted me to do. I prayed He would help me adjust so I could live in the world as a male with my surgically-altered body.

I waited a bit before I told Julie, to be sure this was not fleeting. In late January, I told her what was going on. She was so shocked she was virtually speechless. I told some close friends. They were shocked. Our kids? Shocked. My trans friends at the group Julie and I attend? Shocked.

Since I had been shocked at this new twist, why should they have been any less stunned?

I was a mess, often depressed. It showed, especially when there was no one around but Julie and me. She urged me to see a therapist. I couldn't imagine a therapist would have anything to tell me that I didn't already know. I toughed it out.

In late February, it faltered. That old sense of being two people revisited, male and female competing for dominance. The female sense returned strongly enough I shaved my legs for the first time since early January. I painted my nails, which I hadn't touched in weeks, and was comfortable wearing a skirt and heels to church. Before this happened, I twice found myself unable to attend church. I couldn't bear to dress myself in women's clothes and, since they only knew me at church as Gina, I wasn't ready to go to church in men's clothes.

I found myself relieved to be feeling female again, and figured the previous couple months of feeling male was a blip on the radar. I sighed a huge *Whew!* that I would not have to face undoing my transition.

The female sense lasted but a few days, then I returned to feeling exclusively male. That brief event plunged me back into serious fighting with myself. I was miserable, depressed, and unable to see how I was going to live. As a male? As a female? Going back and forth—gender fluid—depending on what signals my brain was sending me?

Was my brain going to toy with me forever? Could I ever trust it?

I waited for the next crash. I was afraid to blink.

No next crash came. I moved through March hating everything. I had no hope. I feared the future. I cried a lot. Despair took over when I settled down to sleep, the silent darkness giving way to the deafening noise of this battle I had fought for too long.

On the final Sunday in March, as I was spilling my hurting head and heart to Julie, she finally convinced me to see a therapist. I decided I wanted to see someone new, a person who didn't know me. I also didn't want this professional to be one who commonly sees transgender folks, hoping that fresher eyes might see the bigger picture.

Julie found a psychologist who looked like a winner. I called him the next day. He protested, saying he'd never had a client who had gender dysphoria, or one whom he knew to be transgender. I said, "Perfect! When can you see me?" He had openings. I got in that week.

I was in sad shape, so I saw him twice a week the first two weeks, then one time each of the next two weeks. After two sessions I was feeling strong again. By the final session, I went dressed as a guy.

He showed me he knew his stuff, a grizzled veteran of psychology. He asked all the right questions. He made astute observations.

I told him I recognized a connection between being on HRT and these episodes of feeling male (which I outline in the next chapter). I explained my thought that it was all I went through surgically in 2017 which had brought on this new sense of being male, and that I was hopeful it would now stick because I had completed the process.

He suggested I should allow myself to be gender fluid, that perhaps I will always have periods where I feel male, and times of being female, and the overlapping two-person struggle. He found me being too hard on myself, that my sense of things was too black and white, and that if I would go with the flow I might not struggle so much.

I hated his suggestion.

I had no interest in being gender fluid.

He and I debated it in every session.

It is no fun for me to go back and forth. Thinking about my family and friends, and everywhere I go and everything I do—and trying to find a job!—I could not imagine, "Hey, I'm Gina, today," and then, "I'm back to Greg these days." No thanks.

Aside from the gender-fluid suggestion, my sessions with the therapist had me feeling better. The depression lifted. I continued to remain content, with zero days struggling with my gender. After I hit the six-week mark, which is how long supercalifragilisticexpialidocious lasted, every day became the longest I had no gender issues since this began in 1968.

Fifty years.

Wow. I couldn't believe it was fifty years.

I couldn't believe, despite all that had happened to me since 2013, that I could finally say this: I am a man who has no interest in being a woman.

As April progressed, more and more I wore men's clothes. I only dressed as a woman when going somewhere, such as to church, where they knew me as Gina, and I was having a hard time doing it. We had been worshiping at the same LCMS church where the furor over our membership erupted in September 2016. We faithfully attended. We got to know people. We strived to demonstrate that we loved the Lord the same way everyone else in that church did.

I visited one of the pastors in April, to tell him what was happening in me. I was concerned it would be confusing if I abruptly began coming to worship dressed as a man. He was not so concerned. He welcomed me to do so.

As I had done in a few of the half-dozen meetings I had with the pastors, I once again suggested doing some education in the congregation regarding gender dysphoria and being transgender. He replied with the answer I heard every time: "The congregation is not ready." I finally said, "They will never be ready if you don't do anything." I added, "You know, you have at least one other trans person in your church. That person reached out to me." He wasn't surprised. His stance didn't change.

That evening, informing Julie of the meeting, she and I knew it was time to move on. It had been nineteen months since we were forced to resign our membership. I had spoken with a number of pastors in the LCMS, getting nowhere. I had written letters to those pastors who had published in LCMS magazines articles with transgender references, and wrote twice to the president of the LCMS. One replied that there was nothing for us to talk about. From the others I received only silence.

In mid April we received an invitation to the one-hundred-fiftieth anniversary celebration for the ELCA congregation where we had worshiped for the first nine months of my transition. We decided to attend the April 29 event. They received us with warmth and joy. We once again made our church home in that congregation.

They only knew me as Gina, so that's how I presented myself. The next week, still as Gina, I began telling folks I was feeling male. After a third week attending as a female, I walked into church dressed as a male, my long hair pulled into a ponytail.

The church by that time had a new pastor. He'd met me as Gina. He knew nothing of who I was, a former LCMS pastor. I now introduced myself as Greg. He didn't flinch. I said, "I need to talk with you, Pastor." Soon, we went to lunch. I laid it all out. Not only did he not flinch, he quickly became my friend and ally.

As April moved into May and I was feeling so good, I wanted to scream to the world that I was Greg, that I was a man, that I no longer experienced gender questioning. It grew challenging to interact online, where everyone referred to me as Gina.

I had to be patient. I needed to be sure this would last. I needed to be able to explain things well. A lot of people would be confused—*Detransitioning? Is that a thing? Was he ever really transgender?* Some would make fun of me. Others would be convinced I was mentally ill all along ... and still am. My fellow Christians who rejected me would have a field day with this news.

Especially, I needed to protect all who are transgender, that I did not misrepresent them or what it means to be transgender, that this was my experience and no one else's. I simply could not reveal what was going on with me to the harm of another transgender person.

To go public with this, I set my sights on July, which would be six months since the onset. The delay in returning publicly to Greg was helpful, giving me time to proceed cautiously and reflect on what was happening with me.

During those weeks, a light flipped on which allowed me to see why I was suddenly feeling male. Indeed, I found it was not at all sudden. This had been coming for more than four years.

And I had been observing and recording it all along.

47

It was my hormones all along

Soon after I began therapy in 2013, Doc encouraged me to write when I awoke in the night and couldn't return to sleep. While I never made it to my desk, I used the tossing and turning to rehearse my thoughts so I would remember them the next day.

I wrote and kept writing, creating a record for myself. Writing in the moment is not only therapeutic, but also helps one retain specifics.

In chapter sixteen, I wrote about diethylstilbestrol (DES), an artificial estrogen, and the study which showed forty-seven percent of five hundred males, whose mothers took DES when pregnant with them, reported being somewhere on the transgender spectrum. Finding ample evidence to believe my mom was given DES when pregnant with me, I became all but convinced my gender dysphoria was the result of my endocrine system having been disrupted when I was in the womb. Therefore, hormone levels typical for the average male did not fit with me, creating my gender struggle.

As I traced my life since I began hormone replacement therapy (HRT) in September 2013, to what I was experiencing as 2018 opened, it became the final piece in the enigmatic puzzle which was my life: perhaps I suffered gender dysphoria because of my hormones.

Desiring to keep orderly a potentially convoluted and confusing track of time, I present my evidence in diary form. The first five entries summarize ground previously addressed.

November 2013

I came to refer to it as supercalifragilisticexpialidocious, so profound was what I experienced on November 22.

I began HRT on September 27. My doctor said to begin looking at the eight-week mark for signs it was working. Working? I never expected this.

That Friday morning, I felt like a guy. I pondered my women's clothes. I couldn't understand why I ever wanted to wear them. I looked into the mirror and, for the first time in I don't know how long, I liked the man's image which was reflected there.

Since there was only one difference in my life—HRT—Julie and I believed the altering of my testosterone and estrogen was behind this sensation.

Was it possible my physiology works best when my testosterone is lower and my estrogen higher than they typically are in me, which before beginning HRT were in the normal range for a guy my age?

My doctor had never heard a trans person describe what I told him. We would try to maintain it, checking my blood and monitoring my HRT dosage.

Exactly six weeks after the harmony began, my gender dysphoria returned.

June 2014

My brain was on fire, so intense was the male versus female struggle inside me. As May opened, I resumed HRT.

In a month, my sense of being a male returned. It happened so quickly I took the peacefulness as my being days from retiring, that leaving the stress of being a minister was relaxing my brain.

Not wanting my breasts to grow, I again stopped HRT.

So much for retiring being the calm for my mind. Three days after we moved to Indianapolis, a month after being off HRT, my brain was once again on fire.

September 2014

270

The month of July was hell. A male and a female lived in me, battling for dominance. Seeking to calm my brain, the first of August I resumed HRT.

As three months earlier, the sense of my being male returned at the four-week mark. How wonderful was it? I felt so strong, one-hundred-percent male, that I could not imagine ever losing it. I stopped taking the HRT after a month and, you guessed it, in October I crashed, and the rest of the year nearly burned to the ground.

February 2015

In December, I engaged a therapist in Indianapolis. I would need her endorsement to see a doctor for HRT.

I didn't have much of an HRT supply left. I tried to guess when my therapist would endorse me. I restarted HRT in January, hoping I would have enough before I got new prescriptions.

I ran out a few weeks before my first doctor's appointment, but I had taken enough HRT that I thought the male sense might return. In mid February, I had the sense my brain was shifting and the male sense was arriving. Sure enough, the next day it did.

It didn't settle in as firmly as the previous three times. I speculated it was because I wasn't on a full dose of HRT. For days, I would feel male, then female, with the two-person struggle mixed in. I thought I was going to lose my mind.

April of 2015 to April of 2017

I was back on HRT the beginning of April 2015 and remained on it.

Supercalifragilisticexpialidocious did not return. I did, however, experience wild swings which my doctor figured to be hormonal. I could especially tell when my testosterone was not being suppressed. My internal male versus female battle would rage.

The doctor upped, and upped again, the medicine to block my testosterone production. She also increased my estrogen. I switched from pills, to patches, to injections, to achieve the best flow of estrogen into my system.

Eventually, my testosterone was suppressed dependably enough I felt good most of the time. I continued to experience occasions when I wanted to get out of transitioning, but they never persisted for long.

On April 11, 2017, I had gender confirmation surgery. A month before surgery, I had to cease HRT for blood clot concerns, and would not resume it until two weeks after surgery. I feared that by the four-week mark being off HRT, I might crash right before surgery.

Ten days before surgery, I felt my hormones shift, but no crash came. I went into surgery with confidence, feeling fully female.

Late April 2017

Just before resuming HRT post-surgery, another new experience visited me. I felt completely and utterly asexual. I had no sense of being female. Not an inkling of maleness. I looked at women, at men. I felt nothing. I envisioned feminine women's clothes and handsome men's clothes on me. I felt nothing.

I had taken no estrogen for six weeks, and now my testosterone-producing factory had been surgically removed. Both my estrogen and testosterone levels were undoubtedly very low. For me to feel asexual made perfect sense, because my sex hormones had bottomed out.

As my body evened out, a most unexpected thing occurred. I began feeling like Greg again. I don't mean I began feeling male, but returning was the way I had always experienced myself in the world. This had dramatically changed over the previous two years as I evolved into living as a female.

During the two years of transitioning, I gradually felt more female than male. As I pondered my life before 2015, it was as though I were looking at a different person, a phenomena reported by many trans folks. Certain activities, such as jogging and gardening, which before felt masculine, slowly shifted so they no longer brought back memories of being a guy.

Now, in the spring of 2017, I was swinging back to feeling like that person, yet I retained the sense of being female.

I was now the female my brain insisted I should be, yet I regained my sense of the life I had built for sixty years. It was wonderful.

By the time I finished my third and final transitioning surgery in November, I was on top of the world. I had completed my transition. In the process, one of my fears never came to pass: I did not become a different person.

I was elated to feel like my old self, while being my new self. I felt whole. Finally.

August 2017

I saw my endocrinologist. Somewhere in our conversation, she suggested I could reduce my estrogen intake, that I could experiment with the dosage, perhaps beginning by reducing it to eighty percent of what I'd been taking, and even less if I felt good.

Then, she surprised me when she said that, actually, I no longer required it. I had surgically completed my transition. If I wanted to see how I felt, with my adrenal glands producing small amounts of testosterone and estrogen, I could give a shot to no longer giving myself shots.

I immediately reduced my weekly injection of estrogen by twenty-five percent.

A week before my November surgery, for blood clot concerns I had to stop taking estrogen. When I resumed, post-surgery, I reduced my weekly estrogen intake a bit more. I now was injecting about sixty percent of what had been a full dose.

January 2018

By the second week of the new year, I couldn't believe what I was experiencing. I pondered the previous days, and I could see it had been coming for several days, gradually but steadily, the way the sun rises each day.

I felt exclusively male.

I would love to write, as with the previous times this happened, that I enjoyed a marvelous sense of peace. This time, there was no supercalifrag- ilisticexpialidocious, because I had fully transitioned. I fell into a deep depression.

The fully-male sense continued until late February, then slipped for a few days. When I resumed feeling male, I decided it was time to experiment with ceasing my estrogen injections, hoping to achieve consistency in feeling male. The last time I injected was the final Sunday in February.

I struggled with myself during the month of March. I felt male, but I had transitioned. It seemed I had ruined my life. Returning to a therapist was helpful, and by the beginning of April I felt content. By July, except for the few days of dysphoria in February, I hit the six-month mark of feeling male. On July 9, I went public and returned my online profiles to Greg.

I processed this history, each event of the past five years, and it all came together. My theory seemed proven, that my gender dysphoria was the result of my hormones not working for me at levels typical for a male. I hoped my consistently low levels of testosterone and estrogen would keep me constantly feeling male.

Along the way, I came to know a gender-dysphoric man who was on HRT, lowering his testosterone and raising his estrogen for the purpose of easing his dysphoria so he could remain male and, two years into it, it was working for him. More proof for me that, for some, hormones could be the gender-dysphoria culprit.

Now, I had to test this. I had to live it. It had to persist. Not only did this feeling of absolute maleness have to continue, it had to continue every hour, every day, with the weeks running into months.

There is a bit of 2018 remaining as I write this. I am pleased to report that since the blip in February there have been no blips, no bumps, no bruises.

I feel healed.

48

Loose ends and lessons

I have been in love with three women. Somehow, through my gender dysphoria and transitioning, I lost none of them. This amazes me.

Once through the rocky first couple of years after telling my kids about my gender issues and then transitioning, as relationships with my children returned so did my friendship with my first wife, Kim. She proved to be exactly the person I knew her to be from the day we met. She accepted me and was friendly with me as Gina. She's a friend to me as Greg.

I wrote that Lori, my first girlfriend, would become a good friend. I informed her of my gender dysphoria before I went public, feeling she deserved to hear it directly from me. She was, of course, surprised, but she also was concerned and compassionate. She sent the occasional email to check in on how I was. As with Kim, she showed me the person I always knew.

All three women—Julie, Kim, and Lori—have continually demonstrated what moved me to love them. I am filled with thanks and love for each one.

Though I returned to being called Greg, I decided not to bother my grandchildren by having them switch back to calling me Papa. Gigi is not an uncommon nickname for grandmothers, but I find it still works for me—the uncommon grandfather! With my grandkids, I gladly remain Gigi.

While I took every step in transitioning and had every surgery, there is one I did not complete. Despite 103 hours of electrolysis on my face, perhaps thirty percent of my facial hair remains. Since six laser treatments eliminated all of the dark hairs, and because Barb the Impaler concentrated on my chin, it takes three non-shaving days to see my whiskers. And that's about how often I shave. I miss Barb—she's a lovely person and became a friend—but I don't miss her impaling, so I will let this remain the step not completed.

When I began therapy in 2013, I felt if I tried to do away with Gina I would be murdering her. Now, having fully lived as Gina and having put her aside, I do not feel that I killed her. Rather, she's been retired. I lived her fully. She served me well. She got me through the hurricane. I am indebted to her for holding on for dear life with all I put her through.

As I negotiated my crazy path since 2013, I longed to educate, to teach and speak about this subject so many find bewildering. I yearned to foster understanding for transgender people, who are too often rejected, discounted, and misunderstood. With my experience as a minister, I especially wanted to reach pastors and Christian lay folk.

In September 2018, I had my first opportunity to conduct a seminar for a congregation. The group was attentive to all I explained about gender dysphoria and being transgender. There is a hunger and need for this type of talk, not only in churches but also in all facets of life.

As, when I was a pastor, being thrust into the most difficult of situations forced me to learn how to address them, the same happened in my trans years. With every condemnation, I learned how to counter it. When someone thought he nailed me, I did my homework and answered appropriately.

Perhaps the most aggravating illustration given to stifle me was of a person who suffers anorexia nervosa. A pastor, who rejected my position of making use of transitioning as any person uses surgery and medicine for healing, said, "You wouldn't tell an anorexic person not to eat, and that it was okay to starve herself to death."

Dear pastor, of course you want to help the anorexic to eat. But, if she didn't eat, if she could not find the ability to eat and she continued to weaken, and even grow near death, you would continue ministering to her. You

276

certainly would not kick her out of your church.

When I learned about diethylstilbestrol, I came to believe I had a physical malady worthy of addressing medically. Though I proceeded with that mindset to take every step in transitioning, I do not encourage others to do so. When I communicate with gender dysphoric folks, I answer their questions and commiserate with them in their pain, but I never tell them they ought to transition. That decision is theirs.

Although I likely have an intersex condition caused by my endocrine system having been disrupted when my mom was carrying me, there is no *you can test it and see it* evidence to know what causes gender dysphoria. Gender conflict could be hormonal, or another physical condition, or in some cases psychological.

I've learned much about endocrine disruptors, that they permeate our environment, and that they dramatically affect us. Endocrine disruptors are located in chemicals, plasticizers, and pharmaceuticals. Many physical maladies caused by them have been identified. I find it plausible that if chemicals and drugs can cause birth defects and cancerous tumors, they could create gender conflict.

To this end, I came to ask: if a woman takes artificial estrogen when pregnant with a male baby, doesn't it make sense that he could be profoundly affected?

Does the cause of gender dysphoria remain mysterious? Yes. So does the cause of autism, yet no one suggests that a person on the autism spectrum only needs psychotherapy to be healthy, and no pastor would ever accuse an autistic person of having caved in to a sinful temptation.

I discovered the past five years that many Christians don't know what to do with gender dysphoria and with transgender persons. For every lay person or pastor who seeks to learn and display compassion, there is a lay person or pastor who has no capacity for anything good toward us. Instead of leaning in, learning, and loving, they accuse and condemn, erect walls, and walk away.

Sometimes, dissenters discount you so they can dismiss you. Explaining to one pastor the severity of my suffering, he replied, "Surely, it's not that bad."

This, from a man who suffers PTSD, often itself a discounted, dismissed condition.

I found in depression a helpful comparison. Only recently has depression been understood. Go back just one generation to be reminded that our attitude toward it was what one man's continued to be as he told me about his daughter's struggle: "If she would just count her blessings and get out into the sunshine she would feel better."

When I heard one person lament about me, "Why didn't he try harder to remain male?" it came home to me how some view struggles with gender dysphoria as they see depression: you're a weak person, and if you only got your head right you would be okay.

I came to see the topic of transgender as many cutting edge things which have been scoffed at and rejected. When I was young, heart transplants were introduced. Many times I heard someone reject this surgery with, "They're playing God!" Before long, this procedure was widely accepted.

With time and familiarity, concepts and methods that seem outlandish initially become recognized as beneficial.

People find it difficult to wrap their heads around something foreign. As is the case with xenophobia—a fear or dislike of people from different cultures—transgender often elicits a knee-jerk reaction: It's new to me. It's different. It makes me feel icky. It's hard to adjust to it. I shouldn't have to adapt to it. I can't accept it. I fear it. I reject it.

For all the misunderstanding, fear, and rejection I experienced, I retained the desire to educate, to help, to reconnect. The old saying by mountain climbers is they climb because the mountain is there. There is a mountain of transgender education to do with the Christian Church and the world, and because it is there I undertook the climb. Despite the boulders rolled into my path to knock me off the mountain, I have kept climbing. The peak is yet a long trek away, but it is a worthy goal. The very lives of transgender people depend on them being heard and understood.

Rejection might be the biggest boulder rolled into the path of every trans person. I experienced rejection in every fashion. I reckon it might be the number one reason trans folks attempt to kill themselves. Dealing with one's mismatch of identity and body is itself nearly insurmountable. Even if you successfully negotiate that, it can be impossible to abide if you are scorned and disdained by your family.

This kind of rejection attacks your very being. Rejected simply for being who you are. All you desire is wholeness and you are spit on for it. You are criticized and you are ignored. You are told you are not welcome and you are treated as if you no longer exist.

This does not just happen among Christians and those of other religions. I witness it also among those who have no religion, who are agnostics and atheists, and even among those who hold the most liberal political ideologies.

In the two most important areas of my life, I learned the best lessons. The first is in the faithfulness of the Lord Jesus. I continually ran toward Him, to His Word and in prayer. My trust in the Father, through my faith in the Son, by the Holy Spirit who works with my spirit, continually deepened. During the worst times, He strengthened me as He promises to do. He enabled me to hold firm to everything I confessed when I was ordained a minister in the LCMS. Since my faith in Christ is the only thing I can take from this life, nothing can compare with it in importance.

I am humbled and gratified as to how I moved through and came out of my transition, from living as a transgender woman to now as a male who has no questioning of his gender. As all Christians should do, I relied on God's grace in Christ, trusting I am loved and covered by my Lord Jesus' life and death and resurrection and ascension.

One area of grave concern for my fellow Christians was my marriage to Julie. Two pastors even suggested it was my job to divorce her, to set her free from what they saw was the abomination I was foisting upon her.

Our marriage was also of grave concern to us. We never considered divorce, though at my worst moment I told her to divorce me, that she didn't deserve the trouble I was putting her through. A heartbeat later, I begged her not to divorce me. She continually assured me of her love.

And then we lived it. Together, we lived every last bit of it.

We lived our marriage in the privacy of our home. We lived our marriage as Christians. We lived our marriage in front of our family. I continued to see myself as Julie's husband, and I acted toward her in that way. I longed to fulfill my vows to her.

Was it unique? Even, as one friend put it, weird? Yup, it was. Many people find themselves in unique and weird circumstances. What are you going to do when they face you? Honorable people handle them with grace, with love, always providing the compassion they desire from the other and returning it.

I hope the lesson others learned from us is the lesson we taught ourselves. The "for worse" part of "for better or for worse" can be handled when the two people in the marriage are all in with their spouse.

Every situation that provided me with a new experience taught me a lesson. Ultimately, I saw all of them grow me as a person, especially as a Christian. I have been shaped and molded into a person who has a heart for *all people*, no matter their religion, or ethnicity, or political views, or sexual orientation, or how they express their gender.

A challenging section of Scripture, which I loved to teach when I was a pastor, proved true. It's from the fifth chapter of Romans. We are told that we rejoice in our sufferings. *What?* Why? We do so because suffering produces perseverance. Then, perseverance produces character. Next, character produces hope. Finally and ultimately, hope does not disappoint us because God poured out His love to us through the Holy Spirit.

Boy, have I had a lot of Holy Spirit poured into me! All of my suffering has indeed led me to persevere, that perseverance built my character, and in that character came a greater and deeper hope.

My hope in Jesus Christ never disappoints me. His faithfulness, reliably fulfilling His every promise to me, is the best lesson of my life.

49

Coasting

It is amusing that in 2013 Julie came to describe my struggle as my being a chrysalis riding a roller coaster through a hurricane. She enjoys roller coasters. I favor rides such as the Tilt-a-Whirl and the Scrambler and the Ferris Wheel. She can't handle rides that go in circles. I can't stomach the dramatic ups and downs.

Somehow, we both survived the formidable ups and downs and circles and swings of the past five years.

Finishing this final chapter in January 2019, I passed the one year mark since I stopped feeling female, and eight months since resuming living full time as a male. Throughout 2018, a few things were regularly on my mind, the first two as questions.

The natural question I have been asked most often: what if the gender dysphoria returns? I know only one way to reply: if it does, I'll deal with it, just as I dealt with it before.

I don't want ever again to have to deal with it.

Now that I've lived as a male for several months, and because I have loved being a guy, and since I have enjoyed this period with no sense of being, or wanting to be a female ...

I simply can't go back. I don't want to be a woman. Indeed, ask any man, who knows he's a male, whether he wants to be a woman. Of course, he doesn't. Well, that's me, now. Finally, that's me.

I simply can't go back, because going back isn't as simple as living as a female. The miserable aspect is the battle that rages during the transformation, when I feel them both, the male and female warring with each other. The mental distress creates a noise in my mind which I have best described as my brain being on fire. It is exhausting and agonizing.

So, when I've answered the question, what if the dysphoria returns, I've always added this: if it returns I just might tear my house down to the ground with my bare hands. I would be equal parts furious and frazzled.

The second question has been: do you have any regrets for having fully transitioned? My answer came quickly and has not wavered.

I have no regrets.

Sure, I *wish* I didn't have to go through all I did, and I *wish* I didn't have to put my family through all of this, and I *wish* I didn't have this huge investment of time and money and the changes to my body, but I immediately recognized that if I had not accomplished everything with transitioning, I would still be in the process. I believe if I had tried to postpone a surgery, or held back on any one step, that thing would still be before me, and I could not have come to the spot at which I arrived in January 2018.

As much as I believe I can point to my hormones finally coming to rest as causing this phenomenal supercalifragilisticexpialidocious, I find that completing the process was fundamental to what I am now experiencing. Now a year into it, I retain that conviction.

The answers to both questions leads to the thought ringing in my head: I have a profound sense of having been healed.

I speak this carefully and sparingly. I don't want this misconstrued, lest a person would see transgender people as broken, as ill, as inferior. What I am feeling is strictly my experience. By using "healed," I in no way intend it as a commentary on what it means to be transgender.

Though I needed to transition, and though I found that transitioning removed the twin thoughts of suicide and losing my mind, I remained the reluctant trans person.

When I was a kid, I never could dream of being the woman I wanted to be, and as an adult I was utterly unable to conjure the possibility of being rid of my gender identity issues. Now, despite the irreversible surgery to my genitals—not to mention my surgically-altered face and voice, and the legal name I need to have reversed, and the double mastectomy I crave—I feel so completely male I constantly find myself thinking, "I have been healed."

I can still say this even as, in November 2018, I was forced to resume injecting estrogen. Six months earlier, I began having hot flashes. Researching it, I found it could only be what women experience during menopause. Oh, gravy.

While I learned hot flashes really are as nasty as I always heard, they were slight compared with what then happened to my leg muscles. As summer wore on and fell into autumn, I lost strength. I struggled to run five miles. My pace grew slow. My muscle soreness worsened. I experienced joint pain for the first time.

Returning to my endocrinologist, she pinned everything on my now too-low levels of testosterone and estrogen. I expressed alarm over playing with my levels by going back on HRT, that shifting my levels could bring a return of my gender dysphoria. She thought even a small amount of estrogen might resolve my hot flashes and muscle issue. I agreed to restart the once-a-week injections at about thirty percent of what I took previously.

In two weeks, the hot flashes resolved. At four weeks, my muscles strengthened and I resumed running.

In the mean time, I have grown determined the dysphoria will not return. It's almost a stubborn resolve: *I am healed, you nasty gender dysphoria. There's no place in me for you anymore.*

A person can ride a roller coaster only so long. Now that I've arrived where I am, I need to be on solid ground.

Please, Lord, let this wild ride be over.

+ + +

That was supposed to be the end of the book, but it can't be. The ultimate final topic is my Julie.

Far too many spouses escape a marriage when the going gets tough. There's not much more difficult, demanding, or exhausting situation than abiding in the suffering Julie went through with me.

Instead of walking away, Julie got on board and rode the roller coaster by my side.

She remained patient, even as her patience must have worn thin a gazillion times. When I saw a hint of a crack in her longsuffering, she quickly patched it. Her love for me never failed.

She was, as I have gladly said to many, my Jesus in the flesh.

Isn't that how all people should be? Even if you aren't a Christian—shoot, even if you are an atheist—in the person of Jesus is seen the compassion and love and friendship and helpful spirit which we long to see in every human being, especially in those who are closest to us.

For the outcast, Jesus was a friend. For the sick, He was a healer. For sinners, He died.

For me, Julie was everything the Lord Jesus would have her be. She's that way with everyone, everywhere, in every way she has opportunity.

I return to March of 2013. To the morning I told Julie how badly I was hurting. When I revealed I might not survive if I didn't transition. She responded: "We'll figure it out."

We.

Us.

Together.

A few hours later, when she was at work, she texted me. "If I didn't say it earlier, I want you to know I'm not going anywhere."

Indeed, the only *where* she went was with me, by my side, on the roller coaster, through the eye of the storm, all the way to the finish.

Is it any wonder what my favorite name is for Julie? I call her My Heart.

About the Author

Greg Eilers has a Masters of Divinity degree and was a Lutheran pastor for eighteen years. Recognizing that misunderstanding transgender issues is more prevalent than lack of knowledge, he used his blog and public speaking to edify his fellow Christians and secular society. Demonstrating that being transgender is no more a lifestyle than any way of being, he stuck with everything he believed and practiced, including his passions: caring for his family, gardening, and running.

Greg continues to blog at eilerspizza.wordpress.com.

You may email Greg using the *Contact Us* link on the homepage of gregeilers.com., or message him through Facebook. He welcomes your questions and requests for information and assistance.

Made in the USA
Monee, IL
21 October 2022

16318860R00177